The Dutch Oven Cookbook for Camping Chef

Over 300 fun, tasty, and easy to follow Campfire recipes for your outdoors family adventures. Enjoy cooking everything in the flames with your dutch oven and cast iron.

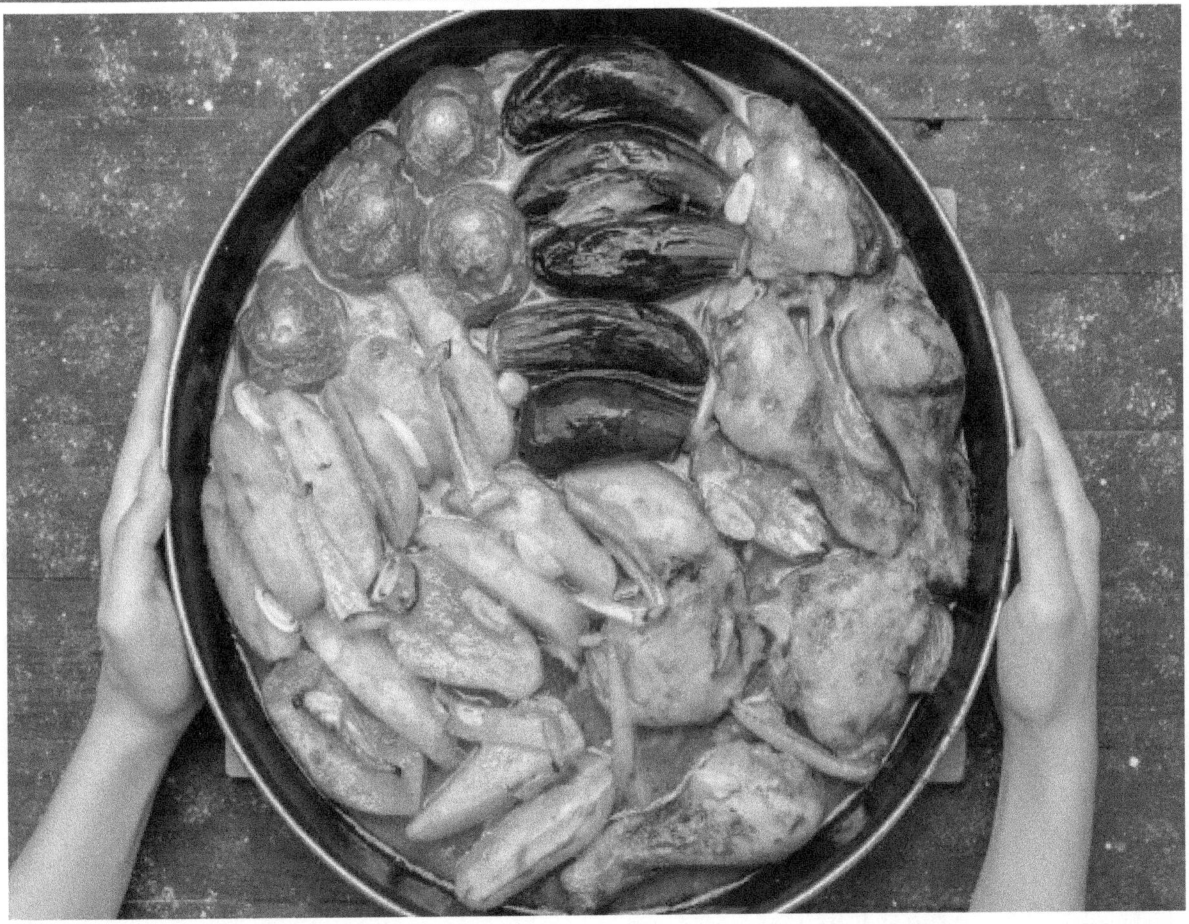

© Copyright 2019 - All rights reserved.

The content contained within this book may not be reproduced, duplicated or transmitted without direct written permission from the author or the publisher.

Under no circumstances will any blame or legal responsibility be held against the publisher, or author, for any damages, reparation, or monetary loss due to the information contained within this book, either directly or indirectly.

Legal Notice:

This book is copyright protected. It is only for personal use. You cannot amend, distribute, sell, use, quote or paraphrase any part, or the content within this book, without the consent of the author or publisher.

Disclaimer Notice:

Please note the information contained within this document is for educational and entertainment purposes only. All effort has been executed to present accurate, up to date, reliable, complete information. No warranties of any kind are declared or implied. Readers acknowledge that the author is not engaged in the rendering of legal, financial, medical or professional advice.

Table of contents

- **Breakfast recipes**..1

  - 1 Corned Beef Hash Browns
  - 2 Mushroom Frittata
  - 3 Baked Oatmeal
  - 4 Dutch Oven Tater Tot Casserole
  - 5 Biscuits and Gravy
  - 6 Breakfast Sausage Casserole
  - 7 Sausage-Hash Morning
  - 8 Ham Cheese Omelet
  - 9 Classic Bacon and Eggs
  - 10 Breakfast Chicken Casserole
  - 11 Raisin and Almond Granola
  - 12 Syrupy Pear Oatmeal
  - 13 Apple Quinoa
  - 14 Butter Toast Casserole
  - 15 Cheesy Broccoli Casserole
  - 16 Cheese Egg Scramble with Salsa
  - 17 Spinach and Mushroom Ham Frittata
  - 18 Bacon and Cheese Potato
  - 19 Beef and Potato
  - 20 Creamy Banana and Berry Oatmeal
  - 21 Roast Garlic Potato.
  - 22 Syrupy Berry Toast Casserole
  - 23 Pecan and Banana Pudding
  - 24 Blueberry and Almond Cheese Cake
  - 25 Pecan Cake
  - 26 Glazed Apple Fritters.
  - 27 Mushroom and Potato Tomato Bake
  - 28 Potato Cheese Crust
  - 29 Cheese Potato Quiche with Salmon
  - 30 Bacon and Apple Cheese Frittata
  - 31 Egg Cheese Chilaquiles with Salsa
  - 32 Creamy Mushroom Bread Pudding
  - 33 Cheesy Zucchini Strata
  - 34 Tomato Cheese Frittata
  - 35 Polenta Cheese Egg
  - 36 Sausage Cheese Casserole
  - 37 Juicy Cranberry and Raisin Oat

- **Soups, Stews, and Chilis Recipes**..18

  - 38 Black Bean and Corn Chili
  - 39 Beer Beef Chili
  - 40 Pork and Bean Chili
  - 41 Pork and Black Bean Chili
  - 42 Turkey Bean Chili with Salsa
  - 43 Beans Chili with Salsa
  - 44 Turkey Bean and Corn Chili
  - 45 Beef and Cabbage Soup
  - 46 Quinoa Chickpea Corn Soup
  - 47 Sweet Potato Soup
  - 48 Pork and Bean Soup
  - 49 Tomato Cream Soup with Basil
  - 50 Chicken Bean Barley Soup
  - 51 Pea and Chicken Rice Soup
  - 52 Tomato Soup with Pancetta
  - 53 Sausage and Kale Bean Soup
  - 54 Mushroom Cream Soup
  - 55 Carrot Soup
  - 56 Collard Green White Bean Soup with Sausages
  - 57 Bacon and Potato Soup
  - 58 Chicken Mushroom Soup
  - 59 Creme Potato Chicken Soup
  - 60 Broccoli Cheese Soup
  - 61 Chicken Tortilla Soup with Avocado
  - 62 Rib Soup with Onion
  - 63 Tomato Chicken Soup

- **64** Sweet Potato and Corn Soup
- **65** Carrot and Lentil Soup
- **66** Beef Cheese Soup
- **67** Tangy Black Bean Soup
- **68** Butternut Squash Soup
- **69** Lemony Cauliflower Potage
- **70** Chickpea and Spinach Stew
- **71** Potato and Beef Stew
- **72** Tomato and Beef Stew
- **73** Beef Stew with Potato
- **74** Shell Bean and Lamb Stew
- **75** Tomato Bean Stew

❖ **Sides and Appetizers Recipes**..38

- **76** Tomato and Cauliflower Antipasto
- **77** Egg and Butter Spaetzle
- **78** Juicy Squash with Walnut
- **79** Bacon and Pea Risi e Bisi
- **80** Lemony Artichok
- **81** Vinegary Cabbage with Apple
- **82** Creamy Cheese Potato
- **83** Potato with Cheese
- **84** Sherry Mushroom
- **85** Green Beans with Bacon
- **86** Creamy Corn Cheese Soufflé
- **87** Corn Cheese Pudding
- **88** Baby Bok Choy and Mushroom
- **89** Tomato and Corn Beans
- **90** Beans with Cilantro
- **91** Mushroom Cheese Cocotte
- **92** Breaded Cheese Risotto
- **93** Beans with Bacon
- **94** Corn Fritters with Chutney
- **95** Raisin and Pistachios Pilaf
- **96** Bulgur and Tomato Pilaf
- **97** Corn Cheese Polenta with Aioli
- **98** Syrupy Parsnip and Turnip
- **99** Apple Cheese Cocottes
- **100** Juicy Cranberry Sauce
- **101** Apple and Mango Chutney
- **102** Golden Onion Rings
- **103** Cheesy Spaghetti Squash
- **104** Golden Cheese Cocotte

❖ **Beef and Chicken**..52

- **105** Beer Braised Beef
- **106** Korean Beef Stew
- **107** Braised Short Ribs
- **108** Short Ribs in Wine
- **109** Carrot Beef Stew
- **110** Chuck Beef Roast.
- **111** Beef Roast and Potato
- **112** Braised Beef Ribs
- **113** Dutch Oven Corned Beef
- **114** Beef Carrot Meal
- **115** Beef Burgundy
- **116** Vegetable Beef Soup.
- **117** Baked Beef Stew
- **118** Beef Pot Roast
- **119** Greek Beef Stew
- **120** Beef Bourguignon
- **121** Indian Beef Stew
- **122** Roasted Chicken and Potatoes
- **123** Turkey Meatballs in Tomato Sauce
- **124** Chicken Fajitas
- **125** One-Pot Chicken Parmesan Spaghetti
- **126** Crispy Fried Chicken Thighs.

- **127** Creamy Parmesan Chicken with Mushroom Sauce
- **128** Creamy Chicken and Rice
- **129** Chicken & Vegetables.
- **130** Wine Braised Chicken
- **131** Garlic Chicken
- **132 Rosemary** & Vegetables
- **133** Whole Chicken Roast
- **134** Lime Chicken
- **135** Chicken Stew
- **136** Soy Chicken & Mushrooms
- **137** Moroccan Chicken
- **138** Arugula Chicken Spaghetti
- **139** Enchilada Penne Chicken…
- **140** Salsa Verde Chicken
- **141** Olive Chicken
- **142** Spiced Chicken Wings
- **143** Parmesan Mushroom Chicken

❖ <u>Pork and Lamb</u>..69

- **144** Tangy Lamb Shanks…
- **145** Lemony Rib Lamb Chops
- **146** Potato and Carrot Lamb Stew
- **147** Lamb Leg with Rosemary
- **148** Lamb Tagine
- **149** Tropical Honey Shanks
- **150** Stew with Veggies
- **151** Braised Lamb Shanks
- **152** Lamb Pie
- **153** Mediterranean Roast
- **154** Lamb Shanks.
- **155** Sweet Lamb Chops
- **156** Pork Carnitas Tacos with Onion.
- **157** Pork Sausage Jambalaya with Shrimp
- **158** Panko Bean Stew with Chorizo
- **159** Pork Chops with Carrot
- **160** Pork Loin with Apple and Cabbage
- **161** Aromatic Pork Shoulder
- **162** Pineapple Pork Roast
- **163** Beer Pork with BBQ Sauce
- **164** Garlicky Pork Belly
- **165** Glazed Pork Tenderloin
- **166** Pork Meatballs with Orange Glaze
- **167** Baked Pork and Eggplant Casserole
- **168** Pork Roast with Tomato

❖ <u>Fish and Seafood Recipes</u>..83

- **169** Lobster Bisque.
- **170** Baked Salmon with Herbs
- **171** Baked Trout with Cherry Tomatoes
- **172** Tilapia Cacciatore.
- **173** Seafood Cioppino.
- **174** Apple Cobbler
- **175** Mussels in Coconut Sauce.
- **176** Shrimp Paell
- **177** Wild Rice Salmon
- **178** Salmon in Creamy Sauce
- **179** White Fish Curry
- **180** Roasted Cod.
- **181** Trout Fennel Curry.
- **182** Seafood Risotto
- **183** Calamari Fra Diavolo
- **184** Seafood Stew
- **185** Pasta with Clams and Pancetta
- **186** Beer Mustard Shrimp
- **187** Tilapia Nuggets
- **188** Salmon with Spinach
- **189** Buttery Grouper
- **190** Whitefish and Oyster Bouillabaisse
- **191** Buttery Tomato Shrimp

- **192** Lemon Halibut with Tomato
- **193** Roast Fish with Lemon
- **194** Beer Catfish Fillet
- **195** Cod Fillet with Beer
- **196** Salmon Fillet with Lemon
- **197** Arugula Cod with Cherry Tomato
- **198** Olive Cod with Lemon
- **199** Mussels with Bacon
- **200** Chives Mussels
- **201** Shrimp and Mussels Paella
- **202** Crab and Clam Cioppino
- **203** Breaded Crab Fish Cheese Casserole
- **204** Panko Shrimp Scampi
- **205** Creamy Shrimp Mushrooms Stroganoff
- **206** Oysters and Shrimp Cream
- **207** Salad Shrimp and Tomato Provençal
- **208** Lemony Salt Snapper
- **209** Baked Salmon Fillet
- **210** Lemon Halibut with Salsa
- **211** Quick Swordfish Steaks
- **212** Panko Crab Cakes
- **213** Mango Shrimp
- **214** Savory Calamari

- ❖ **<u>Vegetarian recipes</u>**..102

- **215** Zucchini and Corn Chowder
- **216** Butternut Squash Soup
- **217** Lentil Coconut Soup
- **218** Italian White Bean Soup
- **219** Vegetarian Chili
- **220** Quinoa Veggies Bowl
- **221** Vegetable Stew
- **222** Bean Basil Bowl
- **223** Pasta e Fagioli with White Beans
- **224** Oven Roasted Cauliflower
- **225** Beans with Chard
- **226** Savory Beans Rice
- **227** Corn and Bean Succotash
- **228** Panko Eggplant
- **229** Navy Beans and Zucchini
- **230** Butternut Squash Risotto
- **231** Cheese Mushrooms Bake
- **232** Cream Mushroom Pasta Bake
- **233** Tomato and Peas Korma
- **234** Rice with Kale and Lentils
- **235** Lentils and Tomato over Rice
- **236** Tofu with Cashews and Spinach
- **237** Kidney Bean and Tomato Pasta Soup
- **238** Peas and Carrot Fried Rice
- **239** Cabbage Noodles
- **240** Asparagus Peas Risotto with Cheese
- **241** Cheesy Spinach Ziti Bake
- **242** Chickpeas Pasta with Cheese
- **243** Cheesy Butter Pasta
- **244** Spaghetti with Cheese
- **245** White Bean and Tomato Chili
- **246** Baked Cheese Pizza
- **247** Rice and Quinoa Stuffed Pepper
- **248** Barley Butternut Squash Risotto
- **249** Barley and Mushroom Casserole
- **250** Corn and Black Bean Couscous
- **251** Roast Chickpeas and Zucchini
- **252** Lentils with Carrot and Turnip
- **253** Cauliflower with Chickpeas

- **254** Spinach and Mushroom Curry
- **255** Okra Corn and tomato Stew
- **256** Ratatouille with Tomato

❖ **<u>Desserts</u>**..123

- **257** Quick and Easy Pop Brownies
- **258** Chocolate Chip Cookies
- **259** Dutch Oven Brownies
- **260** Double Chocolate Cake
- **261** Cinnamon Rolls
- **262** Verry Berry Swirl
- **263** Upside Down Peach Cake
- **264** Cherry Grunt
- **265** S'Mores Cookie Cake
- **266** Dutch Baby Mixed Berry
- **267** Fruity Pebbles Doughnuts
- **268** Peach Cobbler
- **269** Chocolate Cake
- **270** Cheesecake
- **271** Mud Cake
- **272** Buttermilk Cherry Clafoutis
- **273** Pearl Tapioca Pudding
- **274** Butter Brownie Pudding
- **275** Baguette Butter Pudding
- **276** Strawberry and Oats Crumble
- **277** Peach Butter Cobbler
- **278** Buttery Chocolate Chip Cookie
- **279** Fluffy Butter Cheesecake
- **280** Rhubarb and Strawberry Oats Crisp.
- **281** Cherry and Almond Oats Crumble
- **282** Chocolate Bread Pudding
- **283** Brandy Banana Flambé
- **284** Apples with Caramel Sauce
- **285** Almond Butter Cake
- **286** Berry Cream Bake
- **287** Pears with Orange Pee
- **288** Apple and Cashew Toffee Crisp
- **289** Apple Cream Crumble
- **290** Apple and Cranberry Stew.
- **291** Marshmallow Casserole with Chocolate Chips
- **292** Red Wine Pears
- **293** Apple with Vanilla Ice Cream
- **294** Cookies and Cream Ice Cream Cake
- **295** Cherry Pie Cake
- **296** Raisins Rice Pudding
- **297** Chocolate and Walnuts Brownies
- **298** Butterscotch Crumble Cake
- **299** Pineapple Rings and Cherry Cake
- **300** Mango Sushi Rice

Breakfast recipes

1 Corned Beef Hash Browns

Serves 4 | Prep time 10 minutes | Cooking time 30 minutes

Ingredients

- 2 tablespoons olive oil
- 1 onion, diced
- 2 pounds frozen hash browns
- 1 teaspoon dried oregano Salt and pepper to taste
- 4 cups cooked corned beef, chopped
- 8 large eggs

Directions

- Warm the olive oil in the Dutch oven over medium heat.
- Add the diced onion and hash browns.
- Season with oregano and salt and pepper to taste.
- Cook for about 10 minutes. Remove from Dutch oven and set aside.
- Add the corned beef to the greasy Dutch oven and stir-cook for around 5 minutes until lightly browned.
- Stir the cooked hash browns and onions back in.
- Make 8 holes and crack an egg into each hole.
- Cover and cook for 20–25 minutes at 350°F (180°C).
- Serve warm.

2 Mushroom Frittata

Serves 4 | Prep time 10 minutes | Cooking time 30 minutes

Ingredients

- 2 tablespoons olive oil
- 12 green onions, chopped
- ½ pound cremini mushrooms, chopped Salt and pepper to taste
- 8 large eggs
- ½ cup grated Parmesan cheese

Directions

- Warm the olive oil in the Dutch oven over medium heat. Add the diced onion and chopped cremini mushrooms.
- Season with salt and pepper and cook for about 10 minutes.
- Whisk the eggs and Parmesan together and pour over the cooked mushrooms and onions.
- Cover and cook for 20–25 minutes at 350°F (180°C).
- Slice and serve.

3 Baked Oatmeal

Serves 4 | Prep time 10 minutes | Cooking time 35 minutes

Ingredients

- ¼ cup butter
- 2 cups blueberries
- 3 cups old fashioned oats
- 2½ cups whole milk
- 1 cup maple syrup
- 2 teaspoons baking powder Pinch of salt

Directions

- Warm the butter in the Dutch oven and spread the blueberries over the bottom.
- Sprinkle the old fashioned oats on top of the blueberries.
- Whisk the whole milk, maple syrup, baking powder, and salt in a medium bowl.
- Pour over the oats, making sure to cover them completely with the liquid.
- Cover and cook for 35–40 minutes at 350°F (180°C).
- Serve warm.

4 Dutch Oven Tater Tot Casserole

Serves 4 | **Prep time** 10 minutes | **Cooking time** 30 minutes

Ingredients

- 2 tablespoons olive oil
- 1 small onion, diced
- 1 pound ground beef Salt and pepper to taste
- 2 (10½-ounce) cans cream of mushroom soup
- 2 pounds frozen tater tots
- 2 cups grated cheddar cheese

Directions

- Warm the olive oil in the Dutch oven over medium heat. Add the diced onion and ground beef.
- Season with salt and pepper and cook for about 10 minutes.
- Stir in the cream of mushroom soup.
- Arrange the tater tots on top and bake uncovered for about 25 minutes at 350°F (180°C).
- Sprinkle in the cheese and bake for another 5–7 minutes.

5 Biscuits and Gravy

Serves 4 | **Prep time** 10 minutes | **Cooking time** 25 minutes

Ingredients

- 2 tablespoons olive oil
- 1 (16-ounce) can of refrigerated jumbo buttermilk biscuits
- 1 pound pork breakfast sausages
- ¼ cup flour
- 2¼ cups whole milk Salt and pepper to taste

Directions

- Preheat the Dutch oven to 350°F (180°C).
- Grease it well with olive oil or butter. Place the biscuits in the heated Dutch oven, cover, and bake for about 25 minutes.
- Remove the biscuits and set aside.
- Break up the breakfast sausage and cook for about 5 minutes, stirring frequently.
- Stir in the flour, mix well, and pour in the milk.
- Cook for about 5 minutes until a sauce forms. Season with salt and pepper.
- Serve the sausage gravy over the warm biscuits.

6 Breakfast Sausage Casserole

Serves 4 | **Prep time** 10 minutes | **Cooking time** 25 minutes

Ingredients

- 2 tablespoons olive oil
- 2 pounds pork breakfast sausage Salt and pepper to taste
- 2 pounds hash brown potatoes
- 8 large eggs
- ¼ cup heavy cream
- 2 cups shredded mozzarella cheese

Directions

- Preheat the oven to 350°F (180°C).
- Warm the olive oil in the Dutch oven over medium heat.
- Add the pork breakfast sausage, break it up with a wooden spoon, and cook for 5–7 minutes.
- Remove from the Dutch oven and set aside.
- Spread the hash browns evenly in the bottom of the Dutch oven. Season with salt and pepper.
- Gently brown the potatoes and place the cooked sausage on top of them.
- Whisk the eggs with a fork and spread them on top of the potatoes and sausages.

- Sprinkle with grated cheese.
- Cover and bake for 20–25 minutes.
- Serve warm.

7 Sausage-Hash Morning

Serves 6 | **Prep. time** 10–15 minutes | **Cooking time** 25 minutes

Ingredients

- 2 tablespoons olive oil
- ½ pound cooked Spanish chorizo or cooked Andouille sausage, finely chopped
- 4 celery ribs, finely chopped
- 1 medium onion, finely chopped 4 cloves garlic, minced
- ½ teaspoon salt
- ¼ teaspoon pepper
- 4 cups (2–3 medium) sweet potatoes, finely chopped

Directions

- Add the oil to the Dutch oven and heat it over medium-high heat.
- Add the sausage and stir-cook until evenly browned.
- Add the other ingredients and stir-cook.
- Simmer over low heat for about 15–20 minutes until the potatoes are cooked well, stirring occasionally.
- Serve warm.

8 Ham Cheese Omelet

Serves 1 | **Prep. time** 5 minutes | **Cooking time** 5–8 minutes

Ingredients

- 1 tablespoon butter
- 3 eggs
- 3 tablespoons water
- ⅛ teaspoon salt
- ⅛ teaspoon pepper
- ½ cup cooked ham, cubed
- ¼ cup Swiss cheese, shredded

Directions

- Add the butter to the Dutch oven and melt it over medium-high heat.
- Whisk the eggs in a bowl. Add the water, salt, and pepper. Mix well.
- Add the mixture to the Dutch oven and make a thin layer.
- Cook until the eggs are set, then stir without breaking the layer.
- Add the ham on one side and add the cheese on top.
- Fold the other side over the filling.
- Serve warm.

9 Classic Bacon and Eggs

Serves 8 | **Prep. time** 10–15 minutes | **Cooking time** 25 minutes

Ingredients

- 1-pound bacon strips, chopped
- 1¼ pounds hash brown potatoes, refrigerated
- 8 large eggs
- ½ cup half-and-half cream
- ½–1 teaspoon hot pepper sauce (optional)
- 2 cups cheddar-Monterey Jack cheese, shredded

Directions

- Heat the Dutch oven over medium-high heat.
- Add the bacon and cook until crisp. Drain over paper towels and set aside.
- Keep 2 tablespoons of the drippings in the oven. Discard the remaining drippings.
- Add the potatoes.
- Whisk the eggs and cream in a bowl. Add the pepper sauce. Mix well.
- Pour the mixture over the potatoes. Add the bacon and cheese on top.
- Cover the Dutch oven and cook for 20–25 minutes until the eggs are cooked well.
- Serve warm.

10 Breakfast Chicken Casserole

Serves 8 | Prep. time 10 minutes | Cooking time 25 minutes

Ingredients

- ¼ cup butter 12 eggs
- 1-quart whole milk
- 1½ teaspoons Italian herb blend 1 teaspoon salt
- ½ teaspoon pepper 8 slices bread, diced
- 2 chicken breasts, cooked and shredded
- 1-pound cheddar cheese, grated

Directions

- Spread the butter evenly over the inside surface of the Dutch oven.
- Heat the Dutch oven to 350°F (175°C).
- Beat the eggs in a bowl. Add the milk, Italian herbs, salt, and pepper. Mix well.
- Make a layer of bread in the Dutch oven. Cover it with the shredded chicken.
- Pour on the egg mixture.
- Cover the Dutch oven and cook for 20–25 minutes.
- Add the cheese, cover again, and cook for 10–15 minutes more until the eggs are well cooked.
- Serve warm.

11 Raisin and Almond Granola

Prep time: 5 minutes | Cook time: 25 minutes | Makes 3 cups

Ingredients

- 2 tablespoons butter
- 2 cups old-fashioned rolled oats
- 3 tablespoons pure maple syrup
- ½ cup raisins
- ½ cup toasted slivered almonds

Directions

- Preheat the oven to 325°F (163°C).
- In a Dutch oven over medium heat, melt the butter.
- Add the oats, and stir in the maple syrup. Cook, stirring often, for about 5 minutes, until the granola is well coated and golden.
- Bake for 20 minutes, uncovered, until the oats are golden brown.
- Remove from the oven and cool for 10 minutes, then transfer to a large bowl and stir in the raisins and almonds.
- Store in an airtight container.

12 Syrupy Pear Oatmeal

Prep. time: 10 minutes | Cooking time: 50 minutes | Serves 6

Ingredients

- Nonstick cooking spray
- 2 cups old-fashioned rolled oats
- 2½ cups milk, plus more for serving
- ⅓ cup pure maple syrup, plus more for serving
- 1 egg, beaten
- ¼ teaspoon salt
- 2 medium pears, peeled, cored, and chopped

Directions

- Preheat the oven to 350°F (180°C). Spray a Dutch oven generously with nonstick cooking spray.
- In a medium bowl, mix together the oats, milk, maple syrup, egg, salt, and pears.
- Spread the mixture evenly in the Dutch oven. Bake uncovered for 45 to 50 minutes or until most of the liquid is absorbed and the pears are tender.
- Remove from the oven and let cool with the lid on for 5 minutes. This will loosen the oatmeal so it doesn't stick to the pot.
- Serve topped with extra milk or maple syrup, if desired.

13 Apple Quinoa

Prep time: 10 minutes | **Cook time:** 30 minutes | **Serves** 4

Ingredients

- 2 tablespoons butter
- 2 medium apples, peeled, cored, and sliced
- ¼ cup light brown sugar
- 2 cups low-fat milk
- 1 cup quinoa, rinsed

Optional:

- Brown sugar Milk
- Ground cinnamon

Directions

- In a Dutch oven over medium-high heat, melt the butter. Add the apples and sugar. Cook for 5 to 10 minutes, until the apples are soft. Add the milk.
- Bring the milk to a boil, then add the quinoa and return to a boil.
- Reduce the heat to low, stir well, and cover. Simmer on low for 15 minutes, then uncover.
- Cook for about 5 more minutes, until the liquid is absorbed and the quinoa is tender and creamy. You can add more milk if you like a thinner consistency.
- Serve with brown sugar, milk, and cinnamon on top, if desired.

14 Butter Toast Casserole

Prep time: 10 minutes | **Cook time:** 50 minutes | **Serves** 6 to 8

Ingredients

- ¼ cup salted butter
- 1 (16-ounce / 454-g) loaf cinnamon swirl bread, cubed
- 6 eggs
- 2 cups whole milk
- ⅓ cup brown sugar

Directions

- Preheat the oven to 350°F (180°C).
- In a Dutch oven over low heat, melt the butter. Add the bread cubes, toss, and let the bread toast for 3 minutes.
- In a medium bowl, whisk together the eggs and milk. Pour the mixture evenly over the bread.
- Sprinkle the brown sugar over the casserole.
- Bake for about 45 minutes, uncovered, until a fork or toothpick inserted into the middle comes out clean and the top is golden brown.
- Let it cool for 10 minutes, then serve drizzled with maple syrup or dusted with powdered sugar, if desired.

15 Cheesy Broccoli Casserole

Prep time: 10 minutes | **Cook time:** 1 hour | **Serves** 6

Ingredients

- 2 cups whole milk 6 eggs
- 1 teaspoon salt
- ¼ teaspoon freshly ground black pepper 2 tablespoons extra-virgin olive oil
- 1 (16-ounce / 454-g) bag frozen broccoli florets or cuts
- ¾ loaf (12 ounces / 340 g) potato bread, cubed
- 3 cups shredded Cheddar cheese, divided

Directions

- Preheat the oven 350°F (180°C). In a medium bowl, whisk together the milk and eggs. Add the salt and pepper.
- In a Dutch oven over medium heat, heat the olive oil. Add the broccoli and sauté for 2 to 3 minutes, until defrosted. Stir in the bread cubes and 2 cups of the cheese. Mix well.
- Remove the pot from the stove, and pour the milk and egg mixture over the bread mixture. Let it sit for 10 minutes. Sprinkle with the remaining 1 cup of cheese.

- Bake in the oven, uncovered, for 50 to 60 minutes, until the casserole is puffed and golden brown. Cool before serving.

16 Cheese Egg Scramble with Salsa

Prep time: 10 minutes | **Cook time:** 20 minutes | **Serves** 6

Ingredients

- 2 tablespoons extra-virgin olive oil
- 1 red bell pepper, cored and chopped
- 1 small onion, chopped
- 12 eggs
- ¼ cup water
- 1½ cups shredded Cheddar cheese 1 to 2 cups salsa, for serving

Directions

- In a Dutch oven over medium-high heat, heat the olive oil. Add the pepper and onion. Sauté for about 10 minutes, until the vegetables are softened to your liking.
- While the veggies are cooking, in a medium bowl, beat together the eggs and water. Add the eggs to the Dutch oven. They will start to cook in about 30 seconds. Using a heatproof silicone spatula, push them to the center of the pan so they form large curds as they cook. Curds are soft but solid pieces and should not be overcooked. Remove the pot from the heat when there is barely any liquid in it but the eggs are soft. This should only take a few minutes.
- Sprinkle the cheese over the egg mixture and cover the pot. Allow the eggs to sit for a few minutes so the cheese melts.
- Serve the eggs with salsa on the side.

17 Spinach and Mushroom Ham Frittata

Prep time: 10 minutes | **Cook time:** 20 minutes | **Serves** 6

Ingredients

- 2 tablespoons extra-virgin olive oil
- 8 ounces (227 g) mushrooms, sliced
- 1 cup diced cooked ham
- 6 ounces (170 g) baby spinach, chopped
- 8 eggs
- 2 tablespoons water
- ½ teaspoon salt
- ½ teaspoon freshly ground black pepper
- 2 cups shredded Swiss cheese

Directions

- Preheat the oven to 400ºF (205ºC).
- In a Dutch oven over medium-high heat, heat the olive oil. Add the mushrooms and cook for 3 minutes, until they start to soften. Add the ham and spinach. Cook for another few minutes, until the spinach is wilted.
- In a large bowl, beat together the eggs and water. Mix in the salt, pepper, and cheese.
- Pour the egg mixture into the pot and cook, scraping the sides with a silicone spatula. When the eggs have started to cook, turn the heat down to low and cook for about 5 minutes, or until the eggs start to set.
- Transfer the pot to the oven. Bake for 8 to 10 minutes, uncovered, until the frittata is golden and puffy.
- Remove from the oven and let cool for 5 minutes with the lid on to prevent sticking.
- Loosen the edges with a spatula, cut into wedges, and serve.

18 Bacon and Cheese Potato

Prep time: 10 minutes | **Cook time:** 1 hour | **Serves** 6

Ingredients

- 8 ounces (227 g) bacon, chopped
- 2 pounds (907 g) Yukon Gold potatoes, cut into 1-inch cubes
- 1 cup shredded Cheddar cheese
- Salt and freshly ground black pepper, to taste

Directions

- Preheat the oven to 350°F (180°C).
- In a Dutch oven over medium heat, cook the bacon for 10 minutes or until slightly crispy. Drain most of the bacon fat, reserving a few spoonfuls in the pan. Add the potatoes and toss with the remaining bacon fat. Cook for 5 minutes, until the potatoes start to soften.
- Cover the pot and transfer it to the oven; bake for 35 minutes or until the potatoes are tender.
- Carefully remove the lid, top the potatoes with the cheese, and bake uncovered for 10 more minutes, until the cheese is bubbly. Season with salt and pepper, and serve.

19 Beef and Potato

Prep time: 15 minutes | **Cook time:** 40 minutes | **Serves** 6

Ingredients

- 3 cups peeled and cubed Yukon Gold potatoes
- 2 tablespoons extra-virgin olive oil
- 1 small green bell pepper, cored and chopped
- 2 cups cubed corned beef, either leftover or from the deli
- 2 scallions, white and green parts, chopped
- Salt and freshly ground black pepper, to taste

Directions

- Place the potatoes in a Dutch oven, and cover with cold water. Over high heat, bring to a boil. Turn the heat down to a simmer, and cook until the potatoes are slightly softened, about 5 minutes. Drain in a colander.
- In the Dutch oven over medium-high heat, heat the olive oil. Add the pepper and cook for 5 minutes or until softened.
- Add the drained potatoes, and spread them out in an even layer. Cook for about 10 minutes, until the bottoms are starting to brown. Flip them over, and add the corned beef and scallions. Stir with a wooden spoon to combine. Continue to cook for another 10 minutes, allowing the potatoes to evenly brown on the other side.
- Season with salt and pepper before serving.

20 Creamy Banana and Berry Oatmeal

Prep time: 5 minutes | **Cook time:** 3 minutes | **Serves** 4

Ingredients

- 4 cups water
- ¼ teaspoon salt
- 2 cups quick cooking oats
- ¼ cup creamy peanut butter
- 1 ripe banana, sliced
- 4 ounces (113 g) fresh berries of choice Chia seeds, for garnish
- Honey or brown sugar, for serving (optional)

Directions

- Boil the water. In a Dutch oven over high heat, combine the water and salt and bring to a boil.
- Cook the oats. Stir in the oats, reduce the heat to medium, and simmer for 2 minutes, stirring occasionally. Turn off the heat.
- Add the peanut butter and serve with fruit. Stir in the peanut butter. Ladle the oats into serving bowls and garnish with banana slices, berries, and chia seeds. Sweeten with honey or brown sugar (if using).

- Refrigerate leftover oatmeal for up to 2 days. Add a splash of milk when reheating for a creamy texture.

21 Roast Garlic Potato

Prep time: 10 minutes | **Cook time:** 40 minutes | **Serves** 4

Ingredients

- 3 large Yukon gold potatoes, cubed
- Pinch plus ½ teaspoon salt, divided
- 1 tablespoon olive oil
- 1 white onion, roughly chopped
- 1 orange bell pepper, roughly chopped
- 4 garlic cloves, smashed
- 1 teaspoon ground turmeric
- ½ teaspoon smoked paprika
- Freshly ground black pepper, to taste

Directions

- Preheat the oven to 425ºF (220ºC).
- Parboil the potatoes. Fill a Dutch oven with 1 inch of water. Bring the water to a boil over high heat, add the potatoes and a large pinch of salt, and boil for 3 minutes to cook the potatoes partially (a fork should pierce a piece of potato with some resistance). Place a colander in the sink and drain the potatoes. Let the potatoes sit for a few minutes to steam.
- Roast and serve. Place the Dutch oven over low heat and add the oil, onion, bell pepper, and garlic, tossing to coat. Cook for 2 minutes, stirring frequently to prevent browning. Add the potatoes. Stir well and season with the turmeric, smoked paprika, and the remaining ½ teaspoon of salt. Roast, uncovered, in the oven for 28 minutes. Taste and adjust the seasoning with salt and pepper as desired. Refrigerate leftovers for up to 3 days.

22 Syrupy Berry Toast Casserole

Prep time: 10 minutes | **Cook time:** 50 minutes | **Serves** 6

Ingredients

- Unsalted butter, for preparing the Dutch oven
- 1 (1-pound / 454-g) day-old loaf challah bread, sliced
- 4 large eggs
- 1¾ cups half-and-half
- ⅓ cup pure maple syrup, plus more for serving (optional)
- 1 tablespoon brandy
- 1 teaspoon grated orange zest
- ½ teaspoon salt
- 1½ cups frozen mixed berries

Directions

- Preheat the oven to 350ºF (180ºC). Generously coat the inside of a Dutch oven with butter.
- Assemble and bake the casserole. Arrange the bread slices in the Dutch oven, overlapping them. In a medium bowl, whisk the eggs, half-and-half, maple syrup, brandy, orange zest, and salt to combine. Add the berries. Pour the egg mixture over the bread, making sure to get the liquid between the slices. Cover the pot and bake for 40 minutes.
- Remove the lid and cook for 10 minutes more. Serve with maple syrup (if using). Refrigerate leftovers for up to 4 days.

23 Pecan and Banana Pudding

Prep time: 10 minutes | **Cook time:** 40 minutes | **Serves** 6

Ingredients

- 4 large eggs
- 1½ cups whole milk
- 1 teaspoon vanilla extract
- 8 thick slices bread, cut into cubes
- 3 medium bananas, peeled and diced
- ½ cup pecans
- ½ cup (packed) brown sugar 2 tablespoons dark rum
- 4 tablespoons unsalted butter, cut into small pieces

Directions

- In the Dutch oven, whisk together the eggs, milk, and vanilla. Add the bread cubes and stir to coat well. Let soak for at least 30 minutes.
- Preheat the oven to 400°F (205°C).
- In a medium bowl, stir together the bananas, pecans, brown sugar, and rum. Spread over the top of the bread mixture in the Dutch oven. Dot with the butter. Cover and bake for 35 to 40 minutes, until the pudding is cooked through, puffed, and golden on top.
- Serve warm.

24 Blueberry and Almond Cheese Cake

Prep time: 10 minutes | **Cook time:** 55 minutes | **Serves** 8

Ingredients

Cake:

- ¾ cup unsalted butter, at room temperature, plus additional for preparing the Dutch oven
- 2¼ cups all-purpose flour
- ¾ cup sugar
- ½ teaspoon fine sea salt
- 1 large egg
- ¾ cup buttermilk
- ½ teaspoon baking soda
- ½ teaspoon baking powder
- 1 teaspoon vanilla extract Frosting:
- 8 ounces (227 g) cream cheese, at room temperature
- ⅓ cup sugar
- 1 large egg
- 1 teaspoon vanilla extract

Assembling the Cake:

- 1¼ cups fresh blueberries, divided
- ½ cup sliced almonds
- ¾ cup powdered sugar, for a garnish

Make the Cake

- Preheat the oven to 350°F (180°C). Coat the inside of the Dutch oven with butter.
- In a large bowl, mix together the flour, butter, sugar, and salt until the mixture is crumbly. Remove 1 cup of the mixture and reserve for later.
- Add the egg, buttermilk, baking soda, baking powder, and vanilla to the remaining mixture in the bowl. Stir to mix, then transfer the mixture to the prepared pot, smoothing it out into an even layer.

Make the Frosting

- In a small bowl, using an electric mixer, cream together the cream cheese and sugar until smooth. Beat in the egg and vanilla.

Assemble the Cake

- Pour the mixture over the top of the cake, spreading it out in an even layer and leaving a 1½-inch rim around the edge of the cake.
- Scatter 1 cup of the blueberries over the cream cheese mixture.
- In a small bowl stir together the reserved flour mixture and the almonds. Sprinkle this mixture over the top of the cake.
- Bake, uncovered, in the preheated oven for 50 to 55 minutes, or until the center is set.
- Remove from the oven and let cool completely. Sprinkle the powdered sugar over the top and serve, garnished with the remaining ¼ cup of blueberries.

25 Pecan Cake

Prep time: 10 minutes | **Cook time:** 30 minutes | **Serves** 8

Ingredients

Butter or oil for preparing the Dutch oven

Filling:

- 2 tablespoons unsalted butter, softened
- ¾ cup (packed) brown sugar
- 1 large egg, lightly beaten
- ⅓ cup milk
- ⅓ cup chopped pecans

Cake Batter:

- 2 cups all-purpose flour
- ¾ cup sugar
- 1 tablespoon instant coffee
- 2½ teaspoons baking powder
- 1 teaspoon fine sea salt
- 2 large eggs
- ⅔ cup milk
- ½ cup vegetable oil

Directions

- Preheat the oven to 375°F (190°C) and coat the inside of the Dutch oven with butter or oil. Set aside.

Make the Filling

- In a medium saucepan, combine the butter, brown sugar, and egg and stir to mix well. Stir in the milk and cook, stirring, over medium heat, until the mixture thickens and becomes smooth, about 3 minutes. Stir in the pecans. Set aside.

Make the Cake Batter

- In a large bowl, whisk together the flour, sugar, coffee, baking powder, and salt.
- In a separate large bowl, beat together the eggs, milk, and oil. Add the flour mixture to the egg mixture and mix just until combined.
- Transfer the batter to the prepared Dutch oven and spread the filling mixture over the top. Use a knife to swirl the filling into the batter.
- Cover and bake for 25 to 30 minutes, until a tester inserted into the center comes out clean.

26 Glazed Apple Fritters

Prep time: 15 minutes | **Cook time:** 15 minutes | **Makes** 12 fritters

Ingredients

- 2 quarts peanut or vegetable oil, for frying

Glaze:

- 2 cups powdered sugar
- 1 teaspoon vanilla extract 1 taspoon cinnamon
- 2 tablespoons milk, plus additional if needed

Batter:

- 1 cup flour
- 1½ teaspoons baking powder
- ½ teaspoon salt
- 2 tablespoons sugar
- ½ to 1 teaspoon cinnamon (depending on how much you want)
- 1 large egg, beaten
- ½ cup plus 1 tablespoon milk
- 1½ cups (about 3 whole) peeled and diced apples

Directions

- Fill the Dutch oven about half full with oil and heat over medium- high heat until the oil registers 375°F (190°C) on a deep-fry thermometer. Line a plate with paper towels.

Make the Glaze

- While the oil is heating, make the glaze. In a medium bowl, stir together the powdered sugar, vanilla, cinnamon, and milk. If the glaze is too thick, add more milk, 1 teaspoon at a time, until the desired consistency is reached.

Make the Batter

- In a large bowl, whisk together the flour, baking powder, salt, sugar, and cinnamon. Stir in the egg and milk until incorporated. Stir in the apples and mix well.

Assemble the Fritters

- Once the oil is hot, drop the batter by the heaping tablespoonful into hot oil, cooking three or four fritters at a time, being careful not to crowd the pan. Cook until the fritters are deep golden brown, about 2 minutes per side. Using tongs, a slotted spoon, or a spider, transfer the cooked fritters to the prepared plate.
- Once all the fritters have been fried, drop each one separately into the glaze mixture, turn it over to coat the whole thing, and then transfer it to a wire rack set over a baking sheet or a piece of parchment. Let cool completely. Serve at room temperature

27 Mushroom and Potato Tomato Bake

Prep time: 10 minutes | **Cook time:** 30 minutes | Serves 4

Ingredients

- 4 portobello mushroom caps, stemmed
- 2 to 3 large Yukon gold potatoes, cut into thin wedges
- 1 pint cherry tomatoes
- 2 tablespoons olive oil
- 2 garlic cloves, minced
- Kosher salt and freshly ground black pepper, to taste
- 4 large eggs
- 2 tablespoons chopped flat-leaf parsley

Directions

- Preheat the oven to 425°F (220°C).
- In the Dutch oven, toss the mushroom caps, potatoes, and tomatoes with the olive oil and garlic. Season with salt and pepper. Spread the mixture out into an even layer in the pot, and roast in the preheated oven for about 15 minutes.
- Remove the pot from the oven and stir the vegetables. Arrange the mushroom caps so that they are gill-side up. Crack an egg into each cap, season with a little salt and pepper, and return the pot to the oven to bake for another 10 to 12 minutes, until the whites of the eggs are opaque and the yolk is still a bit runny.
- Serve immediately, garnished with parsley.

28 Potato Cheese Crust

Prep time: 10 minutes | **Cook time:** 45 minutes | Serves 8

Ingredients

- Butter for preparing the Dutch oven
- 2 medium sweet potatoes, peeled and sliced into very thin rounds, about 1/16 inch thick
- 6 large eggs
- ½ cup whole milk
- ¼ teaspoon kosher salt
- ¼ teaspoon freshly ground black pepper 4 scallions, thinly sliced
- 2 tablespoons chopped fresh oregano
- 4 ounces (113 g) crumbled Goat cheese

Directions

- Preheat the oven to 350°F (180°C) and coat the inside of the Dutch oven with butter.
- Create a crust with the sweet potato slices by arranging them, slightly overlapping one another, to cover the bottom of the Dutch oven. Trim some of the slices so that you can stand them on their flat edges to form a wall around the sides of the Dutch oven. You will end up with a bottom and sides that are several layers deep with sweet potato slices. Bake the crust for 20 minutes.
- Meanwhile, in a large bowl, whisk together the eggs, milk, salt, and pepper until combined. Stir in the scallions, oregano, and Goat cheese.
- Remove the crust from the oven and increase the oven temperature to 400°F (205°C).

- Pour the egg mixture into the crust and bake for about 25 minutes, until eggs are set in the middle. Let cool for a few

29 Cheese Potato Quiche with Salmon

Prep time: 20 minutes | **Cook time:** 40 minutes | Serves 6 to 8

Ingredients

- 4 medium russet potatoes (about 2 pounds / 907 g), peeled and grated
- 1 teaspoon kosher salt, divided
- ¾ teaspoon freshly ground black pepper, divided 2 tablespoons unsalted butter
- 2 tablespoons vegetable oil
- 6 large eggs, at room temperature
- 4 ounces (113 g) cream cheese, at room temperature
- 1¼ cups half-and-half
- 6 ounces (170 g) smoked salmon, chopped
- 2 tablespoons chopped fresh dill

Directions

- Preheat the oven to 350°F (180°C).
- In a large bowl, toss together the shredded potatoes, ½ teaspoon of salt, and ½ teaspoon of pepper. Transfer the potatoes to a dish towel, and wring out any excess liquid.
- In the Dutch oven, heat the butter with the oil over medium-high heat. Add the shredded potatoes, pressing them into the bottom and sides of the pot to form a crust. Continue to cook, pressing the crust into the pot, until the potatoes begin to brown, about 10 minutes. Remove from the heat.
- In a large bowl, whisk together the eggs and cream cheese until combined. Add the half-and-half, salmon, dill, the remaining ½ teaspoon of salt and ¼ teaspoon of pepper.
- Pour the egg mixture into the potato crust and bake for about 30 minutes, until the egg mixture is set and golden brown on top. Letcool for about 15 minutes before serving. Serve warm.

30 Bacon and Apple Cheese Frittata

Prep time: 15 minutes | **Cook time:** 25 minutes | Serves 6 to 8

Ingredients

- 6 slices bacon
- 12 large eggs
- 1½ cups shredded sharp Cheddar cheese, divided
- ½ teaspoon kosher salt
- ¼ teaspoon freshly ground black pepper
- 2 tablespoons unsalted butter
- 3 tart, crisp apples, like Granny Smith or Fuji, peeled, cored, and thinly sliced

Directions

- Preheat the oven to 450°F (235°C).
- In the Dutch oven, cook the bacon over medium-high heat until crispy, about 5 minutes. Drain the slices on paper towels and then crumble.
- In a large bowl, whisk the eggs, then whisk in 1 cup of Cheddar cheese, the salt, and the pepper.
- Drain the bacon fat from the Dutch oven, but don't wash the oven. Add the butter, and warm over medium heat until the butter is melted. Pour in the egg mixture, and sprinkle the crumbled bacon over the top.
- Arrange the apple slices on top of the egg mixture. Sprinkle the remaining ½ cup of Cheddar cheese over the top. Bake for about 20 minutes, until the eggs are set and the top is golden brown.
- Remove from the oven and run a knife or flexible spatula around the edge of the frittata to loosen it. Carefully invert the frittata onto a cutting board. Slice into wedges and serve warm or at room temperature.

31 Egg Cheese Chilaquiles with Salsa

Prep time: 5 minutes | Cook time: 25 minutes | Serves 6

Ingredients

- 2 tablespoons vegetable oil or olive oil
- 1 to 2 minced chipotle chiles, plus 1 to 2 tablespoons sauce from a can or jar of chipotles in adobo
- 6 cups (about 5 ounces / 142 g) thick-cut tortilla chips
- 3 cups fresh salsa
- 6 large eggs
- ¾ cup shredded Mexican Queso Fresco or Cheddar or Monterey Jack cheese

Optional Garnishes:

- 1 large avocado, sliced
- ½ cup sour cream
- ½ cup chopped cilantro
- ½ cup sliced scallions 1 lime, cut into wedges

Directions

- Preheat the oven to 375°F (190°C).
- In the Dutch oven, heat the oil over medium heat. Add the minced chipotle and sauce. Add the chips, breaking them up a bit in your hands. Cook, stirring, for 2 minutes, then add the salsa. Spread the mixture out into an even layer in the pot and make six wells or divots. Crack an egg into each well.
- Bake, uncovered, for 12 to 15 minutes, until the whites of the eggs are fully set and the yolks are still a bit runny.
- Sprinkle the cheese over the top and return to the oven to bake for about 5 minutes more, until the cheese has melted.

32 Creamy Mushroom Bread Pudding

Prep time: 15 minutes | Cook time: 1¾ hours | Serves 8

Ingredients

- 2 tablespoons olive oil 1 large shallot, minced
- 1 garlic clove, minced
- 1 pound (454 g) mushrooms, such as button, cremini, or shiitake, sliced
- 1 tablespoon fresh thyme leaves
- 2 teaspoons kosher salt, divided
- ½ cup dry white wine
- 9 large eggs, lightly beaten
- 2 cups whole milk
- 1 cup heavy cream
- 2 tablespoons Dijon mustard
- 1 teaspoon freshly ground black pepper
- 1 pound (454 g) day-old or toasted French bread, cut into cubes
- 1 (8-ounce / 227-g) wheel or wedge of Brie cheese, top and bottom rinds cut off and discarded, cut into ½-inch cubes
- ¼ cup freshly grated Parmesan cheese

Directions

- In the Dutch oven, heat the oil over medium-high heat. Add the shallot and cook, stirring frequently, until softened, about 3 minutes. Stir in the garlic and then the mushrooms, thyme, and ½ teaspoon of salt. Cook, stirring occasionally, until the mushrooms soften and begin to brown, about 8 minutes. Increase the heat to high and pour in the wine to deglaze the pot. Bring to a boil and cook, stirring and scraping up any browned bits from the bottom of the pot, until the liquid has evaporated, about 4 minutes.
- Remove from the heat and transfer the mushroom mixture to a bowl.
- In a large bowl, whisk together the eggs, milk, cream, mustard, remaining 1½ teaspoons of salt, and pepper.
- Add half of the bread cubes to the Dutch oven and spread them out into an even layer. Top with half of the mushroom mixture and half

- of the Brie. Top with the remaining bread cubes, the remaining mushroom mixture, and then the remaining Brie. Pour the egg mixture evenly over the top and press down gently to make sure that all the bread is saturated. Cover and refrigerate for 2 hours to overnight.
- Preheat the oven to 350°F (180°C). Let the bread pudding stand at room temperature for 15 minutes before baking.
- Bake the bread pudding, covered, for 60 minutes. Uncover, top with the Parmesan cheese, and bake for an additional 20 to 25 minutes, until the top is puffed and golden brown. Let cool for 10 to 15 minutes before serving.

33 Cheesy Zucchini Strata

Prep time: 20 minutes | **Cook time:** 1¼ hours | **Serves** 8

Ingredients

- 3 tablespoons olive oil
- 1 onion, diced
- 4 scallions, sliced
- 1 medium zucchini, diced
- 3 red or orange bell peppers, cut into thin strips
- 1 teaspoon kosher salt, plus a pinch
- ½ teaspoon freshly ground black pepper, plus a pinch
- 1 pound (454 g) day-old or toasted French or Italian bread, cut into cubes
- 2 cups (about 8 ounces / 227 g) crumbled Feta cheese 1 cup freshly grated Parmesan cheese
- 12 large eggs
- 2½ cups whole milk
- ½ cup pitted and drained Kalamata olives

Directions

- In the Dutch oven, heat the oil over medium-high heat. Add the onion and cook, stirring frequently, until softened, about 5 minutes. Reduce the heat to medium-low and add the scallions, zucchini, bell peppers, a pinch of salt, and a pinch of pepper. Cook, stirring, until the vegetables are tender and beginning to brown, about 10 minutes. Remove from the heat and transfer the vegetable mixture to a bowl.
- Arrange half of the bread cubes in the Dutch oven, spreading them out into an even layer. Top with half of the vegetables, half of the feta, and half of the Parmesan cheese. Repeat this step with the remaining bread cubes, vegetables, and cheese.
- In a large bowl, whisk together the eggs, milk, olives, remaining 1 teaspoon of salt, and remaining ½ teaspoon of pepper. Pour the egg mixture evenly over the bread, pressing down gently to make sure all the bread gets saturated. Cover and chill for at least 2 hours.
- Preheat the oven to 350°F (180°C) and let the strata stand at room temperature for 15 minutes before baking. Bake, uncovered, for about 60 minutes, or until the top of the strata is puffed and golden brown. Let stand for 10 to 15 minutes before serving.

34 Tomato Cheese Frittata

Prep time: 5 minutes | **Cook time:** 40 minutes | **Serves** 6

Ingredients

- 2 tablespoons olive oil
- 1 red bell pepper, seeded and diced
- 1 garlic clove, minced
- 10 large eggs
- 1 cup crumbled Feta cheese
- ¼ cup water
- 2 tablespoons bread crumbs
- ½ teaspoon kosher salt
- ¼ teaspoon freshly ground black pepper
- 1 tablespoon minced fresh oregano, plus additional leaves for garnish
- 1 tablespoon minced fresh basil, plus additional leaves for garnish
- ½ cup sliced black olives, such as Kalamata
- 1 large tomato, diced

Directions

- Preheat the oven to 350°F (180°C).
- In a Dutch oven, heat the oil over medium-high heat. Add the bell pepper and garlic and cook, stirring occasionally, until the peppers begin to soften, about 4 minutes.
- In a large bowl, whisk together the eggs, feta, water, bread crumbs, salt, pepper, oregano, and basil.
- Add the tomatoes and olives to the Dutch oven and stir to combine with the peppers. Poor the egg mixture over the vegetables, stirring. Transfer the Dutch oven to the preheated oven and bake until lightly browned around the edges and set in the middle, about 35 to 40 minutes. Slice into wedges and serve, garnished with the remaining basil and oregano, if desired.

35 Polenta Cheese Egg

Prep time: 10 minutes | **Cook time:** 45 minutes | **Serves** 6

Ingredients

- 4 cups water
- 1 cup heavy cream 1 teaspoon salt
- 2 cups quick-cooking grits or polenta
- 1 tablespoon unsalted butter
- cup shredded sharp Cheddar cheese 6 large eggs
- ½ teaspoon freshly cracked black pepper
- ¼ cup fresh chopped chives (optional)

Directions

- Preheat the oven to 350°F (180°C).
- In a Dutch oven, combine the water, heavy cream, and ½ teaspoon salt. Heat the mixture over high heat and allow to come to a rolling boil. Reduce heat to medium-low and slowly whisk in grits. Once all grits are added turn heat up to medium and cook, stirring constantly with a wooden spoon or heatproof spatula, 5 minutes, or until grits have absorbed all the liquid.
- Remove grits from heat and add butter and cheese. Stir until melted and completely combined.
- Place the cover on the Dutch oven and bake grits 15 minutes. Remove the pot from the oven and remove the lid. Carefully make 6 indentions in grits using back of large ladle or spoon. Crack 1 egg into each indention. Sprinkle eggs with remaining salt and pepper.
- Bake, uncovered, until egg whites have set but yolks are still slightly soft in the center, about 12 to 15 minutes. Garnish with fresh chives, if desired. Serve hot.

36 Sausage Cheese Casserole

Prep time: 15 minutes | **Cook time:** 55 minutes | **Serves** 8

Ingredients

- 2 pounds (907 g) breakfast sausage, mild, spicy, or a mixture of both
- 1 tablespoon unsalted butter
- 1 medium onion, peeled and chopped
- 1 (20-ounce / 567-g) bag shredded hash browns
- ½ teaspoon smoked paprika
- ½ teaspoon freshly cracked black pepper
- ¼ teaspoon salt
- ½ cup shredded Pepper Jack cheese
- ½ cup shredded Cheddar cheese 4 large eggs
- 1 cup whole milk
- ½ cup heavy cream

Directions

- Heat oven to 350°F (180°C).
- Heat a Dutch oven over medium-high heat. Add sausage and cook, breaking sausage into crumbles, until cooked through and browned, about 8 to 10 minutes. Remove sausage from the Dutch oven and drain off all but 2 tablespoons of sausage drippings.
- Add butter to the Dutch oven and once it foams add onion. Cook, stirring constantly, until onion is translucent, about 3 minutes. Remove the pot from heat and add cooked sausage, hash browns, paprika, pepper, salt, and both cheeses. Stir to combine.

- In a medium bowl beat eggs with milk and cream. Pour egg mixture evenly over hash brown mixture.
- Bake 30 to 40 minutes, or until casserole is golden brown on top and the center of casserole is set. Cool 5 minutes before serving.

37 Juicy Cranberry and Raisin Oat

Prep time: 10 minutes | **Cook time:** 15 minutes | **Serves** 8

Ingredients

- 8 cups filtered water
- 2 cups steel-cut oats
- ¼ teaspoon salt
- 1 cup orange juice
- ½ cup dried cranberries
- ¼ cup golden raisins
- Maple syrup or brown sugar, for garnish

Directions

- In a Dutch oven add water, oats, and salt. Bring mixture to a boil and cook 1 minute, then turn off heat and cover with the lid. Let stand overnight in the refrigerator.
- In a microwave-safe bowl combine orange juice, dried cranberries, and raisins. Microwave 1 minute then cover and refrigerate overnight.
- The next morning drain the dried fruit and discard liquid. Remove lid from oats and stir in soaked fruit.
- Place the Dutch oven over medium heat and bring oats to a boil. Turn off heat and add maple syrup or brown sugar. Enjoy warm or at room temperature.

Soups, Stews, and Chilis Recipes

38 Black Bean and Corn Chili

Prep time: 9 minutes | **Cook time:** 21 minutes | **Serves** 2

Ingredients

- 2 to 3 tablespoons vegetable oil
- ½ small onion, diced
- 2 medium garlic cloves, minced
- ½ small red or green bell pepper, seeded and diced Kosher salt, to taste
- 2 tablespoons ancho chili powder 1 teaspoon ground cumin
- ½ teaspoon dried oregano
- ½ cup diced canned tomatoes with their juice
- 1 small chipotle chile in adobo, minced, plus 2 teaspoons of the adobo sauce
- 1 (14-ounce / 397-g) can black beans, drained and rinsed 1 cup frozen corn kernels, thawed
- ½ avocado, diced
- ¼ cup shredded Monterey Jack cheese 2 scallions, diced

Directions

- Place the Dutch oven over medium heat. Add enough oil to coat the bottom of the pot and heat until the oil shimmers. Add the onion, garlic, and bell pepper and season with salt. Cook, stirring, for 4 to 6 minutes, or until browned slightly.
- Stir in the ancho chili powder, cumin, and oregano and cook for a minute or so, until the spices become fragrant. Add the tomatoes and bring to a simmer, scraping up any browned bits from the bottom of the pot.
- Stir in the chipotle, black beans, and corn. Bring to a simmer and cover. Cook for about 15 minutes then uncover the pot. Continue to simmer until the sauce thickens. Taste and adjust the seasoning.
- Ladle into bowls and top with the avocado, cheese, and scallions.

39 Beer Beef Chili

Prep time: 20 minutes | **Cook time:** 70 minutes | **Serves** 2

Ingredients

- 1 pound (454 g) beef shoulder (chuck), trimmed of fat and cut into ¾- inch cubes, divided
- Kosher salt, to taste
- 2 to 3 tablespoons olive or vegetable oil
- 1 medium onion, sliced thin
- 2 garlic cloves, minced
- 2 tablespoons ancho chili powder
- 1 teaspoon ground cumin
- ½ teaspoon dried oregano
- ¼ teaspoon freshly ground black pepper
- ½ cup mild beer, such as lager
- 1½ cups low-sodium beef or chicken stock
- ¼ cup tomato sauce
- 1 chipotle chile in adobo sauce, minced, plus 2 teaspoons adobo sauce

Directions

- Liberally season the beef cubes with salt. Place the Dutch oven over medium heat.
- Add enough oil to coat the bottom of the pot and heat until the oil shimmers. Add half the beef cubes in a single layer and cook for 2 to 3 minutes, without stirring, until the first side is browned. Turn and brown at least one other side of the cubes. Transfer the beef to a plate.
- Add the onion and garlic and cook, stirring, for 4 to 6 minutes, or until browned slightly. Stir in the ancho chili powder, cumin, oregano, and pepper and cook for a minute or so, until the spices become fragrant.
- Pour in the beer and bring to a simmer, scraping up any browned bits from the bottom of the pot. Reduce by about half, then add the stock, tomato sauce, chipotle, and adobo sauce. Add the seared and raw beef and stir to coat. Bring the liquid to a simmer.

- Cover and reduce the heat to simmer over medium-low. Cook for 45 to 60 minutes, stirring occasionally.
- After 45 minutes, check a piece of beef. The beef should be tender enough to cut with a fork; if not, cook for another 15 to 20 minutes.
- When the beef is tender, uncover and let it cool for 15 minutes to let any fat rise to the surface. Spoon or blot it off. Bring the chili back to a simmer to reduce the sauce slightly, until it's the consistency of gravy. Serve with chopped onions, grated cheese, or sour cream, if desired.

40 Pork and Bean Chili

Prep time: 20 minutes | Cook time: 70 minutes | Serves 2

Ingredients

- 1 large or 2 small Anaheim or other mild green chiles, seeded and cut into 3 or 4 fairly flat pieces
- 1 jalapeño pepper, seeded and cut into 3 or 4 fairly flat pieces 1 to 2 tablespoons vegetable or olive oil
- ⅔ cup frozen corn kernels, thawed
- Kosher salt, to taste
- ½ small onion, coarsely chopped
- 1 small carrot, peeled and coarsely chopped 1 cup low-sodium chicken stock
- 1 teaspoon ground cumin
- 2 teaspoons ancho chili powder
- ¼ teaspoon chipotle powder or cayenne pepper
- ½ pound (227g) boneless country-style pork shoulder ribs, trimmed of fat and cut into bite-size pieces
- (14-ounce / 397-g) can cannellini beans, drained and rinsed 2 tablespoons chopped cilantro leaves
- 2 tablespoons sour cream

Directions

- Set the broiler on high, with the rack in the highest position. Place the Anaheim chiles and jalapeño skin-side up on a broiler pan or baking sheet, and broil until they're blackened and their skin puffs. Place in a bowl and cover for 10 to 15 minutes. Peel the skin off and dice.
- While the chiles cool, place the Dutch oven over medium-high heat. Add enough oil to coat the bottom of the pot and heat until the oil shimmers. Add the corn in a single layer and let it cook without stirring for 4 to 5 minutes, or until the corn starts to char. Sprinkle with salt and stir quickly. Pat the corn into a single layer again and let that side brown, 2 to 3 minutes. Turn the heat down to medium.
- Add the onion and carrot and cook for 2 to 3 minutes, or until the onions just start to brown. Add the chicken stock and stir, scraping the bottom of the pot to get up any browned bits.
- Season with salt, and add the cumin, ancho chili powder, and chipotle or cayenne. Bring to a simmer over medium-low heat and add the pork. Cover and cook for 30 minutes, adjusting the heat to keep the mixture at a simmer. Add the beans and cook for another 15 to 20 minutes, or until the pork is tender. Ladle into bowls and garnish with the sour cream and cilantro.

41 Pork and Black Bean Chili

Prep time: 10 minutes | Cook time: 1¾ hour | Serves 6

Ingredients

- 2 tablespoons olive oil
- 2 pounds (907 g) boneless pork shoulder
- 2 teaspoons salt
- 1 teaspoon dried oregano
- 1 teaspoon ground cumin 1 teaspoon onion powder
- 1 teaspoon ground coriander 1 cup salsa verde
- ½ cup sour cream
- 1 (4-ounce / 113-g) can diced green chiles 1 cup filtered water
- 1 (15-ounce / 425-g) can black beans, drained and rinsed

Directions

- Cook the pork. Cut the pork shoulder into cubes, roughly 1 inch thick. In a Dutch oven over medium heat, warm the olive oil. Add the pork and season with the salt. Sear for 3 minutes to brown the meat on all sides, turning it with a spatula.
- Add the spices and other ingredients, then simmer. Stir in the oregano, cumin, onion powder, and coriander. Cook for 30 seconds, until aromatic. Pour in the salsa verde, sour cream, green chiles, and water. Stir to combine, scraping along the bottom of the pot with a wooden spoon or spatula to release any browned bits. Cover the pot and reduce the heat to medium-low. Simmer the soup for 1½ hours or until the pork is tender and shreds easily with a fork.
- Add the black beans, adjust seasonings, and serve. Add the black beans and bring the soup back to a simmer. Taste and adjust the seasoning as desired. Ladle into bowls and garnish with cilantro (if using) and cheese (if using). Refrigerate leftovers for up to 4 days.

42 Turkey Bean Chili with Salsa

Prep time: 10 minutes | **Cook time:** 15 minutes | **Serves** 6

Ingredients

- 2 tablespoons olive oil 1 white onion, chopped
- 2 tablespoons chipotle powder 1 tablespoon ground cumin
- 1 tablespoon garlic powder 1 teaspoon salt
- 1 pound (454 g) ground turkey
- 1 (24-ounce / 680-g) jar chunky mild salsa
- 2 (15-ounce / 425-g) cans red kidney beans, drained and rinsed

Directions

- Sauté the vegetables. In a Dutch oven over medium heat, warm the olive oil. Add the onion and cook for 4 minutes, stirring occasionally, until soft. Stir in the chipotle powder, cumin, garlic powder, and salt. Cook for 1 minute.
- Cook the turkey. Add the ground turkey. Cook for about 3 minutes, stirring to break up the meat, until the juices begin to release.
- Finish the chili. Pour the salsa over the turkey and stir to combine, scraping up any browned bits from the bottom of the Dutch oven. Add the kidney beans, cover the pot, and simmer for 5 minutes. Refrigerate leftovers, which taste even better the next day, for up to 3 days.

43 Beans Chili with Salsa

Prep time: 10 minutes | **Cook time:** 15 minutes | **Serves** 4

Ingredients

- 2 tablespoons olive oil 1 white onion, chopped
- 2 tablespoons chili powder
- 1 tablespoon ground cumin
- 1 tablespoon garlic powder
- 1 teaspoon salt
- ½ teaspoon ground coriander
- 1 (24-ounce / 680-g) jar chunky mild salsa
- 1 (15-ounce/ 425-g) can red kidney beans, drained and rinsed
- 1 (15-ounce/ 425-g) can black beans, drained and rinsed
- 1 (15-ounce/ 425-g) can pinto beans, drained and rinsed Chopped fresh cilantro, for garnish (optional)
- Shredded cheese of choice, for serving (optional)

Directions

- Sauté the vegetables. In a Dutch oven over medium heat, heat the olive oil until hot. Add the onion and cook for 3 minutes, stirring occasionally. Stir in the chili powder, cumin, garlic powder, salt, and coriander. Cook for 1 minute.
- 2. Stew the beans. Pour the salsa over the vegetables and stir to combine, scraping up any browned bits from the bottom of the pot. Add the kidney, black, and pinto beans.

- Cover the Dutch oven and simmer for 7 minutes.
- Serve as-is or top with cilantro (if using) and cheese (if using). Refrigerate leftovers for up to 3 days.

44 Turkey Bean and Corn Chili

Prep time: 15 minutes | Cook time: 1 to 1½ hour | Serves 6 to 8

Ingredients

- 1 tablespoon vegetable oil
- 2 strips bacon, diced
- 1 onion, chopped
- 1 red bell pepper, diced 3 garlic cloves, chopped
- 1½ pounds (680g) ground turkey
- ¼ cup chili powder
- 2 teaspoons ground cumin 2 teaspoons dried oregano
- Salt and freshly ground black pepper, to taste 1 (15-ounce / 425-g) can crushed tomatoes
- 1½ cups low-sodium chicken or vegetable broth or stock
- 1 (15-ounce / 425-g) can pinto beans, drained and rinsed 1 (15-ounce / 425-g) can sweet corn

Directions

- Over medium heat in a Dutch oven, heat the vegetable oil. Add the bacon and cook until the fat is rendered and the bacon begins to get crispy.
- Add the onion and red pepper. Sauté, stirring often, until the vegetables are softened. Add the garlic and stir for about 2 minutes, or until the flavor is released.
- Add the ground turkey and stir until no longer pink, gently breaking up the meat with the back of a spoon. Stir in the chili powder, cumin, and oregano. Season with salt and pepper. Stir in the tomatoes, followed by the broth. Bring the mixture to a boil, then reduce the heat to simmer.
- Simmer, uncovered, for 45 minutes to 1 hour, stirring occasionally.
- Carefully fold in the pinto beans and the corn, and simmer for 15 minutes.

45 Beef and Cabbage Soup

Serves 10 | Prep time 15 minutes | Cooking time 2 hours

Ingredients

- 1 pound beef stew meat, cut into ¾-inch pieces Salt and pepper
- 2 tablespoons olive oil
- 6 cups beef stock, divided
- 1 medium-sized green cabbage, shredded 6 tomatoes, crushed
- 1 large onion, diced 3 cups of water
- 2 cloves garlic, minced
- 1 ½ teaspoon Italian seasoning

Directions

- Pat the beef dry with paper towels and season with salt and pepper.
- Add oil to a large Dutch oven and sear the meat over medium heat on all sides until well browned. Do not overcrowd the oven, work in batches if needed. Place the browned beef on a plate.
- Add about half of the beef stock and bring to a boil. Stir and scrape the brown bits. Return the beef to the Dutch oven.
- Add the cabbage, tomatoes, onion, remaining beef stock, water, garlic, Italian seasoning.
- Bring to a boil over medium-high heat.
- Decrease the heat to medium-low and let cook for 2 hours until the beef is tender and cabbage soft, taking care of stirring a few times.
- Taste and adjust seasoning with salt and pepper.

46 Quinoa Chickpea Corn Soup

Serves 6-8 | **Prep. time** 10 minutes | **Cooking time** 25 minutes

Ingredients

- 1 tablespoon olive oil
- 1 medium red onion, chopped
- 1–2 jalapeño peppers, seeded and chopped (optional)
- 4 cloves garlic, minced
- ¼ teaspoon pepper
- 1 cup red quinoa, rinsed
- 2 quarts vegetable broth
- 3 medium tomatoes, chopped 1 cup fresh or frozen corn
- 2 (15-ounce) cans unsalted chickpeas or garbanzo beans, rinsed and drained
- Chopped fresh cilantro (optional)

Directions

- Add the oil to the Dutch oven and heat it over medium-high heat.
- Add the onion, jalapeño, and garlic. Stir-cook for 3–5 minutes until softened and tender.
- Mix in the quinoa and broth.
- Bring to a boil.
- Reduce heat to low and simmer for about 10 minutes until the quinoa is tender, stirring occasionally.
- Mix in the tomatoes, corn, chickpeas, and continue cooking until warm through, about 10 minutes.
- Serve warm with chopped cilantro on top if desired.

47 Sweet Potato Soup

Serves 8 | **Prep. time** 20 minutes | **Cooking time** 1 hour 30 minutes

Ingredients:

- 4 sweet potatoes, peeled and diced
- 1 onion, minced
- 2 (14-ounce) can of light coconut milk
- 2 cup vegetable broth
- 4 cloves garlic, minced 2 teaspoon dried basil Salt and pepper

Directions:

- Place all the ingredients in the Dutch oven and stir.
- Cover and cook for 1 hour 30 minutes, or until the sweet potatoes are tender.
- Puree with an immersion blender until the soup is smooth.

48 Pork and Bean Soup

Serves 8 | **Prep. time** 15 minutes | **Cooking time** 55 minutes

Ingredients

- 1-quart water
- 3 cups pork roast, cooked and cubed
- 1 (15-ounce) can navy beans, rinsed and drained
- 2 medium potatoes, peeled and chopped
- 1 large onion, chopped
- 1 (14½-ounce) can Italian diced tomatoes with juices
- ½ cup unsweetened apple juice
- ½ teaspoon salt
- ½ teaspoon pepper
- Minced fresh basil (optional)

Note: Cook in two batches if needed; or halve the ingredients to make the soup for 4–5 people.

Directions

- Add the water, pork roast, beans, potatoes, and remaining ingredients to the Dutch oven.
- Bring to a boil.
- Reduce heat to low, cover, and simmer, stirring occasionally, for 40–45 minutes until the roast is cooked to perfection and veggies are tender and crisp.
- Serve warm with minced basil on top.

49 Tomato Cream Soup with Basil

Serves 6 | **Prep time** 15 minutes | **Cooking time** 2 hours

Ingredients:

- 3 large carrots, peeled
- 2 celery stalks
- 2 medium onions
- 4 whole cloves garlic, peeled
- 4 (28-ounce) cans whole peeled tomatoes
- 1-quart chicken broth, low sodium
- ½ cup fresh basil leaves, roughly chopped, more for serving Salt and pepper to taste
- ⅓ Cup heavy cream

Directions:

- Dice the carrots, celery, and onions.
- Combine the carrots, celery, onions, garlic, tomatoes, chicken broth, and basil in the Dutch oven.
- Bring to a boil, cover, reduce heat to low, and cook for 2 hours or until the vegetables are soft and tender. The tomatoes should be soft and easy to puree.
- Use an immersion blender to puree.
- Add the cream and blend it in. Season to taste with salt and pepper.
- Serve garnished with more basil leaves, if desired.

50 Chicken Bean Barley Soup

Serves 8 | **Prep time** 15 minutes | **Cooking time** 3 hours

Ingredients:

- 2 strips thick-cut bacon 1 large onion, diced
- 2 cloves garlic, minced
- 1 cup dried barley, soaked overnight, rinsed, and drained
- 1 ½ cups dried navy beans, soaked overnight, rinsed and drained 6 cups low sodium chicken broth
- 4 cups of water
- 1 pound spinach, washed and roughly chopped
- 1 small rotisserie chicken, skin removed, and meat shredded Salt and pepper to taste

Directions:

- Brown the bacon in the Dutch oven over medium heat. When crisp, drain and transfer to a plate lined with paper towels. Set aside.
- Drain off the drippings, leaving about 1 tablespoon. Sauté the onion and garlic until tender.
- Place the barley and beans in the Dutch oven.
- Pour in the broth and water, and stir.
- Bring to a boil over medium-high heat. Cover, reduce heat to medium-low, and cook 60-75 minutes until beans and barley are tender. Check a few times and add more water if needed.
- Add the spinach and chicken continue cooking for another 20 minutes.
- Crumble the reserved bacon. Serve warm with some of the bacon on top.

51 Pea and Chicken Rice Soup

Prep time: 7 minutes | **Cook time:** 18 minutes | **Serves** 2

Ingredients:

Ginger-Scallion Sauce:

- 3 tablespoons peeled and minced ginger root (2 to 3-inch piece) 1 cup chopped scallions (about ½ bunch)
- ¼ teaspoon hoisin sauce
- ½ teaspoon sherry vinegar or rice vinegar
- ½ teaspoon soy sauce
- 1 tablespoon canola or other neutral vegetable oil

Soup:

- 1 to 2 tablespoons vegetable oil 1 tablespoon finely minced garlic
- 1 tablespoon finely minced fresh ginger 2 tablespoons finely minced onion
- 3 cups low-sodium chicken stock
- ¼ teaspoon kosher salt
- ¼ cup long-grain rice
- 1 small carrot, peeled and cut into thin coins

- 1 small boneless chicken breast, cut into bite-size chunks
- 2 to 3 ounces (57 to 85 g) sugar snap peas or snow peas, strings removed
- ½ cup frozen pearl onions, thawed
- 2 to 3 tablespoons ginger-scallion sauce

Directions:

- Place the ginger in the bowl of a small food processor and process for 30 seconds or so. Add the scallions and continue to process for a minute until the vegetables form a coarse paste (don't over-process, or the scallions can become bitter).
- Add the hoisin, vinegar, soy sauce, and oil, and process until the mixture is smoother but not completely puréed. If the mixture is too thick, add a teaspoon or two of water to thin it out. (If you don't have a small food processor, mince the ginger and scallions as fine as possible and stir in the rest of the ingredients.)
- Place the Dutch oven over medium heat. Add enough oil to coat the bottom of the pot and heat until the oil shimmers. Add the garlic, ginger, and onion and cook, stirring, until fragrant, about 2 minutes. Add the chicken stock and salt and bring to a simmer.
- Pour in the rice and cover the pot. Cook for 7 minutes.
- Add the carrot and chicken breast. Simmer for 5 minutes.
- Add the peas and pearl onions, and simmer for another 3 minutes. Taste the rice; it should be soft but not mushy. If it's still hard in the center of a grain, simmer until tender. Adjust the seasoning, adding more salt if necessary.
- Ladle the soup into two bowls and add about a tablespoon of ginger-scallion sauce to each bowl.

52 Tomato Soup with Pancetta

Prep time: 20 minutes | **Cook time:** 40 to 50 minutes | **Serves** 2

Ingredients:

- 1 tablespoon olive oil
- 2 to 3 ounces (57 to 85 g) pancetta, diced 1 small onion, sliced thin
- 1 garlic clove, minced
- 5 to 6 celery stalks, sliced into ¼-inch pieces (about 2 cups) Kosher salt, to taste
- ⅓ cup dry white wine
- 2½ cups low-sodium chicken stock
- ¼ teaspoon red pepper flakes
- ⅔ cup diced tomatoes with their juice (about half a 15-ounce / 425-g can)
- Freshly ground black pepper, to taste
- ¼ cup celery leaves, roughly chopped (optional)

Directions:

- Place the Dutch oven over medium heat. Add enough oil to coat the bottom of the pot and heat until the oil shimmers. Add the pancetta and stir to break it up. Cook, stirring occasionally, until the pancetta crisps and renders most of its fat. If you like, remove a couple of tablespoons of the cooked pancetta and set aside to garnish the soup.
- Add the onion, garlic, and celery to the Dutch oven and stir to coat the vegetables with the fat in the pot. Season with salt and lower the heat to medium-low. Cook, stirring occasionally, until the vegetables are softened slightly, about 4 minutes.
- Add the wine and bring to a boil. Cook until most of the wine has evaporated and then add the chicken stock, red pepper flakes, and tomatoes. Adjust the heat to keep the soup at a low simmer, and cover.
- Cook for 40 to 50 minutes, or until the celery is very tender. Season with salt and pepper. Garnish with the reserved pancetta and celery leaves (if using).

53 Sausage and Kale Bean Soup

Prep time: 15 minutes | Cook time: 25 minutes | Serves 2

Ingredients:

- 1 tablespoon olive oil
- ½ pound (227g) mild or spicy Italian-style chicken sausage, casings removed
- ½ small onion, chopped (about ½ cup) 1 medium garlic clove, minced
- 3 cups low-sodium chicken stock 1 sprig fresh rosemary
- 1 (14-ounce / 397-g) can cannellini beans, drained and rinsed
- ½ cup tiny shells, macaroni, or other very small pasta
- ½ small bunch kale, tough stems removed and cut into ½-inch ribbons (about 3 cups)
- 1 teaspoon red wine vinegar
- ¼ cup grated Parmigiano-Reggiano or similar cheese

Directions:

- Place the Dutch oven over medium heat. Add the olive oil and heat until it shimmers. Add the sausage, breaking it up into bite- size pieces. Cook until the pieces are browned on the outside, about 3 minutes.
- Add the onion and cook, stirring, for a minute or two, just until the onion pieces begin to separate. Add the garlic and cook for a couple of minutes longer, or until fragrant.
- Add the chicken stock and rosemary and bring to a simmer. Stir in the beans, pasta, and kale and bring back to a simmer. Cook, uncovered, for 20 minutes, stirring occasionally. Check the pasta to make sure it's done, and stir in the vinegar. Taste and adjust the seasoning, adding more vinegar if the soup needs brightening.
- Ladle into bowls and serve with grated Parmigiano-Reggiano.

54 Mushroom Cream Soup

Prep time: 20 minutes | Cook time: 25 minutes | Serves 2

Ingredients:

- 1 pound (454 g) cremini or white button mushrooms
- 3 tablespoons butter, cut into 3 pieces
- Kosher salt, to taste
- ¼ cup dried porcini mushrooms
- 1 large shallot, sliced thin
- ⅓ cup dry or medium dry sherry
- 2½ cups low-sodium vegetable stock
- ¼ cup heavy cream
- Freshly ground black pepper, to taste 1 tablespoon minced chives

Directions:

- Wash the mushrooms and trim the stems, reserving them for later. Quarter the mushrooms if small to medium; cut into eighths if they are large. Pile the mushrooms in the Dutch oven and cover with just enough water to make the mushrooms float. Add the butter chunks and sprinkle generously with salt. Place the pot over high heat and bring to a boil.
- Continue boiling until the water has all evaporated and you can hear the mushrooms begin to sizzle; this can take from 12 to 20 minutes, depending on the amount of water and pan size.
- While the mushrooms cook, measure out ½ cup of the hottest possible tap water into a measuring cup and add the dried porcini mushrooms. Let them soak for at least 15 minutes, pushing them down into the water a few times to make sure they soak and don't float.
- When the mushrooms in the Dutch oven start to sizzle, turn them a few times with a spatula to brown them on several sides. Remove about half of them and set aside.
- Add the shallot and the reserved mushroom stems. Sprinkle with salt and cook, stirring occasionally, until softened, about 5 minutes. Add the sherry and bring to a strong simmer.

- Cook, stirring occasionally, for 5 to 7 minutes, until most of the wine evaporates.
- While the sherry reduces, strain the dried mushrooms from the hot water, filtering out any grit or sand that may accumulate at the bottom, and discard the grit and mushrooms. Add the mushroom water, vegetable stock, and about half the reserved cooked mushrooms, and simmer, covered, for 20 minutes.
- If you have an immersion blender, blend the soup until the texture is as smooth as you like it. (If you don't have an immersion blender, pour the mixture into a blender or food processor and pulse to get the desired texture. Pour the soup back into the Dutch oven.) Add the remaining mushrooms and the cream. Heat to a simmer, season with black pepper, and add half the chives. Taste and adjust the seasoning.
- Ladle into bowls and garnish with the remaining chives.

55 Carrot Soup

Prep time: 20 minutes | **Cook time:** 25 minutes | **Serves 2**

Ingredients:

- 1 tablespoon unsalted butter
- ½ small onion, coarsely chopped (about ⅓ cup)
- 4 large garlic cloves, smashed and peeled
- ½ pound (227g) carrots, peeled and cut into coins
- ¼ teaspoon kosher salt, plus more for seasoning
- ¼ cup dry or medium dry sherry
- 2 cups low-sodium vegetable broth
  ⅛ teaspoon ground cumin (or more for seasoning) Pinch cayenne pepper
  ¼ cup fresh or pasteurized carrot juice
  1 tablespoon heavy cream

Directions:

- Melt the butter in the Dutch oven over medium-low heat. When the butter stops foaming, add the onion and garlic and cook, stirring, for a few minutes until the onion pieces separate and begin to soften. Add the carrots and salt. Cook for about 6 minutes, stirring until the vegetables begin to brown.
- Turn the heat to medium-high and add the sherry. Bring it to a boil and cook for a couple of minutes, until mostly evaporated. Add the vegetable broth and bring to a simmer. Cover and cook for 25 to 30 minutes, or until the carrots are very soft.
- Transfer the soup to a blender and carefully purée until smooth, working in batches if necessary. You can also use an immersion blender, although in my experience it doesn't get the soup as smooth as I like. Return to the Dutch oven and place back over low heat.
- Add the cumin, cayenne, carrot juice, and cream and bring to a simmer. Adjust the seasoning, adding salt as necessary.

56 Collard Green White Bean Soup with Sausages

Serves 6 | **Prep time** 10 minutes | **Cooking time** 2-2 ½ hours

Ingredients:

- 1 pound dried white beans, soaked overnight, rinsed, and drained Water
- Salt and pepper
- ½ pound Cajun Andouille sausages, sliced 1/2 large onion, chopped
- 2 stalks celery, chopped 4 sprigs fresh thyme
- 8 cups chicken broth, low-sodium
- 8 cups collard greens, leaves only, cut into 1-inch pieces 1 tablespoon red wine vinegar

Directions:

- Place the beans in a Dutch oven and cover with water. Season with salt and pepper.
- Bring to a boil over high heat. Reduce heat to medium-low, cover, and cook for 45-50 hours or until the beans are tender. Remove from heat and drain the water.
- Add the sausages, onion, celery, thyme, and chicken broth. Bring a boil over high heat, reduce heat to low, cover and cook for 30 minutes over medium-low heat.

- Remove the thyme stems and drop in the collard greens. Cover and cook 15-20 minutes longer or until the greens are tender.
- Add the vinegar, and season with salt and pepper to taste.

57 Bacon and Potato Soup

Serves 8 | Prep time 15 minutes | Cooking time 60-70 minutes

Ingredients

- 8 strips bacon
- 2 teaspoons bacon drippings or olive oil 1 large onion, chopped
- 3 pounds potatoes, peeled, cut into ¼-inch slices 1 cup of water
- 2 (14 ½-ounce) cans chicken broth, Fat-free, lower-sodium
- ½ teaspoon salt
- ½ teaspoon freshly ground black pepper 2 cups low-Fat milk
- ¾ cup cheddar cheese, shredded, more for serving

For serving

- ½ cup light sour cream (optional)
- 4 teaspoons fresh chives, chopped (optional)

Directions

- Fry the bacon strips in the Dutch oven until crispy over medium heat, about 4-5 minutes. Remove the bacon and place on a plate lined with paper towels.
- Keep about 2 tablespoons of the bacon drippings (or oil) in the Dutch oven. Add olive oil if necessary. Warm the drippings over medium heat, and stir-fry the onions until tender. Remove from heat.
- Place the potato slices in the Dutch oven. Stir in the water, broth, salt, and pepper and stir.
- Cover and cook for 40-45 minutes over medium-low heat or until the potatoes are tender.
- Mash potatoes with a potato masher or blender stick. Stir in milk and cheese. Stir to combine.
- Let simmer over low heat for about 20-25 minutes or until heated through and smooth.
- Serve with sour cream, sprinkled with bacon, chives, more cheese, if desired.

58 Chicken Mushroom Soup

Serves 8 | Prep. time 10–15 minutes | Cooking time 30 minutes

Ingredients

- 2 tablespoons olive oil
- 2 cups fresh mushrooms, sliced 2 medium carrots, chopped
- 2 celery ribs, chopped 1 small onion, chopped 1-quart chicken broth
- ⅓ cup all-purpose flour
- 2 cups cooked chicken, cubed
- 1 (8¾-ounce) package precooked chicken-flavored rice 2 cups Fat-free half-and-half
- ½ teaspoon pepper

Directions

- Add the oil to the Dutch oven and heat it over medium-high heat.
- Add the vegetables and stir-cook until the carrots become soft, crisp, and tender.
- Add the broth and flour to a mixing bowl. Mix well.
- Pour the broth into the Dutch oven and bring to a boil, stirring occasionally.
- Stir-cook for 5–6 minutes until thickened.
- Add the other ingredients and cook over medium-low heat until cooked to satisfaction.
- Serve warm.

59 Creme Potato Chicken Soup

Serves 8 | Prep. time 10 minutes | Cooking time 10 minutes

Ingredients

- 3½ cups water
- 4 cups shredded cooked chicken breast
- 2 (10¾-ounce) cans condensed cream of chicken soup, undiluted 1 pound frozen mixed vegetables, thawed
- 1 (14½-ounce) can potatoes, drained and diced
- 1 pound Velveeta, cubed
- Minced chives (optional)

Directions

- Add the water, chicken breast, chicken soup, vegetables, and potatoes to the Dutch oven. Bring to a boil.
- Reduce heat to low, cover, and simmer for 8–10 minutes until the veggies are tender, stirring occasionally.
- Mix in the cheese.
- Serve warm with minced chives on top.

60 Broccoli Cheese Soup

Prep time: 10 minutes | Cook time: 15 minutes | Serves 2

Ingredients

- 2 tablespoons butter
- 1 small onion, thinly sliced
- ¼ teaspoon kosher salt
- ¼ cup dry white wine
- 2½ cups low-sodium chicken stock
- 8 ounces (227 g) broccoli florets
- 1 teaspoon Dijon mustard
- ⅛ teaspoon celery seed
- ⅛ teaspoon freshly ground white pepper
- 1 ounce (28 g) coarsely shredded or crumbled aged Cheddar cheese
- 1 tablespoon sliced almonds, toasted until golden brown

Directions

- Place the Dutch oven over medium heat and add the butter. When the butter stops foaming, add the onion and season with salt. Stir until the onions are coated with the butter. Cook for about 5 minutes, stirring occasionally, until softened.
- Add the wine and bring to a simmer. Cook, stirring occasionally, for a couple of minutes, until most of the wine evaporates.
- Add the chicken stock and broccoli and simmer, covered, for an additional 5 minutes. Uncover the pan and continue to simmer until the broccoli is tender, 2 to 3 more minutes. Remove from the heat and let cool slightly.
- If you have an immersion blender, blend the soup until the texture is as smooth as you like it. (If you don't have an immersion blender, pour the mixture into a blender or food processor and pulse to get the desired texture. Pour the soup back into the Dutch oven.) Add the mustard, celery seed, and pepper. Taste and add more salt if necessary.
- To serve, put the cheese in a bowl and pour the soup over. Top with the almonds.

61 Chicken Tortilla Soup with Avocado

Prep time: 5 minutes | Cook time: 22 minutes | Serves 2

Ingredients

- 2 to 3 cups vegetable oil
- 2 to 3 corn tortillas, cut into ½-inch strips Fine salt for the tortilla strips
- ½ small onion, finely chopped
- 1 small jalapeño pepper, seeded and minced 1 cup fire-roasted diced tomatoes in juice
- 1 large garlic clove, minced
- 3 cups low-sodium chicken stock
- 1 small boneless skinless chicken breast, cut into ½-inch chunks
- 2 tablespoons chopped fresh cilantro
- 1 teaspoon freshly squeezed lime juice
- ½ ripe avocado, pitted and diced

- ¼ cup shredded Monterey Jack cheese

Directions

- Pour the oil into the Dutch oven and place over medium-high heat. Heat the oil to 350°F (180°C) to 375°F (190°C). When the oil is hot, carefully add a layer of tortilla strips; don't crowd the pan. Cook for 5 minutes or so, separating and turning as necessary, until deep golden brown and crisp. Remove from the oil and drain on a fine grid rack set over a sheet pan, or on paper towels. (If you use paper towels, remove the chips from the towels as soon as they're drained so they don't reabsorb the oil from the towels.) Sprinkle lightly with salt. Repeat with the remaining tortilla strips. Pour out all but a light coating of the oil.
- Place the Dutch oven over medium heat until the oil shimmers. Add the onion and jalapeño and let them cook without stirring for 4 to 5 minutes, or until they begin to brown. Stir in the tomatoes and garlic, and bring to a simmer. Cook for about 15 minutes, or until the mixture has thickened and the vegetables are soft.
- Break up the tomato mixture into a chunky paste with a potato masher or a large fork. Add the chicken stock and bring to a simmer. Add the chicken breast and cover. Cook for 8 to 12 minutes, or until the chicken is cooked. Stir in the cilantro and lime juice and taste, adding more salt if necessary.
- Divide the avocado and cheese between two bowls and ladle the soup over. Top with the tortilla strips.

62 Rib Soup with Onion

Prep time: 15 minutes | **Cook time:** 2 hours | **Serves** 2

Ingredients

- 4 tablespoons butter, divided
- 5 to 6 medium white or yellow onions, sliced thin (about 6 cups), divided
- Kosher salt, to taste
- 1 pound (454 g) bone-in short ribs
- ⅓ cup dry or medium-dry sherry 2½ cups low-sodium beef stock
- ¼ teaspoon dried thyme (or 1 sprig fresh) 1 bay leaf
- 1 teaspoon Worcestershire sauce
- 1 teaspoon sherry vinegar (optional)

Directions

- To make the caramelized onions, place the Dutch oven over medium heat. Add half the butter and melt until it starts to foam. Add about 4 cups of the onions and stir to coat with the butter. Season with salt and cover. Turn the heat down to low. Cook for at least an hour (usually 90 minutes), stirring every 15 minutes or so. The onions will soften, then slowly turn golden and then light amber in color. There should still be a fair amount of liquid in the pot. This process can take longer depending on the moisture level of the onions; be patient and don't try to hasten the process by turning up the heat or you risk burning them.
- Uncover and turn the heat up to medium. Cook the onions, stirring occasionally, until they darken to a deep caramel color and the liquid has evaporated and about ⅔ cup of onions remains. Transfer the caramelized onions to a bowl and set aside.
- While the onions cook, salt the short ribs on all sides. Turn the heat to medium-high and add the rest of the butter to the Dutch oven. When the butter stops foaming, add the remaining sliced onions and stir. Spread them into a single layer, and cook without stirring until they start to brown, 2 to 4 minutes. Stir, and repeat the process, until the onions are mostly browned. Transfer to a bowl and set aside. These onions should be browned but not caramelized.
- Place the short ribs in the Dutch oven and cook for several minutes, or until browned. Repeat until all sides are brown; about 12 to 15 minutes. Transfer the short ribs to a plate.
- Add the sherry to the pot and bring to a simmer, scraping up the browned bits from the bottom. Cook until the sherry has reduced by about half then add the beef stock, thyme,

and bay leaf. Stir in the caramelized onions, reserving the browned onions. Add the short ribs and bring the mixture to a simmer.
- Cover and simmer gently for at least 90 minutes and up to 2 hours, turning the short ribs halfway through. When the meat is tender, remove the ribs and let them cool. Remove the bay leaf and thyme sprig and discard. Strain out the onions and reserve.
- From the surface of the mixture sauce, skim off as much fat as possible and add the caramelized onions back to the soup. Bring to a simmer.
- When the ribs have cooled enough to handle, shred the meat, discarding the bones, tendons, and any remaining fat. Add the meat to the soup along with the browned onions and the Worcestershire sauce. Taste and add salt if necessary. If the soup seems too sweet, add the optional sherry vinegar.

63 Tomato Chicken Soup

Prep time: 15 minutes | **Cook time:** 50 minutes | **Serves** 2

Ingredients

- 1 to 2 tablespoons vegetable or olive oil
- ½ small onion, sliced thin
- 1 large garlic clove, minced
- 1 teaspoon minced or grated ginger Kosher salt, to taste
- ¼ teaspoon red pepper flakes
- 3 cups low-sodium chicken stock
- 1 (14-ounce / 397-g) can diced tomatoes, drained
- 1 to 2 boneless skinless chicken thighs, cut into bite-size pieces
- 1 very small sweet potato, peeled and cut into ½-inch chunks
- ¼ cup peanut butter
- 1 to 2 tablespoons chopped roasted unsalted peanuts

Directions

- Place the Dutch oven over medium heat. Add enough oil to coat the bottom of the pot and heat until the oil shimmers. Add the onion and stir to coat with the oil. Cook, stirring, for a minute or two, just until the onion pieces begin to separate. Add the garlic and ginger and sprinkle with salt. Cook, stirring, for a couple of minutes, or until fragrant. Add the red pepper flakes, chicken stock, and diced tomatoes and bring to a simmer. Cover and cook for about 20 minutes.
- Add the chicken and sweet potato chunks to the mixture. Bring the soup back to a simmer and cover. Cook for another 20 to 25 minutes, or until the sweet potatoes are soft.
- Stir in the peanut butter, and taste for seasoning. Ladle into bowls and sprinkle with chopped peanuts.

64 Sweet Potato and Corn Soup

Prep time: 10 minutes | **Cook time:** 20 minutes | **Serves** 6

Ingredients

- 2 tablespoons olive oil
- 1 sweet potato, peeled and diced
- 1 teaspoon salt, plus more for seasoning 5 garlic cloves, minced
- 1 poblano chile, seeded and chopped
- 2 cups frozen corn
- 1 tablespoon chili powder 1 teaspoon ground cumin
- 1 teaspoon ground turmeric
- ½ cup dry white wine
- 4 cups water
- 1 (14-ounce / 397-g) can coconut milk

Directions

- Sauté the vegetables. In a Dutch oven over medium heat, warm the olive oil. Add the sweet potato and salt. Stir to combine and cook for 7 minutes or until the potato begins to brown. Stir in the garlic, poblano, and corn. Cook for 3 minutes more.

- Deglaze and simmer. Add the chili powder, cumin, and turmeric, and toss to coat the vegetables. Cook for 1 minute. Stir in the white wine and deglaze the pot, scraping along the bottom of the pot to release any browned bits. Add the water and increase the heat to medium-high. Bring the soup to a simmer and cook for about 5 minutes, until heated through.
- Season and serve. Turn off the heat and stir in the coconut milk. Taste and, if the soup is bland, season with salt. Refrigerate leftovers for up to 3 days.

65 Carrot and Lentil Soup

Prep time: 10 minutes | **Cook time:** 25 minutes | **Serves** 6

Ingredients

- 3 tablespoons olive oil 1 onion, chopped
- 2 carrots, chopped
- 2 celery stalks, chopped
- 1 tablespoon garam masala, plus more for seasoning
- 1 tablespoon salt, plus more for seasoning
- 2 teaspoons curry powder, plus more for seasoning
- 1 teaspoon freshly ground black pepper, plus more for seasoning
- 6 cups filtered water
- 2 cups red or yellow lentils

Directions

- Sweat the vegetables. In a Dutch oven over medium heat, warm the olive oil. Add the onion, carrots, and celery. Sweat the vegetables for 7 minutes, stirring occasionally. Stir in the garam masala, salt, curry powder, and pepper. Cook for about 2 minutes, until aromatic.
- Simmer the lentils. Pour the water over the vegetables and add the lentils. Stir, then cover the pot and simmer, stirring occasionally, for about 15 minutes, until the lentils are tender and cooked through.
- Adjust the seasoning and serve. Taste the soup and add more salt or spices as desired. Ladle the soup into bowls and top as desired. Refrigerate leftovers for up to 3 days.

66 Beef Cheese Soup

Prep time: 15 minutes | **Cook time:** 45 minutes | **Serves** 6

Ingredients

- 8 tablespoons (1 stick) unsalted butter
- 4 white onions, thinly sliced
- 1 teaspoon salt, plus more for seasoning 2 garlic cloves, minced
- 3 tablespoons all-purpose flour 1 cup dry red wine
- 2 bay leaves
- 1 teaspoon freshly ground black pepper, plus more for seasoning
- 1 teaspoon dried thyme
- 8 cups beef stock
- 4 cups grated Gruyère cheese Fresh parsley, for garnish (optional)

Directions

- Caramelize the onions. Warm a Dutch oven over medium heat. Add the butter, onions, and salt. Stir and cook for about 20 minutes, monitoring the onions closely, until they are mushy, brown, and have a sweet taste.
- Add the flour and wine. Turn the heat to medium-low. Add the garlic. Cook, stirring, for 1 minute. Stir in the flour and cook with the onions for at least 3 minutes, then add the red wine. Cook for about 1 minute, stirring to scrape up any browned bits from the bottom of the pot, until the wine has reduced by half.3.
- Add the beef stock and simmer. Add the bay leaves, pepper, and thyme. Raise the heat to medium-high and add the beef stock. Simmer for 10 minutes. Using tongs, remove the bay leaves. Taste and season with more salt and pepper as desired.
- Preheat the broiler and melt the cheese. When you're ready to serve, position an oven rack under the broiler so the Dutch oven will fit.

- Top the soup with a thick layer of the cheese, then broil for about 3 minutes or until the cheese is bubbly and golden brown. Ladle the soup with the cheese topping into bowls, and serve with crusty bread for dunking, if desired. Garnish with parsley (if using). Refrigerate leftovers for up to 4 days. To reheat the soup in the Dutch oven, simmer it over medium heat for about 5 minutes to melt the cheese and warm the soup.

67 Tangy Black Bean Soup

Prep time: 10 minutes | **Cook time:** 20 minutes | **Serves** 4

Ingredients

- 3 tablespoons olive oil
- 1 white or yellow onion, chopped
- 1 red bell pepper, chopped
- 2 celery stalks, chopped
- 6 garlic cloves, chopped
- 2 teaspoons ground cumin
- 1 teaspoon chili powder
- 1 teaspoon salt
- 2 (15-ounce / 425-g) cans black beans, drained and rinsed
- 2 cups water
- Grated zest and juice of 1 orange Juice of 2 limes
- Chopped fresh cilantro, for garnish (optional)

Directions

- Sauté the vegetables. Heat a Dutch oven over medium heat. Add the olive oil, onion, bell pepper, and celery. Cook for about 7 minutes, stirring occasionally. Add the garlic, cumin, chili powder, and salt. Stir to coat the vegetables and turn off the heat to avoid burning.
- Simmer the beans. Add the black beans and water. Using a spatula, stir to combine, scraping along the bottom of the pot to release any browned bits. Bring the soup to a simmer over medium heat and cook for 8 minutes.
- Season and serve. Stir in the orange zest, orange juice, and lime juice to taste. (Salt and acid lift the savory flavors of this soup.)
- Garnish with cilantro (if using). Refrigerate leftovers for up to 2 days.

68 Butternut Squash Soup

Prep time: 20 minutes | **Cook time:** 90 minutes | **Serves** 6 to 8

Ingredients

- 4 tablespoons butter
- 1 onion, chopped
- 2 cups chopped carrots
- 4 cups chopped butternut squash
- 1 cup peeled and chopped sweet potato
- 4 cups chicken broth or stock
- 1 cup heavy cream
- 3 tablespoons maple syrup
- Sea salt and freshly ground black pepper, to taste

Directions

- In a Dutch oven, melt the butter over medium-high heat, and add the onion, carrots, squash, and sweet potato. Cook for 15 minutes. Add the broth and bring to a boil. Reduce heat, cover, and simmer for 20 to 30 minutes, or until the vegetables are soft.
- Remove the pot from the heat and cool slightly. Using an immersion blender (or in batches in a traditional blender), purée the soup until smooth.
- Reheat the soup over low heat. Swirl in the cream and maple syrup, and season with sea salt and pepper.

69 Lemony Cauliflower Potage

Prep time: 10 minutes | **Cook time:** 45 minutes | **Serves** 6

Ingredients

- 1 head cauliflower, cut into florets
- 1 tablespoon sea salt, plus more as needed Juice of 1 lemon, divided
- 2 leeks
- 2 tablespoons olive oil 4 cups vegetable stock
- Freshly ground black pepper, to taste 4 tablespoons (½ stick) unsalted butter
- ¼ cup slivered almonds
- Freshly grated nutmeg, for seasoning

Directions

- Boil and drain the cauliflower. Fill a Dutch oven about halfway with water and add the cauliflower, salt, and the juice of ½ a lemon. Bring to a boil and cook for 15 minutes. Place a colander in the sink and drain the cauliflower.
- Sweat the leeks and simmer with stock. Remove the leeks' tough outer green portions. Cut lengthwise down the center of the white stalks but keep the root ends intact. Fan the leeks under running water to wash away any sand. Thinly slice the leeks and discard the roots. In a Dutch oven over medium heat, heat the olive oil. Add the leeks with a pinch of salt. Cook for 15 minutes until very tender, stirring occasionally to prevent browning. Add the cooked cauliflower and vegetable stock and bring to a simmer.
- Blend. Using a slotted spoon, carefully transfer the leeks and cauliflower to a blender. Using a liquid measuring cup, transfer 1 cup of cooking liquid to the blender. Blend on high speed until very smooth. Return the puree to the Dutch oven. Taste and season with salt and pepper. Spritz with the juice of the remaining ½ lemon.
- Brown the butter with the almonds. In a small skillet over medium-low heat, combine the butter and almonds. Cook for about 5 minutes, stirring occasionally, until the nuts turn lightly golden and the butter is browned. Pour the browned butter into the soup, reserving the almonds for garnish. Swirl the butter into the soup. Ladle into bowls and garnish with almonds for crunch and a dash of nutmeg, preferably freshly grated. Refrigerate leftovers for up to 4 days, or let the soup cool and then freeze it in freezer-safe plastic bags for up to 2 months.

70 Chickpea and Spinach Stew

Prep time: 20 minutes | **Cook time:** 45 minutes | **Serves** 2

Ingredients

- Kosher salt, to taste
- ¼ pound (113 g) dried chickpeas
- ½ small onion, diced
- 1 medium garlic clove, minced or pressed
- ½ teaspoon ground coriander
- ¼ teaspoon ground cumin
- ¼ teaspoon freshly ground black pepper
- ⅛ teaspoon ground cinnamon
- ⅛ teaspoon red pepper flakes
- 1 small carrot, peeled and cut into thin coins 1 small tomato, seeded and diced
- cups fresh baby spinach or arugula
- 1 teaspoon lemon zest
- 1 tablespoon minced fresh parsley

Directions

- Dissolve 1 tablespoon salt in 1 quart of water, in a large bowl. Add the chickpeas and soak at room temperature for 8 to 24 hours. Drain and rinse the chickpeas.
- Add the chickpeas, onion, garlic, coriander, cumin, pepper, cinnamon, and red pepper flakes to the Dutch oven and add 4 cups of fresh water. Place over high heat and bring to a boil. Reduce the heat to medium-low and simmer for 45 minutes, or until the chickpeas are almost tender.
- Add the carrot and tomato and simmer for another 10 minutes, or until the carrots and chickpeas are tender. (If the broth is too thin, bring it back to a boil and reduce until thickened.) Stir in the spinach or arugula and cook until wilted, about 1 minute.

- Ladle into two bowls and garnish with the lemon zest and parsley.

71 Potato and Beef Stew

Prep time: 15 minutes | **Cook time:** 2¾ hours | **Serves** 6

Ingredients

- 3 pounds (1.4 kg) boneless beef chuck, cut into bite-size cubes and patted dry
- Salt and freshly ground black pepper, to taste 3 tablespoons olive oil
- 2 white or yellow onions, chopped
- ¼ cup water (optional)
- 4 garlic cloves, minced
- 1½ tablespoons tomato paste
- 3 tablespoons all-purpose flour 2 cups dry red wine
- 2 cups beef bone broth
- 2 teaspoons Italian seasoning
- 1 pound (454 g) small white potatoes (such as baby Yukons), peeled and chopped
- 4 carrots, chopped
- Fresh parsley, for garnish (optional)

Directions

- Brown the beef. Season the beef well with salt and pepper. In a Dutch oven over medium heat, warm the olive oil. Working in two batches to avoid overcrowding the pot, cook the beef for 5 to 10 minutes per side. Allow the beef several minutes of contact with the heat to develop a brown crust before turning it. Once the meat is evenly browned, use tongs to transfer it to a large bowl to retain the juices.
- Add the onions, garlic, tomato paste, and flour. Add the onions to the Dutch oven and cook for about 6 minutes, stirring and scraping along the bottom of the pot with a wooden spoon to loosen any browned bits, until soft. If the onion appears dry, add the water. Stir in the garlic and tomato paste and return the beef with its juices to the pot, along with the flour. Stir well and cook for 2 minutes.
- Add the wet ingredients. Stir in the red wine, bone broth, and Italian seasoning, scraping along the bottom of the pot to loosen any caramelized food. Cover the pot, reduce the heat to low, and simmer for 1 hour and 30 minutes.
- Add the potatoes and carrots. Add the potatoes, the carrots, and a pinch each of salt and pepper to the pot. Re-cover the pot and simmer the stew for 45 minutes more. Serve the stew garnished with parsley (if using) and crusty bread, if desired. Refrigerate leftovers, which taste even better the next day, for up to 4 days.

72 Tomato and Beef Stew

Prep time: 30 minutes | **Cook time:** 2 hours | **Serves** 6 to 8

Ingredients

- 1 head of garlic, papery skin removed and each clove cut in half
- 2 tablespoons extra-virgin olive oil, plus 2 teaspoons, divided
- 3 pounds (1.4 kg) chuck roast, trimmed and cut into 2-inch cubes Salt and freshly ground black pepper, to taste
- 1 cup red wine
- 2 tablespoons minced shallots
- 1 cup peeled and sliced carrots
- 1 cup peeled and sliced parsnips
- 5 ounces (142 g) mushrooms, sliced
- 1 cup low-sodium beef broth or stock
- 1½ tablespoons tomato paste
- Zest of half an orange
- 1 tablespoon herbes de Provence
- 1 bay leaf
- 1 (28-ounce / 794-g) can diced tomatoes

Directions

- Preheat the oven to 300°F (150°C).
- Arrange the garlic in a Dutch oven, and drizzle with 2 tablespoons of olive oil. Cover and place in the pre-heated oven for about an hour, until the cloves start to pop out of their skins. Transfer the garlic to a small plate to cool.

- Once slightly cooled, squeeze the cloves into a shallow bowl, and mash them with a heavy fork.
- Place the Dutch oven on the stovetop, and add the remaining 2 teaspoons of olive oil. Heat on medium-high until the oil is hot but not smoking. Add the beef cubes in batches, stirring them until evenly browned on all sides. Season each batch with salt and pepper, and then transfer to a small platter.
- Add the wine to the pot and bring to a boil, scraping the bottom of the pot with a wooden spoon to loosen the browned bits. Stir in the meat, garlic, shallots, carrots, parsnips, mushrooms, broth, tomato paste, orange zest, herbes de Provence, bay leaf, and tomatoes. Bring to a boil, stir, and cover the pot. Place in the preheated oven.
- Bake for about 2½ hours, or until the meat is tender. Remove the bay leaf before serving.

73 Beef Stew with Potato

Prep time: 40 minutes | **Cook time:** 2 hours | **Serves** 6 to 8

Ingredients

- 3 tablespoons extra-virgin olive oil
- 3 pounds (1.4 kg) lean beef (chuck or round), cut into ½-inch cubes
- 5 leeks, chopped
- ¼ cup all-purpose flour
- 3 carrots, cut into 1-inch lengths 1 parsnip, peeled and chopped
- 1 white turnip, peeled and chopped
- ½ celery root (celeriac), peeled and cut into small cubes 1 bay leaf
- 2 large garlic cloves, thinly sliced
- 1 tablespoon roughly chopped fresh thyme leaves 2½ cups low-sodium beef broth or stock
- Salt and freshly ground black pepper, to taste
- 5 potatoes (about 2 pounds / 907 g), peeled and quartered 1 (28-ounce / 794-g) can crushed tomatoes

Directions

- Preheat the oven to 350°F (180°C).
- Heat the olive oil in a Dutch oven over medium-high heat. Begin adding the beef, a few pieces at a time. Brown on one side, then turn with a pair of tongs. Transfer the browned beef to a bowl, and repeat until all the beef is browned.
- Pour off all but a tablespoon of fat in the pot, then add the leeks, and sauté over medium heat, stirring frequently, until they soften.
- Toss the flour with the browned beef, then add the floured meat to the pot. Add the carrots, parsnip, turnip, celery root, bay leaf, garlic, thyme, and broth. Season with salt and pepper. Stir again and bring to a simmer on medium-high heat.
- Cover, place in the preheated oven, and bake for 15 minutes.
- Reduce the oven temperature to 300°F (150°C), and cook for 1½ hours.
- Uncover the pan and add the potatoes and tomatoes. Cover and cook for 25 minutes, or until the potatoes are tender. Remove the bay leaf before serving.

74 Shell Bean and Lamb Stew

Prep time: 30 minutes | **Cook time:** 1½ to 2 hours | **Serves** 6 to 8

Ingredients

- 2 tablespoons extra-virgin olive oil
- 2 pounds (907 g) lamb stew meat, from the shoulder or leg, cut into 1-inch pieces
- 1 yellow onion, minced
- Salt and freshly ground black pepper, to taste 2 tablespoons all-purpose flour
- 3 cloves garlic, minced
- 1½ cups diced tomatoes (fresh or canned)
- 1 bay leaf
- 4 cups water
- 2 pounds (907 g) fresh shell beans (cannellini beans, cranberry beans, black-eyed peas, or garbanzo beans), shelled
- ½ pound (227g) chorizo, sliced

Directions

- In a Dutch oven, heat the olive oil over a medium-high heat. Add the lamb and onion, and season with salt and pepper. Cook, stirring occasionally, until the lamb is golden on all sides, for 8 to 10 minutes. Sprinkle the flour into the pot and stir. Cook for 2 minutes.
- Add the garlic, tomatoes, bay leaf, and water. Bring to a boil over high heat. Reduce the heat to low, and simmer for 1 hour.
- Add the beans and chorizo, and simmer for 40 minutes. Remove the bay leaf before serving.

75 Tomato Bean Stew with Sausage

Prep time: 20 minutes | **Cook time:** 1 hour | **Serves** 6 to 8

Ingredients

- ¾ cup chopped bacon
- 3 tablespoons extra-virgin olive oil, divided 2 yellow onions, peeled and diced
- ½ pound (227g) hot Italian sausage, removed from casing
- 7 carrots, peeled and chopped
- ¼ teaspoon red pepper flakes
- Salt and freshly ground black pepper, to taste 1 tablespoon tomato paste
- 7 garlic cloves, peeled and chopped
- 1 (28-ounce / 794-g) can diced tomatoes, undrained 4 cups chicken broth or stock
- 1 (16-ounce / 454-g) can white cannellini beans, drained and rinsed

Directions

- In a Dutch oven over medium-low heat, cook the bacon in 1 tablespoon of olive oil for 5 to 6 minutes, stirring occasionally, until most of the fat has been rendered and the bacon is beginning to crisp.
- Add the onions and cook for 6 to 7 minutes, or until they become soft and translucent.
- Add the sausage, carrots, and red pepper flakes. Season with black pepper and continue to cook for 10 minutes, breaking up the sausage into small pieces with the back of a wooden spoon.
- Add the remaining 2 tablespoons of olive oil, stir in the tomato paste and garlic, and cook for 3 minutes. Stir in the diced tomatoes, broth, and beans. Season with salt.
- Increase the heat to high until the soup starts to simmer. Reduce the heat to low, and simmer for 30 minutes.

Sides and Appetizers Recipes

76 Tomato and Cauliflower Antipasto

Prep time: 15 minutes | **Cook time:** 15 minutes | **Serves** 8 to 12

Ingredients

- ¼ cup extra-virgin olive oil
- 1 cup diced celery
- 1½ cups peeled and diced carrots
- 2½ cups diced yellow onion
- 6 cloves garlic, minced
- 4 cups sliced cauliflower florets
- 2 cups diced firm zucchini (the smaller dice the better)
- 2 (6-ounce / 170-g) cans tomato sauce
- ¼ cup tomato paste
- ¼ cup small capers
- 2 (8-ounce / 227-g) jars pearl onions, drained
- ½ cup chopped sweet pickles, ½ cup chopped Kalamata olives
- 1 cup sliced pimento-stuffed green olives
- 2 (2-ounce / 57-g) jars quartered olive oil-marinated artichoke hearts, undrained
- ½ cup red wine vinegar
- ¼ cup sugar
- small tin anchovy fillets, drained and chopped
- 1 cup chopped fresh basil, ½ cup chopped fresh parsley

Directions

- Pour the oil into an enameled Dutch oven over medium heat. Add the celery, carrots, onions, garlic, and cauliflower, and braise in the oil, covered, for 5 minutes. Add the zucchini, and steam, covered, for 3 minutes more. Mix in the tomato sauce, tomato paste, capers, pearl onions, sweet pickle, kalamata and green olives, artichoke hearts, vinegar, sugar, and anchovy fillets.
- Cook, uncovered, for 5 minutes.
- Refrigerate for several days before serving to let the flavors mingle together. Add the basil and parsley just before serving.

77 Egg and Butter Spaetzle

Prep time: 5 minutes | **Cook time:** 10 minutes | **Serves** 4

Ingredients

- 2 cups all-purpose flour 3 large eggs
- ½ cup whole milk
- 1 teaspoon kosher salt, plus more for seasoning 4 tablespoons butter (½ stick), melted
- Freshly ground black pepper, to taste

Directions

- Fill a Dutch oven with water and bring it to a boil over medium- high heat. In a medium bowl mix together with a fork the flour, eggs, milk, and salt.
- Put ½ cup of the noodle dough into the spaetzle maker or a potato ricer (using the large hole disk). Firmly squeeze the squiggly noodles into the boiling water. Use a knife to cut away any remaining noodles. Cook for 2 minutes. Remove the noodles from the water with a large slotted spoon and put them in a colander to drain. Continue this process until all of the dough is gone.
- Transfer the spaetzle to a medium glass baking dish and mix with the butter. Season with salt and pepper. When ready to serve, reheat in the microwave or in a 10- or 12-inch skillet over low heat.

78 Juicy Squash with Walnut

Prep time: 10 minutes | **Cook time:** 50 minutes | **Serves** 8

Ingredients

- 1 kabocha squash, stemmed
- 3 Bosc pears, peeled, cored, and coarsely chopped
- ¼ teaspoon grated nutmeg 5 tablespoons butter, melted
- ¼ cup firmly packed brown sugar
- ¼ teaspoon kosher salt 1 cup apple juice or cider
- ½ cup cranberry sauce

- 2 ounces (57 g) walnuts (about ½ cup coarsely chopped)

Directions

- Preheat the oven to 375°F (190°C).
- To seed the squash, use one hand to hold it steady and the other hand to carefully stick the knife into the center of the squash. Slowly rock or wiggle your knife into the squash on one side, from top to bottom. Turn the squash over and follow the line to the top of the squash, making a complete cut through the squash. Use a fork or dinner knife to pry the squash open. Remove the seeds. Quarter the squash, always putting the flat flesh side down when cutting. Cut each quarter in half crosswise so you have eight crescent-shaped pieces.
- Add the squash to a Dutch oven; add the pears on top of the slices of squash. Sprinkle the nutmeg over the pears, and drizzle with melted butter. Distribute the brown sugar and salt. Pour in the apple juice.
- Bake, covered, for 50 minutes. Remove from the oven. Top each serving with 1 tablespoon each of the cranberry sauce and walnuts.

79 Bacon and Pea Risi e Bisi

Prep time: 10 minutes | Cook time: 30 minutes | Serves 4

Ingredients

- 3½ cups chicken broth
- 2 tablespoons butter
- 1 tablespoon extra-virgin olive oil
- 2 ounces (57 g) pancetta or bacon, diced 1 small yellow onion, finely diced
- 1 cup short-grain rice (such as Italian arborio)
- 8 ounces (227 g) peas, shelled or frozen, thawed 2 tablespoons finely chopped parsley
- 1 tablespoon freshly squeezed lemon juice 2 tablespoons grated Parmesan cheese
- Kosher salt and freshly ground black pepper, to taste

Directions

- In a small saucepan bring the broth to a boil. Turn down the heat and simmer. Meanwhile, add the butter and the oil to a Dutch oven over medium heat. Add the pancetta and cook until most of the fat has rendered. Add the onions and sauté until translucent, about 5 minutes.
- Add the rice and stir until each grain is well coated with the oil. Add 1 cup of the broth and stir occasionally until the broth has been absorbed. Continue to add the broth 1 cup at a time, waiting until each cup is absorbed before adding more. Stir occasionally until al dente, about 15 minutes.
- Gently stir in the peas and cook 5 minutes longer. Remove from the heat and gently stir in the parsley, lemon juice, and Parmesan cheese. Season with salt and pepper and serve in warmed bowls or alongside meat or fish.

80 Lemony Artichoke

Prep time: 10 minutes | Cook time: 50 minutes | Serves 4 to 8

Ingredients

- 4 large artichokes
- ½ lemon
- ¼ cup extra-virgin olive oil
- ½ teaspoon kosher salt 2 bay leaves

Directions

- Trim the artichoke stems, leaving ½ inch on the artichoke. Cut 1 inch off the top of the leaves. Place the artichokes stem side down in a Dutch oven. Rub the tops of the artichokes with the lemon half. Pour in 4 cups of water, then the oil. Add the salt and bay leaves.
- Wrap the lid with a kitchen towel to prevent excess liquid from dripping back into the pot, then put the lid on the pot. Cook over low heat for 50 minutes. Remove the artichokes from the pot and serve warm.

81 Vinegary Cabbage with Apple

Prep time: 15 minutes | **Cook time:** 45 minutes | **Serves** 8

Ingredients

- ½ cup red wine vinegar
- ¼ cup firmly packed brown sugar 1 cup chicken broth
- 1 head red cabbage, outer leaves removed, then quartered, cored, and shredded
- 1 Granny Smith apple, peeled, cored, and chopped
- 1 teaspoon caraway seeds

Directions

- Put the vinegar, brown sugar, broth, cabbage, apples, and caraway seeds in a Dutch oven. Mix gently.
- Place the lid on the pot.
- Simmer the mixture over low heat for 45 minutes.
- Serve warm.

82 Creamy Cheese Potato

Prep time: 15 minutes | **Cook time:** 1 hour | **Serves** 8

Ingredients

- 2 cups heavy cream
- 2 cups whole milk
- 1 clove garlic, peeled and smashed
- 2 tablespoons unsalted butter
- ½ teaspoon salt
- ¼ teaspoon freshly cracked black pepper
- ⅛ teaspoon grated nutmeg
- 6 large russet potatoes, peeled and thinly sliced
- 1 cup shredded Gruyère cheese

Directions

- In an ovenproof Dutch oven, add cream, 2 cups milk, garlic, butter, salt, pepper, and nutmeg. Heat mixture over medium heat, stirring constantly, until it comes to a boil. Add sliced potatoes, reduce heat to low, and simmer 10 minutes.
- Heat oven to 350°F (180°C).
- After 10 minutes, carefully remove potatoes with a slotted spoon to a bowl and set aside. Increase heat to medium, bring milk mixture to a boil and, stirring constantly, let mixture reduce by half, about 8 minutes.
- Turn off heat, return potatoes to the Dutch oven, shaking it gently to evenly distribute potato slices, and top with shredded cheese. Bake 25 to 30 minutes, or until potatoes are bubbling around the edges and cheese has browned. Cool 10 minutes before serving.

83 Potato with Cheese

Prep time: 20 minutes | **Cook time:** 1 hour | **Serves** 6

Ingredients

- 2 tablespoons olive oil
- 1 tablespoon unsalted butter
- 1 small onion, peeled and finely chopped
- 1 large clove garlic, peeled and minced
- 1 tablespoon all-purpose flour
- 1¼ cups milk
- 1½ cups heavy cream
- 1 cup shredded Gruyère cheese
- ¼ teaspoon salt
- ¼ teaspoon freshly cracked black pepper
- 2½ pounds (1.1 kg) potatoes, peeled and sliced ⅛ inch thick
- ¼ cup shredded Parmesan cheese

Directions

- Heat oven to 350°F (180°C) and place a rack in the center of oven.
- Place an ovenproof Dutch oven over medium heat. Once it is heated add olive oil, butter, and onion. Cook 3 to 5 minutes until translucent but not brown. Add garlic and cook 1 minute.
- Add flour to the Dutch oven and stir 1 minute. Slowly add milk, stirring continually to prevent lumps. Slowly add cream, stirring continually until it just comes to a simmer. Reduce heat to low and simmer until slightly thickened, about 5 minutes.

- Add Gruyère cheese and stir until it melts. Turn off the heat.
- Sprinkle salt and pepper on potatoes. Slowly add them to the pan, a few at a time. Use a spoon to push potatoes to the bottom of the Dutch oven and make even layers.
- Once all of potatoes have been added, sprinkle Parmesan cheese on top and bake 45 minutes. Let it rest 10 minutes before serving.

84 Sherry Mushroom

Prep time: 10 minutes | **Cook time:** 35 minutes | **Serves** 8

Ingredients

- 4 tablespoons unsalted butter
- 3 pounds (1.4 kg) sliced fresh button or Cremini mushrooms
- 2 tablespoons all-purpose flour
- ½ teaspoon salt
- ½ teaspoon freshly cracked black pepper
- ¼ teaspoon thyme
- ⅛ teaspoon crushed red pepper flakes
- ⅛ teaspoon grated nutmeg
- ¼ cup sherry
- 2 cups half-and-half
- ¼ cup chopped fresh parsley

Directions

- Heat a Dutch oven over medium heat. Once hot add butter and, once it has melted and starts to foam, add mushrooms and cook, stirring frequently, until mushrooms are tender, about 6 to 8 minutes.
- Add flour, salt, pepper, thyme, red pepper, and nutmeg. Cook until flour mixture is just turning golden brown, about 3 minutes. Add sherry and half-and-half and stir well to combine.
- Bring mixture to a boil, then reduce heat to medium-low and simmer until mushroom mixture is thick, about 8 minutes. Remove from the heat and stir in fresh parsley. Serve immediately.

85 Green Beans with Bacon

Prep time: 15 minutes | **Cook time:** 35 minutes | **Serves** 8

Ingredients

- 12 cups water
- 1 teaspoon salt
- 2 pounds (907 g) fresh green beans, trimmed
- ½ pound (227 g) bacon, chopped 2 tablespoons unsalted butter
- 1 clove garlic, peeled and minced
- 1 teaspoon packed light brown sugar
- ½ teaspoon dry mustard powder
- ¼ teaspoon smoked paprika
- ¼ teaspoon freshly cracked black pepper

Directions

- Bring water to a boil in an ovenproof Dutch oven. Add salt and then green beans. Cook 3 minutes, then drain well and plunge immediately into a large bowl of ice water. Once cool drain well and pat dry with paper towels.
- Heat oven to 375°F (190°C).
- Return the Dutch oven to medium heat and add chopped bacon. Cook, stirring frequently, until the fat has rendered and bacon is crisp. Remove bacon with a slotted spoon to a paper towel-lined plate to drain. Pour off all but 2 tablespoons of bacon drippings.
- Return the Dutch oven to the heat and add butter. Once butter has melted add garlic, brown sugar, dry mustard, paprika, and pepper. Cook until sugar has melted and garlic is fragrant, about 30 seconds. Add green beans and crisp bacon to the Dutch oven and toss to coat.
- Roast in the oven uncovered 20 minutes or until the beans are tender. Serve hot.

86 Creamy Corn Cheese Soufflé

Prep time: 15 minutes | **Cook time:** 55 minutes | Serves 8

Ingredients

- 8 ounces (227 g) sour cream
- 4 tablespoons unsalted butter, melted and cooled
- 2 (10-ounce / 283-g) bags frozen whole kernel corn, thawed and drained
- 1 (15-ounce / 425-g) can cream-style corn 2 large eggs, beaten
- 1 (8½-ounce / 241-g) box cornbread mix
- 1 cup shredded Jack or Queso Quesadilla cheese

Directions

- Heat oven to 350°F (180°C) and lightly spray an ovenproof Dutch oven with nonstick cooking spray.
- In a large bowl combine sour cream, butter, thawed corn, cream corn, and eggs and mix until well combined. Add cornbread mix and mix until the dry ingredients are just moistened. Add shredded cheese and fold until well mixed with no large lumps of dry mix remaining.
- Pour mixture into the prepared Dutch oven and bake 45 to 50 minutes, or until a knife inserted into the center comes out clean. Cool 10 minutes before serving.

87 Corn Cheese Pudding

Prep time: 10 minutes | **Cook time:** 1¼ hours | Serves 8

Ingredients

- 2 tablespoons unsalted butter
- 1 medium onion, peeled and chopped 2 cloves garlic, peeled and minced
- 1 medium green bell pepper, seeded and chopped
- 2 tablespoons all-purpose flour
- ½ teaspoon salt
- ⅛ teaspoon pepper
- 1 teaspoon dried thyme leaves 1 cup milk
- 1 (15-ounce / 425-g) can cream-style corn 1½ cups frozen corn, thawed and drained
- 2 large eggs, beaten
- 1 cup shredded Gouda cheese

Directions

- Heat oven to 375°F (190°C).
- In an ovenproof Dutch oven melt butter over medium heat. Add onion, garlic, and bell pepper and cook until tender, about 5 minutes. Add flour, salt, pepper, and thyme and cook until bubbly, about 3 minutes.
- Add the milk and whisk until thickened and bubbling, about 5 minutes. Remove from heat and stir in cream-style corn, thawed corn, eggs, and cheese.
- Bake 30 minutes, then stir mixture, pulling the browned sides into the center. Return to oven and bake 20 to 30 minutes longer until set and browned.

88 Baby Bok Choy and Mushroom

Prep time: 10 minutes | **Cook time:** 10 minutes | Serves 4 to 6

Ingredients

- 2 tablespoons vegetable oil
- 1 teaspoon fresh grated ginger
- 1 clove garlic, peeled and minced
- 1 carrot, peeled and cut into ⅛-inch slices 1 medium onion, peeled and thinly sliced
- 2 pints fresh shiitake mushrooms, stems removed
- 2 baby bok choy, sliced in half lengthwise
- 1 cup beef broth
- 2 tablespoons oyster sauce
- 1 tablespoon Shaoxing wine or sherry
- 1 teaspoon dark soy sauce
- 1 teaspoon sweet soy sauce, or 1 teaspoon light brown sugar
- 1 tablespoon cornstarch

Directions

- Heat a Dutch oven over high heat. Once hot add oil. When oil shimmers and starts to smoke lightly, add ginger and garlic. Cook until fragrant, about 10 seconds, then add

- carrots and onion and cook, stirring constantly, until just tender, about 2 minutes.
- Add mushrooms and bok choy and cook until bok choy is bright green and mushrooms are starting to soften, about 2 minutes.
- In a small bowl combine remaining ingredients and whisk to incorporate cornstarch. Pour into vegetables, then lower heat to medium-low and cook until sauce is thick and coats the vegetables, about 2 to 3 minutes. Serve immediately.

89 Tomato and Corn Beans

Prep time: 10 minutes | **Cook time:** 20 minutes | **Serves** 8

Ingredients

- 2 tablespoons vegetable oil
- 1 medium onion, peeled and finely chopped
- 2 cloves garlic, peeled and minced
- 1 teaspoon cumin
- 1 (28-ounce / 794-g) can pinto beans, drained and rinsed
- 1 (10-ounce / 283-g) can tomatoes and green chilies, drained
- ½ (10-ounce / 283-g) package frozen cut corn, thawed and drained
- ¼ cup roughly chopped cilantro 1 cup chicken or vegetable broth

Directions

- Heat a Dutch oven over medium heat. Once hot, add oil. When oil shimmers add onion and cook until tender, about 3 minutes. Add garlic and cumin and cook until garlic is fragrant, about 30 seconds.
- Add remaining ingredients and bring to a boil. Reduce heat to medium-low and let beans simmer 15 minutes, or until most of the liquid has evaporated away and beans are hot. Serve hot.

90 Beans with Cilantro

Prep time: 10 minutes | **Cook time:** 2½ hours | **Serves** 12

Ingredients

- 1 pound (454 g) dried pinto beans 2 quarts water
- ½ bunch cilantro, tied with twine
- ¼ cup lard
- 1 medium onion, peeled and finely chopped
- 2 cloves garlic, peeled and minced
- 1 teaspoon cumin
- 1 teaspoon coriander
- ½ teaspoon salt

Directions

- Rinse and sort dried beans in a colander, then transfer to a large bowl. Cover beans with 3-inch cold water, and let beans soak overnight in the refrigerator. Once soaked, drain the beans well.
- Add soaked beans to a Dutch oven along with 2 quarts water and bundle of cilantro and bring the mixture to a boil. Once beans come to a boil reduce the heat to low, cover, and let beans simmer 2 hours, stirring occasionally, until beans are tender. Once tender, reserve 1 cup cooking liquid, discard cilantro bundle, and drain beans. Set aside.
- Return the Dutch oven to medium heat and add lard. Once lard has melted add onion and cook until tender, about 5 minutes. Add garlic, cumin, coriander, and salt and cook until garlic is fragrant, about 30 seconds.
- Add cooked beans to the pot and, with a potato masher, roughly mash beans. Cook until beans are thick and hot, adding splashes of the reserved cooking liquid if beans are too thick. Serve hot.

91 Mushroom Cheese Cocotte

Prep time: 10 minutes | Cook time: 30 minutes | Serves 4

Ingredients

- 1 (16-ounce / 454-g) package frozen puff pastry sheets, thawed
- 2 tablespoons unsalted butter
- 1 onion, thinly sliced 1½ tablespoons sugar
- ¼ cup balsamic vinegar
- Kosher salt and freshly ground black pepper, to taste 3 large eggs
- ⅔ cup half-and-half
- 8 ounces (227 g) mixed wild mushrooms, chopped 1 tablespoon minced fresh sage
- ¼ cup finely grated Parmesan cheese

Directions

- Preheat the oven to 400°F (205°C).
- Lay the pastry sheets on a cutting board and cut out four circles, each about 1 inch larger in diameter than the 12-ounce / 340-g cocottes. Press one circle into each of the four mini cocottes, covering the bottom and partway up the sides. Refrigerate until ready to fill.
- In a medium skillet, melt the butter over medium-high heat. Add the onion and cook, stirring frequently, until softened, about 5 minutes. Stir in the sugar and vinegar and bring to a boil. Cook until the liquid has evaporated, then season with salt and pepper.
- In a medium bowl, whisk together the eggs and half-and-half. Stir in the mushrooms and sage and season with salt and pepper.
- Pour the onion mixture and the egg mixture into the mini cocottes, dividing equally. Bake for about 20 minutes, until the filling is set and the pastry is puffed and golden.
- Sprinkle the Parmesan cheese over the tops of the tarts and place under the broiler for about 2 minutes, until the tops are golden. Serve immediately.

92 Breaded Cheese Risotto

Prep time: 15 minutes | Cook time: 50 minutes | Makes about 16 arancini

Ingredients

Risotto:

- 2 tablespoons olive oil 1 medium shallot, diced
- 1 cup Arborio rice
- ¼ cup white wine
- Pinch of saffron threads
- 4 cups chicken broth, heated and kept warm in a saucepan on the stove
- ½ cup grated Parmesan cheese
- ½ cup grated Fontina cheese
- Kosher salt and freshly ground black pepper, to taste

Arancini:

- Vegetable oil, for frying
- ½ cup all-purpose flour
- 2 large eggs, beaten
- 1 cup herbed bread crumbs

Make the Risotto

- In the Dutch oven, heat the oil over medium-high heat. Add the shallot and cook, stirring frequently, until softened, about 3 minutes.
- Stir in the rice until it is coated with the oil. Add the wine and cook, stirring, until most of the liquid has evaporated. Stir in the saffron.
- Add the hot chicken broth, about ½ cup at a time, stirring after each addition until the broth is absorbed. Once all the broth has been incorporated, remove from the heat, stir in the Parmesan and fontina cheeses, and season with salt and pepper. Transfer the risotto to a bowl and set aside until cool enough to handle.

Make the Arancini

- Meanwhile, wash and dry the Dutch oven and then pour about 3 inches of vegetable oil into it. Heat the oil over medium-high heat until the temperature registers 350°F (180°C) on a

deep-fry thermometer. Line a plate with paper towels.
- Form the risotto into 1½-inch balls. One at a time, roll the balls in the flour, then dunk them in the egg, and roll them in the bread crumbs. Fry the balls, several at a time, being careful not to crowd the pan, until golden brown all over, about 2 minutes per side. Drain on the prepared plate and serve hot.

93 Beans with Bacon

Prep time: 10 minutes | **Cook time:** 2¼ hours | **Serves** 10 to 12

Ingredients

- 1 tablespoon vegetable oil 1 large onion, chopped
- 2 garlic cloves, minced 1½ cups ketchup
- ½ cup (packed) light brown sugar
- ½ cup light molasses
- ½ cup whole-grain mustard
- ¼ cup Worcestershire sauce
- 1 tablespoon hot pepper sauce 2 cups water
- Kosher salt and freshly ground black pepper, to taste
- 3 (15-ounce / 425-g) cans navy or great northern beans, drained and rinsed
- 6 slices bacon, halved crosswise

Directions

- Preheat the oven to 350°F (180°C).
- In the Dutch oven, heat the oil over high heat. Add the onion and garlic and cook, stirring frequently, until softened, about 5 minutes. Reduce the heat to low. Stir in the ketchup, brown sugar, molasses, mustard, Worcestershire sauce, hot pepper sauce, and water. Season with salt and pepper. Bring to a simmer and cook for 10 to 15 minutes, until the sauce thickens.
- Add the beans, and lay the bacon slices on top in a single layer. Cover and bake for about 2 hours, until the liquid is bubbly and thickened. Serve hot.

94 Corn Fritters with Chutney

Prep time: 15 minutes | **Cook time:** 30 minutes | **Makes** about 30 (2-inch) fritters

Ingredients

Chutney:

- 2 cups (packed) cilantro sprigs
- 1 cup (packed) fresh mint leaves
- ½ small onion, chopped
- ¼ cup water
- 1 tablespoon freshly squeezed lime juice
- ½ to 1 fresh green chile, such as serrano or jalapeño, or to taste
- 1 teaspoon sugar

Fritters:

- 2 quarts peanut or vegetable oil, for frying
- ¾ cup all-purpose flour
- ½ cup medium-ground cornmeal 2 teaspoons baking powder
- 1 tablespoon curry powder
- ¾ teaspoon kosher salt
- ¼ teaspoon cayenne pepper
- ¾ cup whole milk 1 large egg
- 4 ears white or yellow corn, shucked and kernels cut from the cob 5 scallions, white and light green parts only, thinly sliced

Make the Chutney

- In a blender or food processor, combine the cilantro, mint, onion, water, lime juice, chile, and sugar, and process until mostly smooth. Set aside.

Make the Fritters

- In the Dutch oven, heat the oil over medium-high heat until the temperature registers 360°F (182°C) on a deep-fry thermometer. Line a plate with paper towels.
- In a large bowl, whisk together the flour, cornmeal, baking powder, curry powder, salt, and cayenne.
- In a small bowl or measuring cup, whisk together the milk and egg.

- Add the egg mixture to the flour mixture and stir to mix well. Add the corn kernels and scallions and stir to incorporate.
- Once the oil is hot, drop the batter by the heaping tablespoonful into the oil, being careful not to crowd the pot. Cook, turning once or twice, until the fritters are golden brown all around, about 4 minutes. Using tongs, a slotted spoon, or a spider, transfer the fritters to the prepared plate as they are finished cooking. Repeat until all the batter has been cooked.
- Serve hot with the chutney alongside for dipping.

95 Raisin and Pistachios Pilaf

Prep time: 10 minutes | **Cook time:** 50 minutes | Serves 8

Ingredients

- 2 tablespoons unsalted butter 1 tablespoon vegetable oil
- 3 large shallots, minced 2 cups wild rice
- 4 cups chicken or vegetable broth
- ½ cup raisins 1 bay leaf
- 2 sprigs fresh thyme sprigs
- ½ teaspoon kosher salt
- ⅛ teaspoon freshly ground black pepper
- ½ cup coarsely chopped pistachios
- ¼ cup minced flat-leaf parsley

Directions

- Preheat the oven to 375°F (190°C).
- In the Dutch oven, heat the butter with the oil over medium-high heat. Add the shallots and cook, stirring frequently, until softened, about 3 minutes. Stir in the rice until the grains are coated with the oil. Add the broth, raisins, bay leaf, thyme, salt, and pepper, and bring to a simmer.
- Cover and bake for about 45 minutes, until the rice is tender and the liquid has been absorbed.
- Remove the bay leaf and thyme sprigs and discard them. Stir in the pistachios and parsley and serve hot.

96 Bulgur and Tomato Pilaf

Prep time: 10 minutes | **Cook time:** 30 minutes | Serves 6

Ingredients

- 2 tablespoons olive oil
- 1 onion, diced
- 1 garlic clove, minced
- 1-inch piece fresh ginger, minced 1½ cups bulgur
- ½ teaspoon ground turmeric
- ½ teaspoon ground cumin
- 2 cups vegetable or chicken broth
- 1 (14½-ounce / 411-g) can diced tomatoes, drained
- 1 cup diced eggplant
- 1 teaspoon kosher salt
- ½ cup (loosely packed) finely chopped fresh mint
- ¼ cup (loosely packed) finely chopped flat-leaf parsley Juice of 1 lemon

Directions

- In the Dutch oven, heat the oil over medium heat. Add the onion and cook, stirring frequently, until softened and beginning to brown, about 7 minutes.
- Add the garlic and ginger and cook, stirring, for 1 more minute. Stir in the bulgur, turmeric, and cumin and cook, stirring, for 1 minute.
- Add the broth, tomatoes, eggplant, and salt and bring to a boil. Reduce the heat to medium-low, cover, and simmer for about 15 minutes, until the liquid has been fully absorbed. Remove the pot from the heat and let stand, covered and without stirring, for 5 minutes.
- Just before serving, stir in the mint, parsley, and lemon juice and serve hot.

97 Corn Cheese Polenta with Aioli

Prep time: 10 minutes | **Cook time:** 1 hour | **Serves** 8

Ingredients

Polenta:

- Butter or oil for preparing the Dutch oven
- 2 cups dry polenta (coarsely ground yellow cornmeal)
- 2 cups sweet corn kernels, fresh (from about 2 ears) or frozen 2 garlic cloves, minced
- 2 teaspoons kosher salt
- 1 teaspoon freshly ground black pepper
- 7 cups chicken or vegetable broth or water
- 1 cup grated Parmesan cheese, plus additional for serving
- ½ cup heavy cream
- 4 tablespoons unsalted butter

Aioli:

- 2 garlic cloves
- 2 teaspoons Dijon mustard 3 egg yolks
- 2 tablespoons fresh lemon juice
- Kosher salt, to taste
- 1 cup neutral-flavored oil, such as grapeseed, safflower, or sunflower seed oil
- 2 cups fresh corn kernels

Make the Polenta

- Preheat the oven to 350°F (180°C) and coat the inside of the Dutch oven with butter or oil.
- In the Dutch oven, combine the polenta, corn, garlic, salt, and pepper. Add the broth and stir to mix.
- Bake, uncovered, for 50 minutes. Stir in the Parmesan cheese, cream, and butter, and return to the oven.
- Bake for an additional 10 minutes.

Make the Aioli

- While the polenta is baking, make the aioli. Chop the garlic in a food processor. Add the mustard, egg yolks, lemon juice, and a pinch of salt. Process for about 2 minutes, until the mixture is fully incorporated and pale yellow. With the motor running, slowly add the oil in a thin stream. Continue to process until the mixture is thick and creamy. Taste and add additional salt if needed. Transfer the mixture to a medium bowl and stir in the corn kernels.
- To serve, cut the polenta into wedges and serve with the aioli for dipping.

98 Syrupy Parsnip and Turnip

Prep time: 15 minutes | **Cook time:** 55 minutes | **Serves** 6

Ingredients

- 4 small parsnips, peeled and cut on the bias into 2-inch lengths
- 3 small turnips, quartered
- 3 small gold beets, halved 3 small red beets, halved 2 leeks, halved lengthwise
- 1 red onion, cut into wedges
- 3 tablespoons olive oil
- Kosher salt and freshly ground black pepper, to taste
- 1 cup pure maple syrup
- ¼ cup balsamic vinegar

Directions

- Preheat the oven to 425°F (220°C).
- In the Dutch oven, toss together the parsnips, turnips, beets, leeks, and onion with the olive oil until well coated. Season with salt and pepper. Bake, uncovered, for 45 to 50 minutes, until the vegetables are tender.
- Meanwhile, in a small saucepan, combine the maple syrup and vinegar and bring to a boil over medium-high heat. Reduce the heat to low and simmer until the mixture has reduced by about half and is thick and syrupy. Remove from the heat.
- Once the vegetables are tender, drizzle the syrup over the top and return the pot to the oven to roast for another 5 minutes. Serve hot.

99 Apple Cheese Cocottes

Prep time: 10 minutes | **Cook time:** 40 minutes | **Serves** 4

Ingredients

- 2 large crisp apples
- 1 (8-ounce / 227-g) wheel or wedge of Brie cheese, top and bottom rinds cut off and discarded
- ½ cup chopped walnuts or pecans (or use a mixture) 2 tablespoons honey
- Pinch of kosher salt
- ¼ teaspoon cinnamon
- Bread or crackers, for serving

Directions

- Preheat the oven to 375°F (190°C).
- Cut the top quarter of the apples off so that you have a flat top. Scoop out the apple cores and then use a thin knife to make two concentric circular cuts around the cores, cutting almost but not all the way through the bottom of the apple. Turn the apple upside down so that it is resting on its flat cut surface. Make several slits in the apple starting about ½ inch below the bottom or stem end of the apple (so that the apple still holds together after the cuts are made).
- Place each apple in a 10- or 12-inch mini cocotte, with the cut side up.
- Split the Brie in half and place one half on top of each apple, pressing it down to shape it over the apple. Bake for 20 minutes.
- Meanwhile, in a small saucepan set over medium heat, toast the nuts until they just begin to brown and release a nutty aroma. Stir in the honey, salt, and cinnamon, coating the nuts well.
- Remove the cocottes from the oven and spoon the nut mixture over the tops of the apples, dividing equally. Bake for an additional 15 to 20 minutes, until the apples are tender.
- Serve hot with bread or crackers.

100 Juicy Cranberry Sauce

Prep time: 5 minutes | **Cook time:** 30 minutes | **Makes about** 3 cups

Ingredients

- 1 pound (454 g) cranberries
- 2 cups sugar
- ½ cup apple juice
- ¼ teaspoon ground cinnamon
- ¼ cup bourbon

Directions

- In the Dutch oven, combine all the ingredients and bring to a boil, stirring frequently, over medium-high heat.
- Reduce the heat to medium-low and simmer, stirring occasionally, for 25 to 30 minutes, until the sauce thickens and the cranberries begin to break down. Cool before serving.

101 Apple and Mango Chutney

Prep time: 10 minutes | **Cook time:** 25 minutes | **Makes about** 2½ cups

Ingredients

- 2 medium apples, peeled, cored, and chopped
- 1 large mango, seeded, peeled, and chopped
- 1 hot red chile, seeded and diced
- ¾ cup sugar
- ½ small onion, diced
- ¼ cup golden raisins
- ¼ cup white vinegar
- 2 tablespoons finely chopped, peeled fresh ginger
- 2 teaspoons freshly squeezed lemon juice
- 1 teaspoon curry powder
- ¼ teaspoon cinnamon
- ¼ teaspoon ground nutmeg
- ¼ teaspoon kosher salt

Directions

- In the Dutch oven, combine the apples, mango, chile, sugar, onion, raisins, vinegar, and ginger and set over high heat. Bring the mixture to a boil and then reduce the heat and

simmer, stirring occasionally, until the fruit softens and the liquid thickens, about 20 minutes. Stir in the lemon juice, curry powder, cinnamon, nutmeg, and salt and continue to boil for another 5 minutes.
- Remove from the heat and cool before serving.

102 Golden Onion Rings

Prep time: 10 minutes | Cook time: 10 minutes | Serves 4 to 6

Ingredients

- 3 large Walla Walla (or Vidalia) sweet onions, peeled and cut into ½- inch-thick slices
- 1 egg, separated
- 1 cup milk
- 8 cups plus 1 tablespoon vegetable oil for deep-frying, divided
- ¾ cup plus 2 tablespoons all-purpose flour
- 2 teaspoons kosher salt
- 1½ teaspoons baking powder Sea salt, for sprinkling

Directions

- Separate the onions into rings. Cover with cold water for 30 minutes. Drain well on paper towels. In a large bowl, mix together the egg yolk, milk, and 1 tablespoon of the oil. In a medium bowl, mix together the flour, salt, and baking powder and add to the liquid mixture, blending into a smooth batter.
- Heat the remaining 8 cups oil in a Dutch oven over medium heat to 360°F (182°C). Meanwhile, beat the egg white until stiff and fold into the batter. Dip the onion slices into the batter and fry in the hot oil until golden, turning once. Drain on paper towels and sprinkle with sea salt. Serve right away!

103 Cheesy Spaghetti Squash

Prep time: 15 minutes | Cook time: 25 minutes | Serves 8

Ingredients

- 4 tablespoons (½ stick) unsalted butter
- 1 medium onion, peeled and finely chopped 1 pint sliced button mushrooms
- 1 clove garlic, peeled and minced
- ½ teaspoon salt
- ¼ teaspoon freshly cracked black pepper
- ¼ teaspoon oregano
- 1 large spaghetti squash, cooked and shredded 3 tablespoons all-purpose flour
- 2 cups half-and-half
- 1 cup shredded Cheddar cheese, divided
- 1 cup shredded Gruyère cheese, divided

Directions

- Heat a Dutch oven over medium heat. Once hot add butter. Once butter melts and starts to foam add onion and mushrooms and cook until they begin to soften, about 5 minutes. Add garlic, salt, pepper, and oregano and cook until the garlic is fragrant, about 30 seconds. Add the cooked spaghetti squash and cook until hot, about 1 minute.
- Add flour and cook until flour is moistened and cooked, about 3 minutes. Reduce the heat to low and slowly stir in half-and-half, making sure to stir out any lumps. Once all half-and-half is added increase heat to medium and let sauce come to a boil and thicken, about 8 to 10 minutes, stirring constantly.
- Reduce heat to low and add cheese in four additions, making sure each addition is melted before the next is added. Serve hot.

104 Golden Cheese Cocotte

Prep time: 10 minutes | **Cook time:** 20 minutes | **Makes about** 3 cups

Ingredients

- Butter or oil for preparing the mini cocottes
- 5 ounces (142 g) Goat cheese, at room temperature 2 ounces (57 g) cream cheese, at room temperature 2 ounces (57 g) Greek yogurt, at room temperature
- ½ cup grated Gruyère cheese, divided 1 tablespoon olive oil
- 1½ teaspoons balsamic vinegar
- 1 tablespoon minced flat-leaf parsley 1 teaspoon minced fresh sage
- 1 teaspoon minced fresh thyme 2 garlic cloves, minced
- Kosher salt and freshly ground black pepper, to taste
- Baguette, pita chips, crackers, or vegetables, for dipping

Directions

- Preheat the oven to 375°F (190°C) and coat two 12-ounce / 340- g mini cocottes with butter or oil. Set aside.
- In a medium bowl, combine the Goat cheese, cream cheese, yogurt, ¼ cup of Gruyère cheese, olive oil, vinegar, parsley, thyme, and garlic. Stir until well combined. Season with salt and pepper.
- Spoon the cheese mixture into the prepared cocottes, dividing equally, and top with the remaining ¼ cup of Gruyère cheese. Bake for about 20 minutes, until the dip is bubbly and golden brown on top.
- Serve hot with sliced baguette, pita chips, crackers, or vegetables for dipping.

Beef and Chicken

105 Beer-Braised Beef

Prep Time 10 min | **Cooking Time** 2 h 45 min | **Servings** 4

Ingredients

- 1-lb. chuck beef, diced
- ½ cup stout beer
- ½ cup beef stock
- ¾ tbsp all-purpose flour
- ¼ tsp garlic paste
- 1 tbsp Tomato paste
- ½ tsp balsamic vinegar
- ¼ tsp black pepper
- Salt to taste

Directions

- Season the beef with salt, pepper, and all-purpose flour.
- In a Dutch oven, add oil and cook the beef for 5 minutes until it gets brown color.
- Remove the beef pieces from the pan and add onion and garlic and cook for 3-4 minutes.
- Add the beef pieces and continue to cook for a minute or two.
- Add the remaining ingredients and simmer the mixture for 2 – 2 ½ hours until the beef is tender.
- Serve with rice

106 Korean Beef Stew

Prep Time 15 min | **Cooking Time** 2 hr 20 min | **Servings** 4

Ingredients

- 1 lb.. chuck beef, diced
- 1 red bell pepper, diced
- 2 medium carrots, sliced
- 2 cloves garlic, crushed
- 1 tsp minced ginger 2 tbsp cooking oil
- ½ tbsp corn starch
- ½ tbsp sesame oil 2 tbsp soya sauce
- 2 tbsp brown sugar
- ¼ tsp red chili flakes
- ¼ tsp black pepper Salt to taste

Directions

- Toss the beef pieces in flour.
- In a Dutch oven, add cooking oil and beef pieces and cook for 8 minutes until it gets a golden color.
- Remove the beef from the Dutch oven and set aside.
- Add bell peppers and carrots and cook for 3 minutes.
- Add sesame oil, ginger, and garlic and cook for another minute.
- Add beef stock and corn flour and let it simmer for 5 minutes.
- Add beef pieces, brown sugar, soy sauce, and red pepper flakes.
- Place the Dutch oven in a pre-heated oven at 350 F and let it cook for 2 hours. Serve with quinoa or rice.

107 Braised Short Ribs

Prep Time 10 min | **Cooking Time** 20 min | **Servings** 4

Ingredients

- 3 pounds beef short ribs, boneless and 2 inches thick
- 1 onion, chopped
- 6 cloves garlic, crushed
- 2 inches fresh ginger root, sliced
- 2 ½ cups red wine, dry
- ½ cup mirin
- 1/3 cup soya sauce
- ¼ cup brown sugar, light
- ¾ cup daikon, peeled and diced into 1-inch cubes
- 2 tbsp. olive oil
- 2 cups of water Salt to taste

Directions

- Season the short ribs with salt and let them sit for 15 minutes.
- In a large Dutch oven, add oil and heat.
- Add the short ribs and cook for 10 minutes until they are brown from all sides.
- Remove the short ribs and add onions, ginger and garlic and cook for 8 minutes.

- Add dry red wine and bring it to a boil.
- Reduce the heat and let it simmer for 10 minutes.
- Add soya sauce, mirin, brown sugar and water.
- Add ribs and bring the mixture to boil.
- Reduce the heat and let it simmer for 2 hours on medium heat.
- Add daikon radishes and let it cook for another hour.
- Serve with rice

108 Beef Short Ribs Braised in Red Wine

Prep Time 10 min | **Cooking Time** 20 min | **Servings** 4

Ingredients

- 4 large beefy short ribs
- 2 medium onions diced
- 6 clove Garlic chopped
- 1 celery stalk diced
- 1 carrot diced
- 1 spring fresh thyme
- 2 bay leaves
- 1 ½ cup red wine, dry
- 1 tbsp. olive oil
- 1 tbsp tomato paste
- 2 tbsp. white flour
- 2 cups of water
- Black pepper to taste
- Salt to taste

Directions

- Season the short ribs with salt and pepper generously and let them sit for some time.
- In a Dutch oven, add olive oil and place the short ribs for 5 minutes on all side until they get a nice brown color.
- Remove from heat and let the ribs rest for some time.
- In the same Dutch oven, add ¾ tbsp. of olive oil and add onions, celery and carrots.
- Cook for about 8 minutes until the vegetables are soft.
- Add chopped garlic and continue to cook for 5-6 minutes.
- Add tomato paste and continue to cook for 5 minutes.
-
- Add white flour and combine for 2 minutes.
- Add in dry red wine and stir well until everything is combined.
- Add bay leaves, thyme and water and bring it to a boil.
- Place the browned short ribs back in the Dutch oven and pour the liquid on them using a spoon.
- Place the Dutch oven in a preheated oven at 425
- °F (220 °C) covered and let it cook for 1 ½ hour.
- Take the Dutch oven out and slip the ribs and add some more water if the mixture is getting dry.
- Cover and place in the oven to cook for 1 ½ more hours.
- Serve hot with your favorite puree or mashed

109 Carrot Beef Stew

Prep Time 20 min | **Cooking Time** 2h 30 min | **Servings** 4

Ingredients

- 1 pound boneless beef, cubes in 1 inch cut
- 4 tbsp. all-purpose flour
- small onion, chopped
- potatoes, peeled and cubed in 1-inch cut
- 2 carrots, sliced
- ½ cup peas, fresh or frozen
- 2 cloves garlic, minced
- 2 cups beef stock
- ½ tsp dried thyme
- ½ tsp black pepper
- ½ tsp salt
- 1 tbsp. canola oil

Directions

- In a bowl, combine 2 tbsp. flour, salt and pepper.
- Add beef and mix well to coat.
- In a Dutch oven, add oil and beef and cook from all sides for 3-4 minutes and set aside.

- In the same Dutch oven, add onions and cook for 5 minutes until softened.
- Add garlic and cook for a minute.
- Add remaining flour and stir.
- Gradually add beef stock and stir well. Add beef, thyme and tomatoes.
- Place the Dutch oven in a preheated oven at 350 °F (180 °C) for 1 ¼ hour.
- Add carrots, peas and potatoes and bake for another hour.

110 Chuck Beef Roast

Prep Time 15 min | **Cooking Time** 4h | **Serves** 4

Ingredients

- 3 pounds chuck beef
- 1 white onion, quartered
- 4 russet potatoes, whole
- 1 medium sweet potato, cut into large cubes
- 6 cloves garlic, whole
- 1 ½ cup beef stock
- ¼ cup red wine
- ½ tbsp. dried thyme 1 tsp black pepper Salt to taste
- 1 tbsp olive oil

Directions

- Sprinkle salt and black pepper on chuck beef in let it sit for a few minutes.
- In a Dutch oven, add olive oil and add beef.
- Cook the beef on each side for 3 minutes until brown.
- Place all vegetables around the beef.
- Pour the beef stock and red wine on it as well.
- Sprinkle dried thyme and cover the Dutch oven.
- Place in a preheated oven at 400 °F (200 °C) and let it roast for 4 hours.

111 Beef Roast and Potato

Serves 8 | Prep. time 15–20 minutes | Cooking time 4 hours

Ingredients

- ½ pound thick-cut bacon, coarsely chopped
- 1 (4–5 pound) beef chuck roast
- Salt and pepper to taste 1 yellow onion, minced
- 3 sprigs thyme or rosemary
- ½ cup dry red wine 2 cups beef broth
- 1 pound small potatoes, halved
- ½ pound carrots, peeled and cut into 2-inch pieces

Directions

- Preheat the oven to 325°F (160°C).
- Season the meat with salt and pepper.
- Heat the Dutch oven over medium-high heat.
- Add the bacon and cook until crisp. Drain over paper towels and set aside. Discard the drippings.
- Place the chuck roast in the Dutch oven and spray with some cooking spray.
- Cook for 5–6 minutes per side until evenly browned. Set aside.
- Keep 1 tablespoon of Fat in the Dutch oven.
- Reduce heat to medium and add the onion, salt, and pepper.
- Stir-cook for 4–6 minutes until softened and light brown.
- Pour in the wine and stir-cook until reduced to half.
- Mix in the broth and thyme/rosemary.
- Return the beef to the Dutch oven and stir to coat well. Bring it to a simmer.
- Cover and bake for about 3 hours.
- Add the bacon, potatoes, and carrots around the roast. Season the veggies with salt and pepper.
- Bake for 1 more hour until the veggies are tender.
- Set aside to settle for 15 minutes.
- Slice and serve warm with braised liquid on top.

112 Braised Beef Ribs

Serves 4 | Prep. time 10–15 minutes | Cooking time 2½ hours

Ingredients

- 3 pounds bone-in beef short ribs 2 tablespoons vegetable oil
- Salt and pepper to taste 1 large onion, sliced
- 4 cloves garlic, minced
- 3 cups cooking liquid (wine, beer, or low-sodium broth) 3–4 sprigs fresh rosemary or thyme

Directions

- Coat the short ribs with oil and season with salt and pepper.
- Add the ribs to the Dutch oven and heat it over medium-high heat.
- Stir-cook for 7–8 minutes per side until evenly brown.
- Add the onion and garlic; stir-cook for 4–5 minutes until softened and fragrant.
- Add the cooking liquid and bring to a simmer.
- Add the herb sprigs.
- Cover and cook over medium heat for about 2 hours until the meat flakes easily.
- Set aside for 20 minutes to settle.
- Serve warm with onion sauce on top.

113 Dutch Oven Corned Beef

Serves 8 | Prep. time 10 minutes | Cooking time 3 hours

Ingredients

- 1 (3–4 pound) corned beef brisket with a spice packet, trimmed
- 1 medium onion, sliced
- 1 celery rib, sliced
- ¼ cup butter, cubed
- 1 packed cup brown sugar
- ⅔ cup ketchup
- ⅓ cup white vinegar
- 2 tablespoons prepared mustard
- 2 teaspoons prepared horseradish

Directions

- Add the seasoning pack and beef to the Dutch oven and cover with water.
- Add the celery and onion. Bring to a boil.
- Reduce heat to low, cover, and simmer for about 2½ hours until the meat is tender.
- Drain the liquid and remove the vegetables.
- Transfer the beef to a shallow greased roasting pan. Set aside to cool.
- Clean the Dutch oven. Add the butter and melt it over medium-high heat.
- Add the remaining ingredients; stir and cook for 25 minutes until the sauce is thickened.
- Slice the beef, pour the sauce over it, and serve warm.

114 Beef Carrot Meal

Serves 4 | Prep. time 25 minutes | Cooking time 1½–2 hours

Ingredients

- ½ cup red wine or water
- ½ (6-ounce) can tomato pastes with garlic, basil, and oregano
- 1–1½ pounds boneless beef short ribs, fat trimmed and cut into bite-sized chunks
- Salt and pepper to taste
- 10 cloves garlic, peeled and smashed
- 1 pound Roma tomatoes, chopped
- ½ pound fresh baby carrots, peeled and chopped Fresh basil (optional)

Directions

- Add the water/wine and tomato paste to a mixing bowl. Mix well.
- Season the beef chunks with salt and pepper.
- Add the beef chunks over the bottom of the Dutch oven.
- Add the garlic, tomatoes, and carrots. Pour in the tomato paste mixture.
- Cover and cook for 1½–2 hours until cooked to satisfaction.
- Serve warm with basil leaves on top.

115 Beef Burgundy

Serves 6 | Prep. time 10 minutes | Cooking time 1, 20 h

Ingredients

- 5 slices bacon (chopped)
- 1 cup yellow or white onions (chopped)
- 3 medium carrots (cut
- into 1/4-inch slices) 1/4 cup celery (finely chopped)
- 2 pounds beef chuck (cubed)
- 1/2 teaspoon salt
- 1/4 teaspoon ground black pepper
- 2 teaspoons dried parsley
- 1/2 teaspoon dried
- thyme
- 1/4 teaspoon dried crushed rosemary
- 1/16 teaspoon ground allspice (scant pinch) 1 tablespoon all-purpose flour
- 1 teaspoon tomato paste 1 cups mushrooms (cleaned, coarsely chopped)
- 1 cup burgundy (or dry red wine)
- 1/2 cup beef stock

Directions

- Gather the ingredients.
- In a large saucepan over high heat, cook the bacon until it turns crisp. Transfer the bacon to a paper-towel-lined plate to drain.
- Pour all but 2 tablespoons of bacon grease from the pan. Saute the onions, carrots, and celery in the bacon grease for 5 minutes, until the vegetables turn soft. Transfer them to a bowl with a slotted spoon and set it aside for a moment.
- Season the beef with the salt and pepper and brown it in the remaining bacon grease.
-
- Once all sides of the beef are browned, sprinkle the parsley, thyme, rosemary, allspice, and flour over the beef.
- Stir in the tomato paste and cook the spiced beef for 1 minute.
- Add the mushrooms, cooked vegetables, crisped bacon, red wine, and beef stock, into the pan with the beef, and then cook the mixture over low heat, covered, for 1 hour and 15 minutes.
- Though this is the quick version and ready to eat the day it is made, it will richen by being left overnight and rewarmed and eaten the next day.
- Serve and enjoy!

116 Vegetable Beef Soup

Serves 8 | Prep. time 20 minutes | Cooking time 1, 30 h

Ingredients

- 1 tablespoon olive oil
- 1 ½ pounds beef top sirloin, cut into bite-sized pieces
- 3 ribs celery, chopped 1 small onion, chopped 4 cups water
- 2 (14 ounce) cans beef broth
- 1 (14 ounce) can petite diced tomatoes
- 1 (14 ounce) can diced tomatoes
- 2 eaches potatoes, cut into bite-sized pieces
- 10 eaches baby carrots, chopped
- 2 teaspoons garlic powder
- 2 eaches small bay leaves 1 cup frozen corn
- 1 cup frozen green beans
- 2 teaspoons hot pepper sauce

Directions

- Heat olive oil in a large Dutch oven over medium-high heat. Saute beef in hot oil until completely browned, about 5 minutes. Remove browned beef with a slotted spoon to a plate, retaining beef drippings in the Dutch oven.
- Saute celery and onion in the beef drippings until tender, about 5 minutes. Return beef to the Dutch oven; add water, beef broth, petite diced tomatoes, diced tomatoes, potatoes, baby carrots, garlic powder, and bay leaves.
-
- Place a cover on the Dutch oven, bring the mixture to a boil, reduce heat to low, remove cover from the pot, and simmer the mixture until thick, about 45 minutes.

- Stir frozen corn, frozen green beans, and hot pepper sauce into the mixture in the pot. Place cover on the pot and cook at a simmer until the corn and green beans are just cooked through, about 30 minutes.

117 Baked Beef Stew

Serves 8 | Prep. time 30 min | Cooking time 2, 15 h

Ingredients

- 2 lbs stewing beef, cubed
- ¼ cup flour
- salt and pepper
- 2 cups beef stock
- ½ cup red wine
- 1 (14 ounce) can tomatoes, with juice
- 5 carrots, sliced
- 2 onions, sliced
- 1 cups mushroom, sliced
- ½ teaspoon dried rosemary

Directions

- Toss the beef in the flour and place on a cookie sheet and bake for
- 10-15 minutes in a 500F degrees oven.
- Let the meat get lightly browned.
- Meanwhile, in a large Dutch oven combine all the other ingredients and bring to a boil.
- Put the browned meat in the pot, cover and bake in a 300F degrees for about 2 hours (until the beef is tender).

118 Beef Pot Roast

Serves 8 | Prep. time 30 min | Cooking time 2 h

Ingredients

- 1 boneless beef roast
- 1/2-3 lb, cut to fit pot or crockpot (chuck, shoulder or round)
- 2 tablespoons oil
- salt and pepper, to taste
- 1 tablespoon Worcestershire sauce
- 1 teaspoon instant beef bouillon
- 1 teaspoon dried basil, crushed
- ¾lb new potatoes or 2 medium sweet potatoes
- 1 lb carrots or 6 medium parsnips, peeled, cut into 2- inch pieces
- 2 onions, cut into wedges
- 2 celery ribs, bias-cut in 1-inch pieces
- ¼ cup flour

Directions

- Trim fat from meat. Brown meat on all sides in hot oil in a 4- to 6-quart Dutch oven. Drain fat.
- Mix 3/4 cup water, Worcestershire sauce, bouillon, basil and salt and pepper to taste.
- Pour over roast. Bring to boil. Reduce heat and simmer, covered, 1 hour.
- Peel a strip of skin from center of each new potato or peel and quarter sweet potatoes.
- Add potatoes, carrots, onions and celery to pot. Return to boil. Reduce heat.
- Simmer covered, until tender, 45 to 60 minutes. Add water as needed.
- Transfer meat and vegetables to platter. Reserve juices.
- To prepare gravy, measure juices, skim off fat, and add enough water to make 1 1/2 cups. Return to Dutch oven.
- In a small bowl, stir 1/2 cup water into flour. Stir into pan juices. Cook, stirring, on medium heat until thickened, then 1 minute more. Season to taste. Serve with pot roast.
- For oven cooking: After browning meat and adding liquid mixture to pan, bake, covered, for 1 hour at 325 degrees. Prepare potatoes as directed. Add vegetables to meat. Bake, covered, until tender, 45 to 60 minutes.

119 Greek Beef Stew

Serves 3 | Prep. time 30 min | Cooking time 2,15 h

Ingredients

- 3 tablespoons extra virgin olive oil
- 1 lb stewing beef
- 1 (6-ounce) can tomato paste
- 3 tablespoons red wine vinegar
- 2 cups water

- ¼ teaspoon cinnamon
- 2 onions, chopped
- 2 cloves garlic, minced
- ½ teaspoon ground black pepper
- ¼ teaspoon ground cloves
- 2 teaspoons salt

Directions

- Heat oil in large stewing pot.
- Add meat.
- Brown the meat slightly on all sides.
- Add all remaining ingredients.
- Bring stew to a boil, then reduce heat, cover, and simmer two hours (or longer for a thicker sauce)

120 Beef Bourguignon

Serves 4 | **Prep. time** 10 min | **Cooking time** 35 min

Ingredients

- 1 tbsp olive oil
- 2 lb. beef brisket, 2-inch cut
- ½ cup bacon, chopped
- 1 medium white onion, diced
- 1 medium carrot, sliced
- ½ lb. white mushrooms, quartered
- 4 cloves garlic, crushed
- 1 ¼ tbsp flour
- 1 ¼ tbsp tomato paste 2 cups red wine
- 3 cups beef stock 1 ½ tbsp butter
- ½ tsp dried thyme
- ½ tsp black pepper powder
- Salt to taste

Directions

- In a Dutch oven, add oil and sauté bacon for 3 minutes until it is crisp. Remove from the Dutch oven and set aside.
- Add beef and cook for 5 minutes until it gets a golden color. Remove from the pot and set aside.
- Add onions and carrots and sauté for 3-4 minutes until onions are soft.
- Add ½ of the garlic cook for a minute.
- Discard extra fat leaving 1 tbsp in the Dutch oven.
- Add bacon and beef and season it with salt and pepper.
- Add flour and cook for 4-5 minutes.
- Add red wine, tomato stock, herbs, and Bring the mixture to a boil and let it simmer for 5 minutes.
- Place the Dutch oven in a pre-heated oven at 350 F for 3-4 hours.
- In a pan, add butter, garlic, and mushroom. Sautee for 5 minutes and season with salt and pepper.
- Strain the beef mixture to get to separate the sauce from beef.
- Add the meat back into the Dutch oven and add mushrooms.
- Simmer the stock until it is reduced to 2-2 ½ cup.
- Pour the sauce over meat and serve with mashed potatoes or rice.

121 Indian Beef Stew

Serves 4 | **Prep. time** 15 min | **Cooking time** 2,10h

Ingredients

- 1-lb.. beef, boneless and cut into cubes
- 1 cup baby carrots, diced
- 2 cups baby potatoes, dices
- 1 onion, sliced
- 1 tbsp ginger, crushed
- 2 tomatoes, chopped
- 1 jalapeno pepper, de- deeded and chopped
- ½ cup sour cream
- 1 tsp turmeric powder
- 1 tsp all-spice powder
- 1 tsp cayenne powder
- 1 tsp salt

Directions

- Blend onion, garlic, ginger, tomatoes, sour cream, jalapeños, all- spice powder, cayenne, and salt.
- In a Dutch oven, add cooking oil, beef, and potatoes and cook for 5- 7 minutes.
- Pour the blended spice paste and mix well.

- Add ¼ cup water and place the Dutch oven in a pre-heated oven at 350 F for 60 minutes.
- Add carrots and bake of another 60 minutes until the meat gets tender.
- Serve with naan.

122 Roasted Chicken and Potatoes

Serves 4 | **Prep time** 10 minutes | **Cooking time** 60 minutes

Ingredients

- 1 (4-pound) whole chicken Salt and pepper to taste
- 4 cloves garlic, minced
- 5 tablespoons butter, softened
- 2 tablespoons basil, freshly chopped Juice and zest of 1 lemon
- 1½ pounds baby potatoes

Directions

- Preheat the oven to 450°F (220°C).
- Wash the chicken and pat dry with paper towels.
- Season with salt and pepper.
- Mix the butter with the freshly chopped basil and lemon zest.
- Brush the chicken with the butter, rubbing it under the skin with your hands.
- Place the lemon juice inside the chicken. Crush the garlic and place it inside the chicken as well.
- Arrange the baby potatoes in the Dutch oven. Sprinkle with butter and season with salt and pepper.
- Place the whole chicken in the center of the Dutch oven.
- Cover and bake for 20–25 minutes.
- Remove the lid and reduce the heat to 350°F (180°C). Bake uncovered for about 40 minutes.
- Serve warm

123 Turkey Meatballs in Tomato Sauce

Serves 4 | **Prep time** 10 minutes | **Cooking time** 20 minutes

Ingredients

- 2 pounds ground turkey Salt and pepper to taste
- 1 egg yolk
- ¼ cup breadcrumbs
- ¼ cup grated Parmesan cheese 3 tablespoons butter
- 2 cups tomato sauce

Directions

- Add the ground turkey to a large mixing bowl and season with salt and pepper.
- Stir in the egg yolk, breadcrumbs, and Parmesan.
- Mix well with your hands.
- With wet hands, form Ping-Pong-ball-sized meatballs.
- Warm the butter in the Dutch oven over medium heat. Add the meatballs.
- Cook for about 5 minutes on each side.
- Cover and cook for about 5 more minutes to reduce the juices.
- Pour in the tomato sauce and cook for 10 more minutes uncovered.
- Serve warm.

124 Chicken Fajitas

Serves 4 | Prep time 10 minutes | Cooking time 20 minutes

Ingredients

- 3 tablespoons olive oil 3 bell peppers
- 1-pound chicken boneless breasts
- ½ onion cut into half-moons 4 8-inch flour tortillas
- ¼ cup sour cream
- Salt and pepper to taste

Directions

- Warm the Dutch oven over medium heat and pour in the olive oil.
- Dice the bell peppers and cut the chicken into strips.
- Cook the onion in the hot oil for 2 minutes until tender and then stir in the peppers and chicken.
- Cook for about 10 minutes.
- Season with salt and pepper.
- Serve on tortillas topped with a dollop of sour cream and sprinkled with pepper.

125 One-Pot Chicken Parmesan Spaghetti

Serves 4 | Prep time 5 minutes | Cooking time 15 minutes

Ingredients

- 2 tablespoons olive oil
- 1 pound chicken breast, diced into 1-inch pieces Salt and pepper to taste
- 1 pound spaghetti
- 2½ cups marinara sauce 2 cups of water
- 1 cup grated Parmesan cheese 1½ teaspoons Italian seasoning

Directions

- Add the olive oil to the Dutch oven and heat over medium heat.
- Add the chicken pieces and season with salt and pepper.
- Stir in the spaghetti, marinara sauce, water, and Italian seasoning.
- Bring to a boil and reduce the heat to low.
- Cover and cook for 10–15 minutes until all the liquid is absorbed.
- Stir in the Parmesan.
- Serve in bowls with a drizzle of olive oil and an extra sprinkle of Italian seasoning.

126 Crispy Fried Chicken Thighs

Serves 4 | Prep time 10 minutes | Cooking time 15 minutes

Ingredients

- ½ cup buttermilk
- 2 teaspoons dried paprika (divided) Salt and pepper to taste
- 2 pounds chicken thighs
- 1 cup + ½ teaspoon all-purpose flour
- ¼ cup olive oil
- 1 teaspoon dried garlic
- ¼ cup of water

Directions

- Add the buttermilk to a medium mixing bowl. Stir in 1 teaspoon of the paprika and season with salt and pepper.
- Place the chicken thighs in the buttermilk mixture and let them sit for 5 minutes.
- On a plate, mix the 1 cup of flour, salt and pepper to taste, the remaining 1 teaspoon of paprika, and the garlic.
- Warm the olive oil in the Dutch oven over medium heat.
- Shake excess liquid off the chicken thighs and coat them with the flour mixture.
- Fry the chicken thighs fry in the heated oil for about 8 minutes on each side.
- Remove the chicken thighs and stir in the ½ teaspoon of flour. Cook for 1 minute.
- Stir in the water and whisk with a wire whisk until a creamy sauce/gravy develops.
- Serve the sauce on top of the fried chicken thighs.

127 Creamy Parmesan Chicken with Mushroom Sauce

Serves 4 | Prep time 10 minutes | Cooking time 25 minutes

Ingredients

- 3 tablespoons butter
- 1½ pounds chicken breast Salt and pepper to taste
- 1 pound mushrooms, diced 2 cloves garlic, minced
- 1 cup heavy cream
- ½ cup grated Parmesan cheese

Directions

- Warm the butter in the Dutch oven over medium heat.
- Season the chicken breast with salt and pepper to taste.
- Add the diced mushrooms to the Dutch oven. Season with salt and pepper and cook for 7–10 minutes.
- Remove the mushrooms and cook the chicken breast for 7–10 minutes on each side.
- Return the mushrooms to the Dutch oven and stir in the garlic.
- Pour in the heavy cream and cook for 5 minutes.
- Just before serving, sprinkle the Parmesan on top, cover, and let sit for 5 minutes.

128 Creamy Chicken and Rice

Serves 4 | Prep time 10 minutes | Cooking time 30 minutes

Ingredients

- 3 tablespoons butter
- 1 pound chicken breast, diced into 1-inch pieces Salt and pepper to taste
- 1 cup arborio rice 3 cups of water
- ½ cup white wine
- ½ cup grated Parmesan cheese
- ¼ cup parsley, freshly chopped

Directions

- Warm the butter in the Dutch oven over medium heat.
- Season the chicken breast with salt and pepper to taste.
- Cook for 5 minutes on each side.
- Stir in the rice and season with salt and pepper.
- Stir in the wine and water and bring to a boil.
- Reduce the heat to low and cook, covered, for 20–25 minutes without opening the lid.
- Stir in the Parmesan cheese and freshly chopped parsley.
- Serve in bowls.

129 Chicken & Vegetables

Serves 4 | Prep time 15 minutes | Cooking time 1,15 h

Ingredients

- 4 chicken thighs, with bone and skin
- 1 medium onion, chopped
- 3 potatoes, diced
- 4 carrots, sliced
- 1 ½ cup chicken stock
- ¼ cup white wine 1 tbsp olive oil
- 1 tbsp all-purpose flour
- 2 tbsp fresh thyme 2 tbsp fresh parsley 1 tsp paprika
- 1 tsp black pepper
- Salt to taste

Directions

- Season the chicken with salt and black pepper.
- In a Dutch oven, add oil and place chicken pieces.
- Cook the chicken for 5 minutes on each side until it gets golden brown color.
- Transfer the chicken to a plate.
- In the same Dutch oven, add onion and cook for a minute.
- Add carrots, potatoes, a pinch salt, and pepper and cook for 5 minutes until the vegetables get some color.
- Add all-purpose flour and cook for a minute.

- Add white wine and cook until the alcohol evaporates.
- Add chicken stock and paprika, mix well and let the stock simmer for 3-4 minutes.
- Add chicken to the Dutch oven and bring it to boil.
- Place the Dutch oven in a pre-heated oven at 350 F for 40 minutes.
- Sprinkle thyme and parsley and serve with rice.

130 Chicken Braised in Wine

Serves 4 | **Prep time** 10minutes + 2h marinade | **Cooking time** 1,15 h

Ingredients

- 4 chicken thighs, with bone and skin
- ½ tsp dried rosemary
- ½ tsp paprika
- ½ coriander powder
- ¼ tsp black pepper
- ¼ tsp all-spice powder
- 1 tbsp olive oil
- 2 tbsp tomato paste
- 2 medium onions, sliced
- 1 cup white mushrooms, sliced
- 3 cloves garlic, crushed
- ¼ cup red wine, dry 1 cup chicken stock

Directions

- In a bowl, mix dried rosemary, paprika, coriander powder, all-spice powder, black pepper powder, salt to taste, and rub on the chicken using your hands.
- Marinade the chicken for 2 hours.
- In a Dutch oven, add olive oil and chicken and cook it for 4 minutes on both sides until it gets color.
- Remove the chicken and add onion and garlic. Cook for 5 minutes until onion is soft.
- Add tomato paste, chicken stock, and dry red wine and let it simmer for 5 minutes. Stir in rice and cook for 5 minutes more.
- Place chicken in the pot and bring it to boil.
- Place the Dutch oven in a pre-heated oven at 350 F for 40 minutes.
- Meanwhile, in a frying pan, add a dash of olive oil and sauté mushrooms for 4- 5 minutes.
- Add the mushroom into the Dutch oven after 30 minutes of cooking.
- Remove the chicken from the oven and serve with rice.

131 Garlic Chicken

Serves 4 | **Prep time** 10minutes | **Cooking time** 45 min

Ingredients

- 3 lb. chicken, cut into 8 pieces
- 2 tbsp cooking oil
- 10 cloves garlic, whole
- 1 cup white wine, dry
- 1 cup chicken stock
- 2 tbsp butter
- 2 tbsp all- purpose flour
- ¼ tsp black pepper powder
- Salt to taste

Directions

- Sprinkle chicken with salt and pepper.
- In a Dutch oven, add oil and chicken and cook for 8 minutes until they get brown color.
- Remove the chicken from pot and set aside.
- In the same Dutch oven, add garlic, and cook until brown.
- Add flour and cook for a minute.
- Place the chicken in the pot and cover.
- Place the Dutch oven in the pre- heated oven at 400 F for 5 minutes.
- Remove the pot from the oven and remove chicken pieces.
- Place the Dutch oven on a stove, add the wine and let it simmer for a minute.
- Add chicken stock and let it boil for 3 minutes.
- At butter and whisk until the sauce gets thick.
- Pour the sauce over chicken and serve hot.

132 Chicken, Rosemary and Vegetables

Serves 4 | Prep time 10 minutes | Cooking time 35 min

Ingredients

- 2 boneless chicken breasts, cut into half
- 2 cups baby potatoes, quartered
- 1 cup baby carrots
- 3 tbsp olive oil
- 2 tbsp fresh rosemary, chopped
- 1 tsp garlic powder
- ½ tsp paprika powder
- 1 tsp black pepper powder
- Salt to taste

Directions

- In a bowl, mix chicken breast with ½ tsp garlic powder, paprika powder, ½ tsp black pepper and salt and marinate for 1 hour.
- In another bowl, add baby carrots, potatoes, 2 tbsp olive oil, 1 tbsp rosemary, salt and black pepper. Mix well and set aside.
- In a Dutch oven, add 1 tbsp olive oil and place chicken breasts. Cook the chicken on both sides until slightly browned.
- Once the chicken is slightly brown, add the mixed vegetables in the Dutch oven and sprinkle the remaining rosemary.
- Cover the pot and place it in the oven preheated to 425 °F (220 °C) for 30 minutes.
- Serve immediately.

133 Whole Chicken Roast

Serves 4 | Prep time 15 minutes | Cooking time 1,30h

Ingredients

- 4 lbs. whole chicken
- 2 onions, sliced
- 2 lemons
- 4 tbsp unsalted butter
- 2 tbsp fresh rosemary, chopped
- 1 rosemary spring
- 3 cloves garlic, crushed
- 2 cloves garlic, halved
- 1 tbsp black pepper
- Salt to taste

Directions

- In a bowl, melt butter and add chopped rosemary, crushed garlic, and lemon zest of two lemons, black pepper and salt. Mix well and set aside.
- Clean the chicken and pat it dry.
- Rub the chicken with butter using your hands so that you cover every part of the chicken with the butter.
- Stuff the chicken cavity with lemon rinds, rosemary spring and halved garlic cloves.
- Place sliced onions in the bottom of the Dutch oven and place the chicken on it.
- Pour the lemon juice on the chicken.
- Preheat the oven to 425 °F (220 °C) and place the Dutch oven in it for 30 minutes uncovered.
- Reduce the heat to 350 °F (180 °C) and let it cook for 60 minutes.
- Check its internal temperature using a kitchen thermometer, and if the chicken reaches 165 degrees, it means it is ready.
- Take the Dutch oven out and let the chicken rest for 10 minutes before serving.

134 Lime Chicken

Serves 4 | Prep time 15 minutes | Cooking time 1,20h

Ingredients

- 8 small chicken thighs
- 3 tablespoons extra virgin olive oil
- 20 black olives, pitted
- 1 onion, chopped
- 1 lime juice and zest
- 1 lime, sliced
- 1 teaspoon curry
- ½ teaspoon paprika
- 1 tablespoon cilantro, chopped
- Salt and pepper, to taste
- Approx. 3 tablespoons heavy cream

Directions

- Heat extra virgin olive oil in a Dutch oven over medium-high heat and brown the meat.
- Reduce the heat, cover, and cook the chicken over low heat for 1 hour. Add some vegetable broth if needed.
- Transfer the chicken onto a plate and add onions in the Dutch oven.
- Cook and stir until golden.
- Add in lime juice and zest, olives, powders, salt, pepper, and cilantro. Simmer for 5 minutes.
- Stir in heavy cream and return the chicken to Dutch oven.
- Cover it with lime slices, cover with the lid and cook over low heat for an additional 5 to 7 minutes.

135 Chicken Stew

Serves 4 | **Prep time** 10 minutes | **Cooking time** 1,45 h

Ingredients

- 2 lbs. chicken thighs or drumsticks
- 3 garlic cloves, minced
- 20 oz. large tomatoes, diced
- 1 cup green beans
- 2 ½ cups chicken broth
- 1 rosemary sprig
- 8 basil leaves, chopped
- 1 tablespoon cilantro, chopped
- Salt and pepper, to taste

Directions

- Preheat your oven to 320°F.
- Season chicken thighs with salt and pepper.
- Heat extra virgin olive oil in a Dutch oven over medium heat.
- Brown the meat on each side.
- Add in the rest of the ingredients, and place in the oven.
- Cook covered for an hour and then uncovered for an additional 30 minutes.

136 Soy Sauce Chicken with Shitake Mushrooms

Serves 4 | **Prep time** 30 minutes | **Cooking time** 45 h

Ingredients

For the Marinade:

- 1/3 cup soy sauce 1/3 cup water
- 3 Tbsp dark soy sauce
- 4 Tbsp brown sugar

For the Chicken:

- 4 chicken thighs (skin removed)
- 6 dried shiitake mushrooms
- 2 Tbsp Chinese rice wine 2 Tbsp olive oil (or dry sherry)
- One and half green onions (washed and finely chopped)
- 3 slices ginger
- 2 cloves garlic (crushed)
- 1 small onion (peeled and chopped)
- Extra salt, and freshly ground black or white pepper, to taste

Directions

- Mix together the marinade ingredients. Make 2 or 3 diagonal cuts on each side of the chicken thighs. Place the thighs in a large resealable plastic bag and add the marinade. Marinate the chicken in the refrigerator for 4 hours or longer, moving the bag occasionally.
- While the chicken is marinating, soften the dried shiitake mushrooms by soaking in hot water for about 30 minutes. Squeeze out any excess water. Cut off the stems and cut the caps in half.
- In a large saucepan, heat the olive oil over medium heat. Add the chicken thighs and cook for 5 to 6 minutes until browned, turning over once. Add the onion and saute until softened (about 5 minutes). At the same time, you are browning the chicken and cooking the onions, bring the reserved marinade to boil in a small saucepan. Boil the marinade for 5 minutes.

- Add the marinade and the dried mushrooms to the chicken and onions. Season with salt and freshly ground black or white pepper if desired. Simmer, uncovered, on low heat for 30 minutes, or until the chicken is cooked through, adding water if needed. Serve soy sauce chicken hot over steamed rice.

137 Morrocan Chicken with Preserved Lemon and Olives

Serves 4 | Prep time 15 minutes | Cooking time 1,30 h

- 1 whole chicken, skin on or removed, cut into pieces
- 1/3 cup vegetable oil (or a mix of vegetable oil and olive oil; or a mix of oil and butter)
- 2 very large white or yellow onions (1 lb or 1/2 kg), sliced as thinly as possible
- One small handful of fresh cilantro, chopped
- One small handful of fresh parsley, chopped
- 2 or 3 cloves of garlic, finely chopped or pressed
- 2 Tsp ginger
- 1 Tsp pepper
- 1 Tsp turmeric
- ½ Tsp salt
- 1/2 Tsp saffron threads, crumbled (divided; optional)

For the Sauce

- 1/2 to 1 teaspoon smen (Moroccan preserved butter - optional)
- 1 handful green or red olives, or mixed
- 1 preserved lemon, quartered and seeds removed

Directions

Cook the Chicken:

- Ahead of time if possible, combine the chicken with the onion, garlic, herbs, and spices, including half of the saffron.
- When ready to cook, transfer the chicken and onions (scrape every last bit out of your bowl) to a Dutch oven. Cover and cook the chicken over medium or medium-low heat, gently stirring and turning the chicken every 15 minutes.
- When the chicken is cooked, carefully transfer it to a plate and cover.

Reduce the Sauce:

- Continue cooking the onion mixture and sauce over medium-low heat, stirring occasionally, until the liquids evaporate and the onions can be mashed into a blended mass which separates from the oils.
- Add the preserved lemon, olives, the rest of the saffron, and a few tablespoons of water, and simmer gently for 5 to 10 minutes. Return the chicken to the pot to heat through, or place under the broiler to brown the skin.
- Place the chicken on a serving platter, pour the onion sauce over the top and sides, and garnish the top of the chicken with the quartered lemon and some olives.

138 Arugula Chicken Spaghetti

Serves 4 | Prep. time 10 minutes | Cooking time 20 minutes

Ingredients

- ½ pound bucatini or spaghetti 2 tablespoons butter
- 1 cup Parmesan cheese, grated
- 2 cups warm rotisserie chicken, diced 4 cups baby arugula
- Salt and pepper to taste
- Grated Parmesan cheese for serving

Directions

- Boil salted water in the Dutch oven and cook the spaghetti until cooked well. Drain and set aside. Reserve 1¼ cups of the pasta water.
- Add the butter and some pepper to the Dutch oven and melt the butter over medium-high heat for about 1 minute.
- Pour in the pasta water and simmer. Mix in the Parmesan and cooked pasta. Season with salt and pepper.
- Simmer over low heat until the cheese melts.
- Mix in the chicken and arugula; stir-cook until the arugula is wilted.

- Serve warm with grated Parmesan cheese.

139 Enchilada Penne Chicken

Serves 6 | **Prep. time** 10 minutes | **Cooking time** 25 minutes

Ingredients

- 2 tablespoons olive oil
- ½ small sweet onion, chopped 2 cloves garlic, minced
- 2 large chicken breasts, diced 1 tablespoon taco seasoning
- 2 (10-ounce) cans red enchilada sauce (you can also use homemade enchilada sauce)
- 2 cups chicken broth
- ½ pound penne pasta
- 1½ cups shredded cheddar cheese
- Chopped cilantro or chopped green onions for garnish (optional)

Directions

- Add the oil to the Dutch oven and heat it over medium-high heat.
- Add the onion and stir cook for 1 minute until softened and translucent.
- Add the garlic and stir cook for 3–4 minutes until fragrant.
- Add the diced chicken and taco seasoning and stir-cook until cooked through.
- Mix in the chicken broth, enchilada sauce, and noodles.
- Bring to a boil.
- Reduce heat to low, cover, and simmer for about 10 minutes.
- Uncover and simmer the mixture for about 10 minutes, until the noodles are cooked well and the sauce is reduced to half.
- Remove from heat and mix in 1 cup of the cheese until melted.
- Top with the remaining ½ cup of cheese and serve with chopped cilantro or chopped green onions on top.

140 Salsa Verde Chicken

Serves 4 | **Prep. time** 10 minutes | **Cooking time** 30–45 minutes

Ingredients

- 4 boneless, skinless chicken breasts Salt and pepper to taste
- 1 chopped red onion
- 1 jar salsa verde
- 2 teaspoons ground cumin

Directions

- Season the chicken breasts evenly with salt and pepper.
- Arrange the chicken breasts over the bottom of the Dutch oven.
- Top with the onion, salsa, and cumin.
- Cover and cook for 30–45 minutes until the chicken is easy to shred.
- Remove the chicken, shred it, and mix it back into the sauce.
- Serve warm with cilantro on top.

141 Olive Chicken

Serves 4 | **Prep. time** 10 minutes | **Cooking time** 50–60 minutes

Ingredients

- 6–8 boneless, skinless chicken thighs Salt and pepper to taste
- 1 cup pitted olives (green or black)
- ½ cup low-sodium chicken broth
- ¼ cup unsalted butter Lemon juice to taste

Directions

- Season the chicken breasts evenly with salt and pepper.
- Arrange the chicken thighs over the bottom of the Dutch oven.
- Top with the broth, butter, and olives.
- Cover and cook for 50–60 minutes until the chicken is tender.
- Mix in some lemon juice and serve warm.

142 Spiced Chicken Wings

Serves 8 | Prep. time 10–15 minutes | Cooking time 60 minutes

Ingredients

- 16 chicken wings (about 3 pounds)
- ¾ cup bottled plum sauce 1 tablespoon butter, melted
- 1 teaspoon five-spice powder Green onions, slivered (optional)

Directions

- Preheat the oven to 375°F (190°C). Line a 15×10-inch baking pan with foil.
- Cut the tips off the wings and slice the wings into halves.
- Arrange the wings over the baking pan and bake for 20 minutes. Drain.
- Add the plum sauce, butter, and five-spice powder to the Dutch oven.
- Add the chicken wings and stir to coat well.
- Cover and cook for 50–60 minutes until the chicken is tender.
- Serve warm with some slivered green onions on top.

143 Parmesan Mushroom Chicken

Serves 4 | Prep. time 15 minutes | Cooking time 1–1½ hours

Ingredients

- 6–8 bone-in, skin-on chicken thighs Salt and pepper to taste
- 1 Parmesan rind
- 1 garlic head, halved
- ½ cup low-sodium chicken broth
- ½ pound cremini mushrooms, quartered

Directions

- Season the chicken thighs evenly with salt and pepper.
- Arrange the chicken thighs over the bottom of the Dutch oven.
- Add the Parmesan rind, garlic, and chicken broth.
- Cover and cook for 1–1½ hours until the chicken is tender.
- Remove the chicken, shred it, and mix it back into the sauce.
- Serve warm with grated Parmesan on top.

Pork and Lamb

144 Tangy Lamb Shanks

Prep time: 15 minutes | **Cook time:** 2 hours | **Serves** 6

Ingredients

- 4 pounds (1.8 kg) lamb shanks (about 4½ pounds / 2 kg) Kosher salt and freshly ground black pepper, to taste
- 2 teaspoons cinnamon
- 1 teaspoon ground cardamom 1 teaspoon grated nutmeg
- 1 teaspoon turmeric
- ¼ teaspoon crumbled saffron threads Juice of 2 limes
- ½ cup warm water 1 cup vegetable oil
- 1 large onion, roughly chopped Zest of 1 lime
- Zest of 1 orange 3 thyme sprigs
- 2 fresh bay leaves
- 6 cups chicken broth

Directions

- Preheat the oven to 350°F (180°C).
- Season the lamb shanks generously with salt and pepper. In a small bowl, combine the cinnamon, cardamom, nutmeg, and turmeric and rub the mixture into the lamb shanks.
- In a small bowl, combine the saffron and lime juice with the water.
- Fill the Dutch oven with about ½ inch of oil and heat it over medium-high heat. Brown the lamb shanks in two batches until browned on all sides, about 5 minutes per batch. As the shanks are browned, transfer them to a plate.
- Drain most of the oil from the Dutch oven, leaving just about 2 tablespoons, and set the pot over medium heat. Add the onion and cook, stirring frequently, until softened and golden, about 8 minutes. Add a bit of salt, the lime zest, orange zest, thyme, bay leaves, and saffron mixture, including the liquid. Return the lamb shanks to the pot, add the broth, and bring to a boil.
- Remove the pot from the heat, cover, and transfer to the oven. Cook until the meat is very tender, about 1½ hours.
- Transfer the meat to a serving platter and strain the sauce through a fine-meshed sieve, discarding the solids. Skim off any visible fat, and taste and adjust the seasoning if needed. Remove and discard the thyme sprigs and bay leaves.
- Serve the meat in chunks, with the juices spooned over.

145 Lemony Rib Lamb Chops

Prep time: 5 minutes | **Cook time:** 10 minutes | **Serves** 4

Ingredients

- Juice of 1 large lemon
- 2 tablespoons extra-virgin olive oil, divided
- 1 teaspoon dried oregano
- 1 teaspoon garlic powder
- 1 teaspoon seasoned salt
- 8 rib lamb chops (about 2 pounds / 907 g total) Freshly ground black pepper, to taste
- 2 tablespoons chopped fresh parsley

Directions

- In a large zip-top bag, mix together the lemon juice, 1 tablespoon of the olive oil, and the oregano, garlic powder, and seasoned salt. Add the lamb chops, seal the bag, and turn the bag so the lamb chops are well coated with the marinade. Let the lamb sit for 15 minutes at room temperature, turning the bag halfway through.
- In a Dutch oven over medium-high heat, heat the remaining 1 tablespoon of olive oil. Remove the lamb chops from the marinade and add them to the pot. Cook for about 3 minutes per side, until they reach the desired doneness.
- Season the chops with salt and pepper, and garnish with the chopped parsley before serving.

146 Potato and Carrot Lamb Stew

Prep time: 10 minutes | **Cook time:** 1¾ hour | **Serves** 6

Ingredients

- 2 tablespoons extra-virgin olive oil
- 1½ to 2 pounds (680 to 907 g) lamb shoulder, cut into bite-size cubes
- 1 small yellow onion, chopped 3 tablespoons all-purpose flour 4 cups beef broth
- 1 pound (454 g) red potatoes, cut into 2-inch cubes
- 1 (12-ounce / 340-g) package frozen peas and carrots Salt and freshly ground black pepper, to taste

Directions

- Preheat the oven to 350°F (180°C).
- In a Dutch oven over medium-high heat, heat the olive oil. Add the lamb and cook for 5 minutes, until it's starting to brown. Add the onion and cook for 5 minutes, until translucent. Sprinkle the flour over the lamb and onion, stirring well, and continue to cook for 5 more minutes. Add the broth to the pot and stir well. Cover the pot and transfer it to the oven.
- Bake for 1 hour. Remove from the oven and add the potatoes and frozen vegetables. Mix well. Cover and return to the oven. Cook for 30 minutes, until the meat and vegetables are tender.
- Season with salt and pepper before serving.

147 Lamb Leg with Rosemary

Prep time: 20 minutes | **Cook time:** 3½ hours | **Serves** 8 to 10

Ingredients

- 1 teaspoon salt
- ½ teaspoon freshly ground black pepper
- 1 tablespoon dried rosemary
- 2 tablespoons chopped garlic
- 1 bone-in leg of lamb (about 4 to 5 pounds / 1.8 to 2.3 kg)
- 2 tablespoons extra-virgin olive oil
- 2 cups white wine
- 1 cup vegetable broth

Directions

- Preheat the oven to 325°F (163°C).
- In a small bowl, combine the salt, pepper, rosemary, and garlic. Rub the lamb all over with the olive oil and seasonings.
- Heat a Dutch oven over medium heat until hot. Add the lamb and sear on all sides for about 10 to 12 minutes, until browned all over. Transfer the lamb to a large plate.
- Add the wine and broth and cook for 2 to 3 minutes or until the liquid comes to a boil. Deglaze the pan, scraping up the browned bits from the bottom of the pot with a wooden spoon.
- Place the lamb back in the pot and cover it with the lid. Bake for 3 hours or until it reaches your desired tenderness, basting occasionally.
- Transfer the lamb to a platter, cover it loosely with foil, and allow it to rest for 10 minutes. Strain the sauce in the Dutch oven through a fine-mesh sieve into a measuring cup. Skim any extra fat from the top. Place the sauce back in the pot, and cook it over high heat for 10 minutes, until it reduces. Season the lamb with salt and pepper and serve with the sauce.

148 Lamb Tagine

Prep time: 20 minutes | **Cook time:** 2 hours | **Serves** 4

Ingredients

- 2 pounds lamb shoulder, boneless, 2 inches cut
- 1 large onion, chopped
- 1½ inches fresh ginger, grated
- 4 cloves garlic, sliced
- 2 tbsp. tomato paste
- ⅓ cup almonds
- ¼ cup raisins
- 2 bay leaves

- 3 tbsp. olive oil
- 1 tsp cinnamon powder
- 1 tsp cumin powder
- ¼ tsp cardamom powder
- ½ tsp turmeric powder
- ½ tsp red pepper flakes, crushed
- 6 cups of water
- 1 cup fresh mint leaves
- Salt to taste

Directions

- Season the lamb with salt and store in the fridge overnight or for 6-8 hours uncovered.
- In a large Dutch oven, add olive oil and lamb pieces and cook for about 15 minutes until the pieces get brown colour.
- Remove from The Dutch oven and set aside.
- In the same pot, add onions with a splash of water and cook for 10 minutes until they are soft.
- Add garlic, ginger, raisins, bay leaves, and almonds and cook for 3-4 minutes.
- Add the browned lamb pieces, tomato paste, cumin powder, cinnamon powder, turmeric, cardamom powder and red pepper flakes.
- Cook for about 4-5 minutes until everything is mixed together.
- Add water and bring the mixture to boil.
- Reduce the heat and let the mixture simmer for 1 ½ hour.
- Once the lamb is tender, and the sauce thickens, reduce from heat and garnish with mint leaves.

149 Lamb Tropical Honey Shanks

Prep time: 10 minutes | **Cook time:** 1,30 hours | **Serves** 4

Ingredients

- 2 lb. lamb shanks
- 8 cup water
- 1 tbsp honey
- Sea salt to taste
- 2 tsp garlic powder
- 1 tbsp coconut oil
- 1/2 tsp turmeric powder
- 3 tsp red chili powder
- 2 tsp ginger powder
- 1 tbsp rosemary, minced
- 2 cloves

Directions

- In a Dutch oven add the coconut oil and sear the lamb shanks for 5 minutes.
- Add the garlic, turmeric, red chili powder, cloves, ginger, sea salt, honey and 1 cup of water.
- Cover and cook for 30 minutes. Add the remaining water and cook for 50 minutes.
- Add the rosemary and cook for 10 minutes.
- Serve hot

150 Lamb Stew with Veggies

Prep time: 15 minutes | **Cook time:** 1,30 hours | **Serves** 6

Ingredients

- 2 lb lamb, cut into chunks, boneless
- 1 cup potatoes cut into wedges
- 4 cup water
- 1 cup corn, cut into chunks
- 1 tbsp apple cider vinegar
- 1 tsp dried oregano
- Sea salt to taste
- 1 tsp garlic powder
- 1/3 tsp dried sage
- 2 tbsp grass-fed butter
- 2 tsp red chili powder
- ½ tsp dried cinnamon
- 1 tsp ginger powder

Directions

- In a Dutch oven, add the butter and toss the lamb pieces until they are slightly brown.
- Add the garlic, ginger, red chili powder, cinnamon, sea salt, sage, oregano, and apple cider vinegar.
- Cover and cook for 20 minutes.
- Add the water and cook for 40 minutes.
- Add the potatoes, corn and cook for 30 minutes.
- Serve hot.

151 Braised Lamb Shanks

Prep time: 25 minutes | **Cook time:** 3,30 hours | **Serves** 4

Ingredients

- 3 tablespoons olive oil (divided)
- 1 tablespoon butter
- 1 large onion (coarsely chopped)
- 1 rib of celery (coarsely chopped)
- 1 medium carrot (coarsely chopped)
- 4 cloves garlic (sliced) 4 lamb shanks
- Dash of salt and freshly ground black pepper
- 1 cup dry red wine
- 3 tablespoons tomato paste
- 2 cups chicken broth
- 1 cup beef broth
- 1/4 cup cider vinegar 4 sprigs of fresh thyme
- 1 bay leaf

Directions

- Gather the ingredients.
- Preheat the oven to 325 F.
- In a large skillet or Dutch oven, heat 1 tablespoon of olive oil with 1 tablespoon of butter. Add the chopped onion, celery, and carrot. Cook, stirring until onion is softened.
- Add the garlic and cook, stirring, for 2 minutes more. Remove to a large baking pan, roasting pan, or Dutch oven. Add 2 more tablespoons of olive oil to the pan. Sprinkle the lamb shanks with salt and pepper; saute over medium heat for about 8 minutes, turning to sear all sides.
- Add to the Dutch oven or pan with the chopped vegetables. In the same skillet, deglaze with the red wine. Simmer for 2 minutes.
- Add the tomato paste, chicken broth, beef broth, and vinegar. Bring to a boil. Reduce heat and simmer for 5 minutes. Pour over the lamb shanks and add the fresh thyme and bay leaf.
- Cover the pan tightly and bake for 1 hours. Remove the foil or lid and continue baking for 2 hours longer, turning the shanks occasionally. The lamb should be very tender.
- Serve with mashed potatoes and your favorite steamed vegetables.

152 Lamb Pie

Prep time: 6,15 h | **Cook time:** 6,15 hours | **Serves** 6

Ingredients

- 3 tablespoons olive oil
- 2 lbs lamb shoulder meat, diced
- 1 pinch salt and pepper 1 onion, finely chopped
- 2 celery ribs, finely chopped
- 2 carrots, finely chopped
- 3 garlic cloves, finely chopped
- 1 cup red wine
- 34 ounces beef stock
- 2 bay leaves
- 3 sprigs thyme
- 2 rosemary, stalks
- 1 cup ricotta cheese
- 2 large sweet potatoes, peeled and chopped
- 1 tablespoon butt

Directions

- Preheat oven to 300 F.
- Season lamb meat with a pinch of salt & pepper, before adding 2 Tbsp of oil to a dutch oven on medium-high heat. Brown Meat until golden brown all over, you may do this in batches.
- Remove meat from pan add remaining olive oil along with the onion, garlic, celery and carrots. Cook for 5-7 minutes or until browned.
- Add meat back to the pan along with red wine, cook for 1-2 minutes until wine reduces to bubbles, pour in stock and add the bay leaves, thyme rosemary and a pinch of salt & pepper.
- Bring to a boil cover with a lid and place in the oven to cook for 4-6 hours or meat falls apart.

- Remove from the oven and cook on stove top with lid off until sauce reduces by a third.
- Meanwhile, bring another pot of water to a boil add a pinch of salt and cook potatoes for 8-10 minutes or until easily pierced with a knife. Drain and mix in a bowl with 1 tbsp of butter and season with salt and pepper.
- Turn your broiler or grill on, spoon ricotta on top of lamb mix, followed by potato mix, and cook for 5-7 minutes or until slight little bits of golden color appear on the surface. Take straight to the table.

153 Mediterranean Lamb Roast

Prep time: 15 min | **Cook time:** 2,15 hours | **Serves** 4

Ingredients

- 4 lb. lamb leg, boneless
- ¼ cup olive oil
- 12 cloves garlic
- 1 bunch fresh oregano
- 2 springs fresh thyme
- 3 springs fresh rosemary
- 1 ½ tbsp sumac spice
- ¾ tbsp dried mint
- 2 tbsp lemon juice
- 2 onions, quartered
- 3 potatoes, quartered
- 2 carrots, sectional cut
- Salt to taste

Directions

- Score the top of the lamb in a crisscross manner using a sharp knife.
- Rub the lamb with 4 tbsp of salt and let it sit for 30 minutes.
- In a food processor, add garlic, oregano, thyme, rosemary, dried mint, lemon juice, and olive oil and process till you get a fine paste.
- Rub the paste on lamb using your hands.
- Roll the lamb and secure with kitchen twines.
- In a Dutch Oven, place lamb and put vegetables around the lamb.
- Cook the lamb on a medium flame for 5-10 minutes until it gets brown color.
- Add the remaining paste and add ¼ cup of water.
- Place the Dutch Oven into a pre-heated oven at 375 F and cook for about 2 hours until the internal temperature of the lamb reaches 150 degrees.
- Let the lamb sit for 20 minutes before serving.

154 Lamb Shanks

Prep time: 10 min+30 marinade | **Cook time:** 2 hours | **Serves** 4

Ingredients

- 4 Lamb Shanks
- 3 Jalapeno peppers, de-seeded and sliced
- 1 Red bell pepper, de-seeded and sliced
- 1 large Onion, sliced
- 4 garlic cloves, sliced
- 1 tsp tomato paste
- 2 tsp red chilli powder
- ¼ tsp Cinnamon powder
- 1 ½ cup Chicken stock
- ¼ cup Cilantro, chopped
- 1 tbsp. Vegetable Oil Salt to taste

Directions

- Season lamb shanks with black pepper and salt and let it sit for 30 minutes.
- In a Dutch oven, add oil and place lamb shanks.
- Cook the shanks for 3 minutes on each side so that they get a nice brown colour.
- Remove the shanks from the Dutch oven and get rid of excess fat in the pot so that only 1 tbsp. remains.
- Add onion and garlic and cook for 5 minutes until onions get soft.
- Add tomato paste, chilli powder, cinnamon powder and stir.
- Add 1 cup of chicken stock in the pot and bring it to boil.
- Place the lamb shanks in the mixture, cover the Dutch oven and place in a preheated oven at 425 F (220 °C) for 1 ½ hour.

- Remove the Dutch oven from the oven and add jalapeno and red bell peppers along with ½ cup of remaining chicken stock.
- Bring the mixture to boil on the stove and place it in the oven for 20 more minutes.
- Once the lamb is tender, remove from the oven and garnish with cilantro.

155 Sweet Lamb Chops

Prep time: 15 min | **Cook time:** 15 min | **Serves** 4

Ingredients

- 4 lamb chops
- 1/4 tsp garlic powder
- 1 tbsp honey Sea salt to taste
- 2 tsp grass-fed butter
- ¼ tsp paprika
- ½ tsp lime juice
- ¼ tsp dried thyme
- ¼ tsp dried mint
- 1/4 tsp ginger powder

Directions

- Marinate the lamb chops using ginger, mint, honey, sea salt, paprika, garlic, and thyme.
- Let it marinate for 1 hour.
- In a Dutch oven add the butter and place the lamb chops.
- Cover and cook on low heat for 20 minutes. Flip the lamb chops and cover again.
- Cook for 20 minutes. Serve hot.

156 Pork Carnitas Tacos with Onion

Prep time: 15 minutes | **Cook time:** 1¾ hour | **Serves** 8

Ingredients

Carnitas:

- 4 pounds (1.8 kg) bone-in pork butt, cut into 2-inch-thick slabs
- 1 teaspoon kosher salt
- ⅓ cup water

Pickled Onions:

- 1 large red onion, halved and thinly sliced
- 1½ teaspoons kosher salt
- ½ cup lime juice (from about 6 limes)

Tacos:

- 16 corn tortillas, warmed
- 1 cup salsa
- ½ head green cabbage, shredded

Make the Carnitas

- Preheat the oven to 375°F (190°C).
- Season the pork slabs on all sides with the salt. Pour ⅓ cup of water in the bottom of the Dutch oven, arrange the meat in the pot in a single layer, if possible. Cover and bake for 1 hour.
- Remove the lid from the pot and increase the oven temperature to 450°F (235°C). Roast uncovered until the water is completely evaporated and the fat has rendered from the meat, about 30 minutes.
- Continue to roast, turning the meat a few times over the next 20 to 25 minutes, until the meat falls apart. Remove the meat from the oven and shred it with two forks, removing and discarding the bones.

Make the Pickled Onions

- In a large heatproof bowl, add the sliced onions and pour boiling water over them. Let sit for about 20 seconds and then drain in a colander. Transfer the onions to a bowl, stir in the salt and lime juice, and let sit for at least 30 minutes.

Assemble the Tacos

- Place some of the meat down the center of each of the tortillas. Top with a bunch of pickled onions, a spoonful of salsa, and a handful of cabbage. Serve immediately.

157 Pork Sausage Jambalaya with Shrimp

Prep time: 15 minutes | **Cook time:** 40 minutes | **Serves** 6

Ingredients

- 2 tablespoons unsalted butter
- 2 pounds (907 g) smoked pork loin, cut into cubes 12 ounces (340 g) Andouille sausage, sliced
- 2 medium onions, diced
- 2 green bell peppers, diced 4 celery stalks, diced
- ½ teaspoon salt
- ½ teaspoon pepper
- 6 garlic cloves, minced 2 bay leaves
- ¼ to ½ teaspoon cayenne pepper
- 1 (28-ounce / 794-g) can diced tomatoes 1 cup long-grain white rice
- 2 cups water
- 1 pound (454 g) peeled and deveined shrimp 4 scallions, thinly sliced, for garnish

Directions

- Preheat the oven to 350°F (180°C).
- In the Dutch oven, melt the butter over medium-high heat. Add the smoked pork and the sausage to the pot and cook, stirring frequently, until browned, about 5 minutes. Transfer the meat to a bowl.
- Add the onions, bell peppers, celery, salt, and pepper to the pot and cook, stirring occasionally, until the vegetables soften, about 8 minutes.
- Add the garlic, bay leaves, and cayenne and cook, stirring, for about 6 minutes more, until the vegetables are golden brown.
- Stir in the tomatoes, rice, water, and reserved pork and sausage and bring to a boil. Reduce the heat to medium and simmer, uncovered, until the rice is tender, about 20 minutes.
- Stir in the shrimp and cook until the shrimp are cooked through, 3 to 4 minutes more.
- Taste and season the jambalaya if needed. Serve hot, garnished with the scallions.

158 Panko Bean Stew with Chorizo

Prep time: 10 minutes | **Cook time:** 45 minutes | **Serves** 4

Ingredients

- 3 tablespoons olive oil, divided, plus more for drizzling
- 3 links (about 12 ounces / 340 g) Spanish chorizo, sliced
- 1 onion, diced
- 4 garlic cloves, minced
- 2 sprigs fresh thyme 1 tablespoon paprika
- 1 bay leaf
- ½ teaspoon cayenne pepper
- ½ teaspoon kosher salt
- ¼ teaspoon freshly ground black pepper
- 2 (15-ounce / 425-g) cans cannellini beans, drained and rinsed
- 2 cups chicken broth
- 1 tablespoon sherry vinegar
- 2 cups Panko bread crumbs
- ½ cup grated Parmesan cheese
- ¼ cup chopped flat-leaf parsley, for garnish

Directions

- Preheat the oven to 400°F (205°C).
- In the Dutch oven, heat 1 tablespoon of oil over medium heat. Add the chorizo and cook, stirring occasionally, until browned, about 10 minutes. Using a slotted spoon, transfer the sausage to a plate.
- Add 1 tablespoon of oil to the Dutch oven and heat over medium heat. Add the onion, garlic, and thyme, and cook, stirring frequently, until the onion softens, about 5 minutes. Stir in the chorizo, paprika, bay leaf, cayenne, salt, pepper, beans, broth, and vinegar.
- In a small bowl, stir together the bread crumbs, Parmesan cheese, and the remaining 1 tablespoon of olive oil. Sprinkle the bread crumb mixture evenly over the beans.
- Bake, uncovered, in the preheated oven, for about 30 minutes, until the broth is hot and bubbling and the topping is browned and

crisp. Remove and discard the bay leaf. Serve hot, garnished with the parsley.

159 Pork Chops with Carrot

Prep time: 10 minutes | **Cook time:** 30 minutes | **Serves** 4

Ingredients

- 4 (1-inch-thick) bone-in pork loin chops
- 1¾ teaspoons kosher salt, divided
- 1 teaspoon paprika
- 2 tablespoons olive oil 1 onion, chopped
- 2 garlic cloves, thinly sliced
- ½ teaspoon freshly ground black pepper
- 2 carrots, peeled and cut into 2-inch sticks
- 2 celery stalks, cut into 2-inch sticks
- 1 red bell pepper, seeded and cut into 2-inch slices
- ½ cup chicken broth
- ½ cup dry vermouth 3 sprigs fresh thyme
- 1 teaspoon Dijon mustard
- ½ teaspoon finely grated lemon zest
- 1 teaspoon freshly squeezed lemon juice

Directions

- Pat the pork chops dry with paper towels. Season them all over with ¾ teaspoon of salt and the paprika.
- In the Dutch oven, heat the oil over medium-high heat. Sear the pork chops for about 3 minutes per side, until golden brown (do this in two batches to avoid crowding the pot). As the pork chops are browned, transfer them to a plate.
- Reduce the heat to medium. Add the onion and garlic, along with the remaining ¾ teaspoon of salt and the pepper. Cook, stirring frequently, until the onion begins to soften, about 3 minutes.
- Add the carrots, celery, and bell pepper. Stir in the broth and vermouth and cook, stirring and scraping up any browned bits from the bottom of the pot, for about 3 minutes more.
- Add the browned chops back to the pot, along with any juices that have accumulated and the thyme. Reduce the heat to low, cover, and simmer for about 8 minutes, until the pork chops are cooked through.
- Transfer the chops to a plate and tent loosely with aluminum foil. Let the meat rest for 10 minutes.
- While the chops rest, raise the heat under the pot to medium-high and let the sauce simmer, uncovered, for 6 to 8 minutes, until it thickens a bit and the vegetables are tender.
- Remove the pot from the heat and stir in the mustard and lemon zest and lemon juice. Remove and discard the thyme sprigs.
- Serve the chops along with the vegetables and sauce.

160 Pork Loin with Apple and Cabbage

Prep time: 10 minutes | **Cook time:** 55 minutes | **Serves** 6

Ingredients

- 1 (2½-pound / 1.1-kg) pork loin
- 1½ teaspoons salt
- ½ teaspoon freshly ground black pepper 1 tablespoon unsalted butter
- 1 tablespoon olive oil 1 onion, diced
- 3 tart apples, peeled, cored, and cut into wedges
- 1 head red cabbage, cored and thinly sliced
- ½ cup apple cider vinegar 1½ cups apple cider
- 1 cup chicken broth

Directions

- Preheat the oven 350°F (180°C).
- Season the pork loin with salt and pepper. In the Dutch oven, heat the butter and oil over medium-high heat. Add the pork and cook, turning occasionally, until it is browned on all sides, about 8 minutes total. Transfer the meat to a bowl.
- Reduce the heat to medium, add the onion, and cook, stirring occasionally, until softened, about 5 minutes.
- Add the apples, cabbage, vinegar, cider, and broth and return to a boil over high heat.

- Reduce the heat to medium, cover, and simmer for 7 minutes.
- Return the pork to the pot along with any accumulated juices, nestling the roast into the apples and vegetables. Roast, uncovered, for 35 to 40 minutes, until an instant-read thermometer registers 140°F (60°C).
- Transfer the pork to a cutting board, tent with foil, and let it rest for at least 10 minutes.
- To serve, slice the pork and serve it on top of the vegetables and apples, drizzling the pan juices over the top.

161 Aromatic Pork Shoulder

Prep time: 10 minutes | **Cook time:** 3 hours | **Serves** 8

Ingredients

- 1 (3-pound / 1.4-kg) pork shoulder
- ½ teaspoon cumin
- ½ teaspoon coriander
- ½ teaspoon salt
- ½ teaspoon freshly cracked black pepper
- 2 tablespoons vegetable oil
- 1 large onion, peeled and sliced 1 fennel bulb, sliced
- 2 cloves garlic, peeled and minced
- ¼ teaspoon crushed red pepper flakes 2 cups white wine
- 2 bay leaves
- Water, to cover

Directions

- Pat pork shoulder dry with paper towels. In a small bowl combine cumin, coriander, salt, and pepper. Rub spices on all sides of pork shoulder. Set aside.
- In a Dutch oven over medium heat add oil. Add pork and brown well on all sides, about 5 minutes per side. Remove to a plate to rest.
- Heat oven to 350°F (180°C).
- To the Dutch oven add onion and fennel. Cook until vegetables are tender, about 5 minutes. Add garlic and crushed red pepper flakes and cook until fragrant, about 30 seconds.
- Add wine to the pot and, with a wooden spoon or heatproof spatula, scrape any browned bits off the bottom of the Dutch oven. Add pork shoulder back to the Dutch oven along with bay leaves and enough water to come halfway up the side of the roast. Cover and bake 1 hour, then turn pork over and cook another hour.
- Turn pork roast back over, uncover, and roast another 30 to 45 minutes, or until pork is fork tender and braising liquid has reduced. Remove pork from the liquid and allow to rest on a cutting board tented with foil 10 minutes.
- Once rested slice pork and arrange on a platter. Skim any excess fat from the braising liquid, remove bay leaves, and pour liquid over pork slices. Serve hot.

162 Pineapple Pork Roast

Prep time: 10 minutes | **Cook time:** 3¼ hours | **Serves** 8

Ingredients

- 1 (3-pound / 1.4-kg) pork roast
- ¼ cup all-purpose flour
- ½ teaspoon salt
- ½ teaspoon freshly cracked black pepper
- 2 tablespoons vegetable oil
- 1 medium onion, peeled and sliced 2 cloves garlic, peeled and minced 1 teaspoon fresh grated ginger
- 1 (16-ounce / 454-g) can pineapple chunks in juice, undrained 2 tablespoons soy sauce
- 2 tablespoons mirin, or 1 tablespoon sugar mixed with 1 tablespoon sake
- Water, to cover

Directions

- Pat pork roast dry with paper towels. In a small bowl combine flour, salt, and pepper. Coat the roast with flour mixture, reserving any remaining mixture. Set aside.
- Heat oven to 375°F (190°C).
- In a Dutch oven over medium heat add oil. Once it shimmers add roast and brown well

on all sides, about 5 minutes per side. Remove roast to a plate to rest.
- To the Dutch oven add onion and cook until tender, about 5 minutes. Add garlic and ginger and cook until fragrant, about 30 seconds. Add any reserved flour and stir to coat onions.
- Add pineapple chunks with their juice, soy sauce, and mirin. With a wooden spoon or heatproof spatula, scrape up any browned bits from the bottom of the Dutch oven. Add roast back to the pot and add enough water so it comes halfway up the side of roast. Cover and bake 1 hour, then flip the roast and cook another hour.
- Remove the lid and cook another 40 to 50 minutes, or until roast is tender and sauce has thickened slightly. Remove roast from the liquid and allow to rest, tented with foil, 10 minutes, before slicing and arranging on a platter. Pour the braising liquid over the pork. Serve hot.

163 Beer Pork with BBQ Sauce

Prep time: 10 minutes | **Cook time:** 3½ hours | Serves 8

Ingredients

- 1 (3-pound / 1.4-kg) pork shoulder
- 1 teaspoon cumin
- ½ teaspoon smoked paprika
- ½ teaspoon salt
- ½ teaspoon freshly cracked black pepper
- 2 tablespoons vegetable oil
- 2 large onions, peeled and sliced
- 2 cloves garlic, peeled and minced
- 2 cups beer, ale or lager
- 1 cup barbecue sauce, divided Water, to cover

Directions

- Pat pork shoulder dry with paper towels. In a small bowl combine cumin, smoked paprika, salt, and pepper. Rub spices on all sides of pork shoulder. Set aside.
- In a Dutch oven over medium heat add oil. Brown pork well on all sides, about 5 minutes per side. Remove to a plate to rest.
- Heat oven to 350°F (180°C).
- To the Dutch oven add onion. Cook until onions are tender, about 5 minutes. Add garlic and cook until fragrant, about 30 seconds.
- Add beer to the pot and, with a wooden spoon or heatproof spatula, scrape any browned bits off the bottom of the Dutch oven. Stir in half of barbecue sauce. Add pork back to the Dutch oven and coat the top with reserved barbecue sauce. Add enough water to come halfway up the side of roast. Cover and bake 1 hour, then turn pork over and cook 1 hour more.
- Turn pork roast back over, uncover, and roast another 45 to 55 minutes, or until pork is fork tender and braising liquid has reduced. Remove pork from liquid and allow to rest on a cutting board tented with foil 10 minutes. Once rested shred pork with two forks and place on a platter. Keep warm.
- Heat the Dutch oven with the braising liquid over high heat. Bring the liquid to a boil and reduce until thick, about 8 to 10 minutes. Pour over shredded pork.
- Serve hot.

164 Garlicky Pork Belly

Prep time: 25 minutes | **Cook time:** 2½ hours | Serves 4

Ingredients

- 1¼ pounds (567g) skinless, boneless pork belly
- ¼ cup salt
- ½ cup sugar
- 4½ cups water, divided
- 2 cups ice
- ½ cup chicken broth
- 5 cloves garlic, peeled
- 10 peppercorns

Directions

- Rinse pork belly and remove any loose pieces along the edges.
- Place salt, sugar, and 4 cups water into a small saucepan over medium heat. Stir

frequently until the salt and sugar are dissolved. Place the pork belly into a sealable container that is deeper than the pork belly, but not much wider. Stir ice into the pan of water. Once ice is melted, pour mixture over pork. Refrigerate 12 to 24 hours.
- Heat oven to 300°F (150°C).
- Remove pork from the brine and rinse it. Pat it dry and cut it into four even pieces. Place pieces in the bottom of Dutch oven. Pour in ½ cup water and broth. Sprinkle garlic cloves and peppercorns around the pan. Cover with a lid, place in the middle of the oven, and cook 2½ hours. The pork should be very tender.
- Remove the pork from the Dutch oven, then drain the liquid and peppercorns from the pan. Save garlic cloves. Return the pork to the Dutch oven so it is fat-side down. Smear a garlic clove over the meaty side of each slice of pork. Place the Dutch oven over high heat and cook about 3 to 5 minutes, or until fat is crispy and golden brown. Serve immediately.

165 Glazed Pork Tenderloin

Prep time: 25 minutes | **Cook time:** 30 minutes | **Serves** 6

Ingredients

- ½ cup low-sodium soy sauce
- 2 tablespoons hoisin sauce
- 2 tablespoons honey
- 3 cloves garlic, peeled and minced
- 1 cup chicken broth, divided
- 1 tablespoon brown sugar
- 1 tablespoon grated gingerroot
- ¼ teaspoon pepper
- 2 (1-pound / 454-g) pork tenderloins 2 tablespoons unsalted butter

Directions

- In a large zip-top bag, combine soy sauce, hoisin sauce, honey, garlic, ½ cup broth, brown sugar, gingerroot, and pepper. If necessary, pull the silver skin off pork and discard.
- Add pork to the bag, close, and massage the bag to mix marinade into pork. Place in casserole dish and refrigerate 12 to 24 hours.
- Heat oven to 425°F (220°C).
- Pour tenderloin and marinade into a Dutch oven lightly coated with nonstick cooking spray. Bake 20 to 30 minutes, or until a meat thermometer registers 155°F (68°C).
- Remove pork and cover to keep warm. Place the Dutch oven on stovetop over medium heat and add ½ cup chicken broth. Bring to a boil, scraping to remove pan drippings, until reduced by half. Add butter, swirl to coat, and pour over pork. Serve immediately.

166 Pork Meatballs with Orange Glaze

Prep time: 20 minutes | **Cook time:** 50 minutes | **Serves** 8

Ingredients

- 2 pounds (907 g) ground pork
- ½ cup Panko bread crumbs
- ½ medium onion, peeled and finely chopped
- 1 large egg
- 1 teaspoon salt
- ½ teaspoon ground fennel
- ½ teaspoon oregano
- ¼ teaspoon freshly cracked black pepper
- ¼ cup olive oil, divided
- ½ cup orange marmalade
- ¼ cup orange juice
- 1 teaspoon packed light brown sugar

Directions

- In a large bowl combine ground pork, bread crumbs, onion, egg, salt, fennel, oregano, and pepper. Mix until well combined. Shape meat mixture into 16 balls and place on a parchment-lined baking sheet. Refrigerate uncovered 1 hour.
- Heat oven to 350°F (180°C).
- In a Dutch oven add half the oil. Brown meatballs on all sides in batches, adding additional oil as needed to prevent sticking, about 2 minutes per side. Once all the

meatballs are browned add them all back to the Dutch oven.
- In a small bowl combine marmalade, orange juice, and sugar.
- Pour mixture over the meatballs and toss gently to coat. Cover and bake 30 minutes, then uncover and bake 10 minutes more, stirring the meatballs every 3 minutes, until they are coated in the orange glaze and cooked through. Serve hot.

167 Baked Pork and Eggplant Casserole

Prep time: 15 minutes | **Cook time:** 1¼ hour | **Serves** 8

Ingredients

- 2 pounds (907 g) lean ground pork
- 2 tablespoons peanut or extra-virgin olive oil
- 2 large yellow onions, peeled and chopped
- 3 celery stalks, chopped
- 1 green pepper, seeded and chopped
- 6 cloves garlic, chopped
- 4 medium eggplants, cut into ½-inch dice
- ⅛ teaspoon dried thyme, crushed
- 1 tablespoon freeze-dried parsley
- 3 tablespoons tomato paste
- 1 teaspoon hot sauce, optional
- 2 teaspoons Worcestershire sauce
- ½ teaspoon salt
- ½ teaspoon freshly cracked black pepper
- 1 large egg, beaten
- ½ cup bread crumbs
- 1 tablespoon melted unsalted butter

Directions

- Heat oven to 350°F (180°C).
- Place Dutch oven over medium-high heat. Add ground pork and fry until done, breaking it apart as it cooks. Remove from pan and keep warm.
- Drain off and discard any pork fat from the pan, then add the oil over medium heat. Once the oil is hot and starts to shimmer add onion, celery, and green pepper; sauté until onion is transparent, about 5 minutes. Add garlic, eggplant, thyme, parsley, and tomato paste. Stir to combine. Cover and sauté, stirring often, 20 minutes or until vegetables are tender.
- Return ground pork to pan. Add hot sauce (if using), Worcestershire sauce, salt, pepper, and egg; stir to combine. Sprinkle bread crumbs over the top and drizzle with melted butter. Bake 40 minutes, or until the crumb topping is lightly browned and casserole is hot in the center.

168 Pork Roast with Tomato

Prep time: 15 minutes | **Cook time:** 2½ hours | **Serves** 6 to 8

Ingredients

- 1 teaspoon cinnamon
- ½ teaspoon ground ginger
- ½ teaspoon cumin
- ½ teaspoon cayenne 1 teaspoon paprika
- 1 teaspoon kosher salt
- ¼ teaspoon cardamom
- 2 pounds (907 g) boneless pork roast, cut into 2-inch cubes
- 2 tablespoons olive oil
- 1 large onion, peeled and diced
- 3 cloves garlic, peeled and minced
- ¼ teaspoon saffron
- ¼ cup hot water
- 1 (16-ounce / 454-g) can diced tomatoes, undrained 1 tablespoon brown sugar
- 2 cups chicken or pork broth
- 8 dried apricots, quartered
- ¼ cup minced fresh cilantro

Directions

- Combine cinnamon, ginger, cumin,
- cayenne, paprika, kosher salt, and cardamom, then sprinkle half of the spice mixture over the pork cubes.
- In a Dutch oven heat oil over medium-high heat. Brown pork on all sides, about 3 minutes per side, then remove to a platter. Add onion and garlic, and cook until tender, about 5 minutes.

- Dissolve saffron in hot water. Add saffron, tomatoes, and brown sugar to the pot, and stir well. Return pork to pot, and add broth and apricots. Stir in remaining spices, and then bring to a boil.
- Reduce heat to medium-low, cover, and simmer 2 hours, adding more liquid if necessary.
- Stir in cilantro. Remove from heat and let stand 10 minutes.

Fish and Seafood Recipes

169 Lobster Bisque

Serves 4–6 | Prep. time 10–15 minutes | Cooking time 70 minutes

Ingredients

- 2 (1-pound) live lobsters
- 3 tablespoons butter
- 1 medium onion, chopped
- 2 medium carrots, peeled and chopped
- 2 tablespoons tomato paste
- 2 cloves garlic, minced
- ¾ cup sherry or white wine
- 1-quart seafood stock
- ⅔ cup long-grain rice, uncooked
- 2 cups heavy whipping cream
- 1½ teaspoons salt
- 1 teaspoon pepper
- Minced fresh parsley(optional)

Directions

- Boil 2 inches of water in the Dutch oven. Add the lobsters and cook, covered, for 8 minutes. Remove the lobsters and reserve the water.
- Remove the meat from the lobsters. Reserve the juice and shells; discard the claws and tail.
- Add the butter to the Dutch oven and melt it over medium-high heat.
- Add the onion and carrots and stir-cook for 6–8 minutes until softened and translucent.
- Mix in the tomato paste and cook for 5 minutes.
- Add the garlic and stir cook for 50–60 seconds until fragrant.
- Pour in the wine and cook until the liquid reduces to half.
- Pour in the seafood stock along with the reserved water, juice, and shells. Reserve the meat.
- Simmer for 1 hour; strain to remove solids and shells.
- Heat the strained liquid in the Dutch oven. Add the rice and cook for 25–30 minutes until softened.
- Puree the rice in a blender until it becomes smooth.
- Mix in the pepper, salt, and cream.
- Add the lobster meat and simmer over low heat until cooked well.
- Season with parsley and pepper.
- Serve warm.

170 Baked Salmon with Herbs

Serves 4 | Prep time 10 minutes | Cooking time 35 minutes

Ingredients

- 2 tablespoons olive oil 1 lemon, sliced
- 2 bunches of dill
- 2 pounds salmon fillet
- ¾ cup white wine
- Salt and pepper to taste

Directions

- Arrange the lemon slices on the bottom of the Dutch oven.
- Arrange the dill on top of the lemon and place the salmon fillet on top of that.
- Pour in the white wine and season with salt and pepper.
- Cover and cook at 350°F (180°C) for about 10 minutes.
- Remove the lid and continue cooking for another 20–25 minutes.

171 Baked Trout with Cherry Tomatoes

Serves 4 | Prep time 10 minutes | Cooking time 45 minutes

Ingredients

- 2 tablespoons olive oil
- 2 tablespoons butter
- 1-pound potatoes, sliced
- 1 pound cherry tomatoes
- 2 pounds whole trout Salt and pepper to taste
- 1 lemon, sliced

Directions

- Coat the Dutch oven with butter.

- Arrange the potato slices and cherry tomatoes in the Dutch oven and season with salt and pepper.
- Bake at 350°F (180°C) for about 20 minutes.
- Meanwhile, season the cleaned trout with salt and pepper and stuff it with lemon slices.
- Place the trout on top of the potatoes and cherry tomatoes and drizzle some olive oil on top of the fish.
- Cover and bake for about 20 minutes more.
- Remove the lid and cook for another 10 minutes.

172Tilapia Cacciatore

Serves 4 | **Prep time** 10 minutes | **Cooking time** 30 minutes

Ingredients

- 2 tablespoons olive oil 2 pounds tilapia fillets Salt and pepper to taste 2 cups tomato sauce
- 2 teaspoons Italian seasoning
- ¼ cup white wine
- ¾ cup diced Kalamata olives

Directions

- Warm the olive oil in the Dutch oven over medium heat.
- Season the fish fillets with salt and pepper. Add them to the heated oil and cook for about 5 minutes on each side.
- Pour in the white wine and cook uncovered for about 5 minutes.
- When half of the wine has evaporated, pour in the tomato sauce and season with Italian seasoning.
- Stir in the diced Kalamata olives and cook, covered, for 15–20 minutes.
- When the tomato sauce has thickened and the fish is cooked, serve on plates.

173Seafood Cioppino

Serves 6 | **Prep time** 25 minutes | **Cooking time** 55 minutes

Ingredients

- 1 lb little neck clams
- 2 lb mussels
- 2 tbsp organic unsalted butter
- 1 small yellow onion, finely chopped
- 2 stalks celery, chopped
- ½ bulb fennel, cored and thinly sliced
- 3 cloves garlic, minced
- ½ tsp each sea salt and ground black pepper
- ¼ tsp each whole celery seed and red pepper flakes
- 1½ tbsp unsalted tomato paste
- 1 cup dry white wine (such as pinot grigio)
- 2 cups unsalted diced tomatoes, with juices
- ½ cup clam juice
- ½ cup low-sodium chicken or
- vegetable broth
- 8 oz firm white fish
- 1 lb large shrimp, peeled, deveined and tails removed
- ¼ cup chopped fresh flat-leaf parsley
- 6 slices whole-grain baguette, toasted, optional

Directions

- To clean clams, tap each gently on counter and discard any that do not close or have broken shells. Place in a large bowl and cover with cold water. Let stand at least 20 minutes. Place mussels in a colander and rinse thoroughly, removing grit from shells by rubbing with a towel under running water. Discard any mussels with cracked shells or any that do not close when tapped. Return mussels to a large bowl filled with ice; refrigerate until ready to use.
- Meanwhile, melt butter in a Dutch oven on medium heat. Add onion and cook, stirring occasionally, until golden, 2 to 3 minutes. Add celery and fennel and cook, stirring occasionally, until slightly softened, 7 to 9 minutes.

- Remove clams from water (do not drain but pluck them from water) and scrub any remaining sand from the shells. Increase heat to medium and add clams; cover and cook 5 minutes.
- Add mussels, fish and shrimp. Cover and cook, stirring seafood occasionally to aid in even cooking, until clams and mussel shells have opened, fish is opaque and shrimp is pink, 7 to 9 minutes more. Discard any unopened clams or mussels. Garnish with parsley and reserved fennel fronds, if desired.
- Add garlic and cook 1 minute. Sprinkle with salt, black pepper, celery seed and pepper flakes. Add tomato paste and cook 1 minute, stirring. Add wine, tomatoes, clam juice and broth, scraping up browned bits from bottom of pan; bring to a simmer. Reduce heat to low and simmer until liquid reduces by half, 20 to 25 minutes.

174 Apple Cobbler

Serves 4 | Prep time 10 minutes | Cooking time 20 minutes

Ingredients

Apple Filling:

- 1 ½ lbs apples, sliced
- 1/4 cup granulated sugar
- 1 tablespoon cinnamon
- Cobbler Topping:
- 1 cup flour, (120 grams)
- 1/4 cup granulated sugar
- 1 teaspoon baking powder
- 1 teaspoon cinnamon
- 1/4 teaspoon salt
- 1/4 cup butter, cold
- 1/3 cup milk

Directions

- Prepare 21 coals and line a 10" (4 quart) Dutch oven with parchment paper.
- Make the filling: Core the apples and cut into slices. Add them to the Dutch oven and sprinkle with ¼ cup sugar and 1 tablespoon cinnamon. Stir to coat the apples in the cinnamon and sugar.
- Make the topping: Combine the dry ingredients (flour, baking powder, ¼ cup sugar, 1 tsp cinnamon, salt) in a mixing bowl. Cut the butter into small pieces and add to the bowl. Using your fingers, rub the butter into the dry ingredients until a crumbly meal begins to form. Add the milk and gently combine to create a dough.
- Assemble the cobbler: Tear off bits of dough and place on top of apples. You want little pockets of dough spread evenly around, not one large blob of dough in the middle.
- Bake the cobbler: Set the lid on the Dutch oven. Place the Dutch oven on a ring of seven coals, then evenly space 14 coals on top of the lid (this will create equivalent heat of a 350°F oven). Bake for 30-40 minutes, until the topping is golden brown.
- Remove from heat & serve!

175 Mussels in Coconut Sauce

Serves 4 | Prep time 20 minutes | Cooking time 20 minutes

Ingredients

- 1 lb. mussels
- 2 cup coconut milk 1 tbsp lime juice
- 1 tomato, chopped
- 1 tsp tamarind paste 1 tbsp honey
- Sea salt to taste
- Pepper to taste
- 1 tbsp lemongrass, chopped
- 2 garlic cloves, minced
- 1 tsp red chili powder
- 1 tbsp scallion, chopped
- 1 tsp grass-fed butter

Directions

- In a Dutch oven, melt the butter and fry the garlic for 2 minutes.
- Add the tomatoes and toss for 2 minutes.
- Add the tamarind paste, red chili powder, lemongrass, honey, salt, pepper, and coconut milk.

Cover and cook for 10 minutes.

- Add the mussels and cover again. Cook for 10 minutes.
- Add the scallion, lime juice and serve hot.

176 Shrimp Paella

Serves 6 | **Prep time** 35 minutes | **Cooking time** 35 minutes

Ingredients

- 4 cup long grain rice
- 2 cup large shrimp, peeled, cleaned
- ½ tsp saffron 1 cup milk
- 6 cup fish stock
- Salt and pepper to taste
- 1/3 tsp turmeric powder
- 1 tsp paprika
- 1 tsp mixed herbs
- 4 garlic cloves, sliced
- ½ cup scallion, chopped
- 1 tbsp parsley, chopped
- 2 tbsp grass-fed butter

Directions

- Combine the saffron with the milk. Let it soak for 10 minutes.
- In a Dutch oven, add the butter and toss the garlic for 1 minute.
- Add the rice and toss for 5 minutes.
- Add the milk, fish stock, mixed herbs, paprika, turmeric, salt, pepper, and stir well.
- Cover and cook on high heat for 20 minutes.
- Add the shrimp, scallion, parsley, some more salt and pepper and cook for 8 minutes.
- Serve hot.

177 Wild Rice with Mushroom and Salmon

Serves 4 | **Prep time** 30 minutes | **Cooking time** 30 minutes

Ingredients

- 2 ½ cup wild rice
- 1 cup mushroom, sliced
- 1 cup salmon fillet, boneless, cut into 2 inch chunks
- Salt and pepper to taste
- 1 tsp red chili powder
- 1 tsp lime juice
- 1 tsp garlic paste
- 1 tsp ginger paste
- 1 tbsp parsley, chopped
- 1 cup coconut milk
- 1 cup mushroom stock
- 1 tbsp soy sauce
- 1 tsp grass-fed butter

Directions

- In a Dutch oven, add the butter and toss the wild rice for 5 minutes.
- Add the salt, pepper, soy sauce, ginger, garlic, red chili powder and pour in the mushroom stock.
- Cover and cook for 10 minutes. Add the coconut milk and cook for 10 minutes.
- Add the salmon, mushroom, and parsley. Cover and cook for 10 minutes.
- Serve hot with lime juice on top.

178 Salmon and Baby Potato in Creamy Sauce

Serves 4 | **Prep time** 25 minutes | **Cooking time** 25 minutes

Ingredients

- 2 cup baby potatoes, halved
- 4 salmon fillets, boneless
- 1 tbsp basil, chopped
- 1 tomato, chopped
- 1 tbsp oil
- 2 cup coconut milk
- 3 garlic cloves, sliced
- 1-inch ginger, sliced
- 1 onion, chopped
- 1 tsp mixed herbs Sea salt to taste
- 1 tsp red chili powder

Directions

- In a Dutch oven, add the oil and toss the onion, garlic and ginger for 2 minutes.
- Add the tomato, red chili powder, and toss for 1 minute.

- Add the coconut milk and cook for 5 minutes.
- Add the mixed herbs, baby potatoes, salmon pieces, salt, and cover.
- Cook for 15 minutes. Serve hot with basil on top

179 White Fish Curry

Serves 4 | Prep time 20 minutes | Cooking time 20 minutes

Ingredients

- 4 white fish steak
- 1 cup water
- 1 tbsp soy sauce
- 2 tomatoes cut into wedges
- 1 tbsp fish sauce Sea
- salt to taste
- 1/3 tsp turmeric powder
- 1 tsp cumin
- 1 tbsp parsley, chopped
- 1 tbsp scallion, chopped
- 1 tsp red chili powder
- 1 tbsp oil

Directions

- In a Dutch oven, add the oil and fry the tomatoes for 2 minutes.
- Add the red chili powder, salt, cumin, turmeric, fish sauce, soy sauce and water.
- Cook for 5 minutes. Add the fish steaks and cover. Cook for 10 minutes.
- Serve hot with scallion and parsley on top.

180 Roasted Cod

Serves 4 | Prep time 20 minutes | Cooking time 20 minutes

Ingredients

- 1 lb whole cod, cleaned
- 1 tbsp honey
- 1 tbsp fish sauce
- ½ tsp dried sage
- ½ tsp dried oregano
- 1 tbsp oil
- Sea salt to taste
- ½ tsp red chili powder
- ½ tsp lime juice
- 1/3 tsp garlic powder

Directions

- Marinate the fish using lime juice, fish sauce, sage, oregano, sea salt, red chili powder, garlic and honey.
- Let it sit for 30 minutes. In a Dutch oven add the oil. Place the fish with its juice.
- Cover and cook on low heat for 20 minutes.
- Serve hot.

181 Trout Fennel Tomato Curry

Serves 4 | Prep time 30 minutes | Cooking time 30 minutes

Ingredients

- 1 lb. trout, cut into medium pieces
- 1 cup fennel bulb, halved
- 1 cup tomato, halved
- 2 cup vegetable stock
- 1 tbsp fish sauce
- Sea salt to taste
- Pepper to taste
- 1 tsp dill, minced
- 1 tsp rosemary, minced
- 1 tsp butter
- ¼ tsp red chili powder
- 1/3 tsp garlic powder

Directions

- In a Dutch oven, add the butter and sear the fish for 3 minutes.
- Add the fennel, tomato, garlic, red chili powder, fish sauce, sea salt and pepper.
- Cover and cook for 5 minutes. Pour in the vegetable stock and cook for 10 minutes.
- Add the dill, rosemary and serve hot.

182 Seafood Risotto

Serves 4 | Prep time 10 minutes | Cooking time 40 minutes

Ingredients

- 2 tablespoons olive oil
- 2 tablespoons butter
- 1 onion, diced finely
- ½ pound frozen seafood mix
- 1½ cups arborio rice
- Salt and pepper to taste
- ½ cup white wine
- 3 cloves garlic, minced 1-quart water

Directions

- Warm the olive oil and butter in the Dutch oven over medium heat.
- Stir in the onion and cook for about 5 minutes or until tender.
- Stir in the seafood mix and cook for about 5 minutes.
- Stir in the rice and cook for 5 more minutes.
- Season with salt and pepper and pour in the white wine.
- While stirring constantly, pour in the water, ½ cup at a time, mixing well so the mixture remains creamy but not too watery.
- The risotto is done when the rice is cooked through.
- Serve while it's still creamy with a dash of pepper on top.

183 Calamari Fra Diavolo

Serves 4 | Prep time 10 minutes | Cooking time 40 minutes

Ingredients

- 2 tablespoons olive oil
- 2 pounds fresh squid, cut into rings
- Salt and pepper to taste
- ½ cup red wine
- ½ cup of water
- 1 (28-ounce) can tomato sauce
- 2 teaspoons chili flakes
- 3 cloves garlic, minced

Directions

- Warm the olive oil and butter in the Dutch oven over medium heat.
- Stir in the squid rings and cook for about 5 minutes.
- Season with salt and pepper and chili flakes.
- Pour in the wine, water, and tomato sauce.
- Cover and cook for 30 minutes.
- When the mixture is almost thick and most of the liquid has evaporated, serve alone or on top of pasta or crusty bread.

184 Seafood Stew

Serves 4 | Prep time 10 minutes | Cooking time 40 minutes

Ingredients

- 2 tablespoons olive oil
- 1 medium onion, diced
- 3 cloves garlic, minced
- 1 (14-ounce) bag of frozen vegetables
- 2 pounds seafood mix
- 2 tablespoons tomato paste
- Salt and pepper to taste
- 1-quart water

Directions

- Warm the olive oil in the Dutch oven over medium heat.
- Cook the diced onion and garlic for about 5 minutes until tender.
- Stir in the frozen veggies and seafood and cook for 10 minutes.
- Stir in the tomato paste and season with salt and pepper.
- Pour in the water and cook for 30 minutes.
- Serve with bread if desired.

185 Pasta with Clams and Pancetta

Serves 4 | Prep. time 10 minutes | Cooking time 55 minutes

Ingredients

- 3 tablespoons extra-virgin olive oil

- 2 ounces pancetta, thinly sliced and chopped
- 1 medium onion, finely chopped
- 4 cloves garlic, thinly sliced
- ¾ teaspoon red pepper flakes, crushed
- 1 (28-ounce) can whole tomatoes, peeled and crushed 2 cups of water
- 24 littleneck clams, scrubbed
- 4 ounces (about 1 cup) ditalini pasta or other short cut pasta A handful of torn basil leaves (optional)

Directions

- Add the oil to the Dutch oven and heat it over medium heat.
- Add the pancetta and stir-cook for 4–5 minutes until it begins to crisp.
- Add the onion and stir cook for 6–8 minutes until softened.
- Add the garlic and stir cook for 4–5 minutes until fragrant.
- Mix in the red pepper flakes.
- Add the crushed tomatoes.
- Over medium-high heat, simmer and cook for 12–15 minutes until liquid is reduced to half.
- Add the water and clams. Cover and simmer over low heat for 8–10 minutes.
- Uncover and remove the opened clams.
- Cover again and cook the remaining clams for 15 more minutes. Discard any unopened ones; remove the opened clams.
- Add the pasta and cook for 8–10 minutes until al dente.
- Mix the clams back into the Dutch oven. Add the fresh basil if desired.
- Serve warm.

186 Beer Mustard Shrimp

Serves 4 | Prep. time 10 minutes | Cooking time 10–15 minutes

Ingredients

- 1 cup whole-wheat pastry flour or all-purpose flour
- 1 teaspoon Dijon mustard
- 1 cup pale ale or light-colored beer
- ½ teaspoon salt (divided) 2 tablespoons canola oil
- 1 pound (13–15 pieces) raw shrimp, peeled and deveined, tails left on
- Pepper to taste

Directions

- Add the flour, mustard, beer, and ¼ teaspoon of the salt to a mixing bowl. Mix well to make a smooth batter.
- Cook shrimp in two batches.
- Add 1 tablespoon of the canola oil to the Dutch oven and heat it over medium-high heat.
- Dip the shrimp in the batter, holding them by their tails.
- Add the shrimp one at a time and stir-cook for 3–4 minutes until evenly brown. Drain over paper towels.
- Repeat with the remaining 1 tablespoon of oil and the other half of the shrimp.
- Season with the remaining salt and pepper.
- Serve warm.

187 Tilapia Nuggets

Serves 6–8 | Prep. time 10–15 minutes | Cooking time 10–12 minutes

Ingredients

- 1½ cups all-purpose flour
- 2 pounds tilapia fillets, cut into bite-sized chunks 1 tablespoon onion powder
- 2 cups dry pancake mix 1-pint club soda
- 1 tablespoon seasoned salt 2 cups of vegetable oil Tartar sauce to taste

Directions

- Add the flour to a bowl. Coat the fish chunks with flour. Place them over paper towels and set aside for 5 minutes.
- Add the onion powder, pancake mix, soda, and seasoned salt to a mixing bowl. Mix well to make a smooth batter.
- Coat the fish chunks with the batter.

- Add the oil to the Dutch oven and heat it to 400°F (200°C).
- Add the coated fish chunks and fry for 3 minutes per side until evenly brown.
- Drain over paper towels and serve warm.

188 Salmon with Spinach

Prep time: 10 minutes | **Cook time:** 15 minutes | Serves 6

Ingredients

- 3 tablespoons unsalted butter
- 2 pounds (907 g) fresh baby spinach 4 shallots, minced
- 6 salmon fillets
- 3 tablespoons fresh lemon juice
- Sea salt and freshly ground black pepper, to taste
- 2 teaspoons finely chopped fresh rosemary leaves
- 6 lemon wedges, for garnish
- Horseradish cream sauce, for garnish

Directions

- Preheat the oven to 325°F (163°C).
- Coat the bottom of a Dutch oven, with the butter. Spread the spinach leaves evenly over the butter, and sprinkle with the minced shallots. Place the salmon fillets on the spinach, skin-side down, and drizzle with the lemon juice. Season with the salt, pepper, and rosemary.
- Cover, place in the heated oven, and bake for 8 to 10 minutes. Uncover the pot and check the fish for doneness. If needed, finish the cooking with the pot uncovered for 3 to 5 minutes, or until the fish is opaque and the salmon flakes. Garnish with lemon wedges or a dollop of horseradish sauce.

189 Buttery Grouper

Prep time: 20 minutes | **Cook time:** 50 minutes | Serves 4 to 6

Ingredients

- 2 pounds (907 g) grouper
- 2 tablespoons extra-virgin olive oil
- 1 fennel bulb, thinly sliced
- 2 celery stalks, thinly sliced
- 6 shallots, skinned and chopped
- Salt and freshly ground black pepper, to taste
- 4 ounces (113 g) butter, cut into small chunks
- 2 teaspoons chopped fresh dill

Directions

- Remove the fine membrane covering the grouper. Remove the central bone (if the fish is not already deboned), and cut the fish into 1½-inch-thick diagonal slices.
- In a Dutch oven over medium heat, heat the olive oil. Add the fennel, celery, and shallots, and cook until they begin to soften. Transfer to a small bowl.
- Brown the fish in the oil and transfer to a plate. Return the vegetables to the pot, then lay the fish on top. Season with salt and pepper.
- Cover the Dutch oven and cook over a low heat for 5 minutes. Transfer the vegetables to a serving platter, and cover to keep warm. Cover the Dutch oven, and cook the fish for 30 to 40 minutes, or until tender.
- Transfer the fish to the serving platter with the vegetables.
- Place the Dutch oven back over the heat. Return the liquid to a boil, and stir in the butter. Add the dill and cook, stirring until thickened. Season with salt and pepper, and pour the butter sauce over the fish.

190 Whitefish and Oyster Bouillabaisse

Prep time: 30 minutes | **Cook time:** 1 hour | Serves 4 to 6

Ingredients

- 3 tablespoons extra-virgin olive oil
- 6 garlic cloves, minced
- 1 to 2 onions (about ¾ pound / 340 g), diced
- 1 shallot, minced
- 1 celery stalk, minced
- 1 carrot, diced

- 1½ tablespoons tomato paste
- ½ teaspoon saffron
- 1 teaspoon minced basil or 1 fresh basil leaf
- 2 tablespoons minced fresh parsley
- Salt and freshly ground black pepper, to taste
- 1 (28-ounce / 794-g) can diced tomatoes, undrained 2 cups clam juice
- 1 (8-ounce / 227-g) jar fresh oysters, juice reserved
- 1-pound (454 g) whitefish (cod, halibut, or trout), cut into bite-size pieces
- 2½ pounds (1.1 kg) seafood mix (shrimp, clams, mussels, lobsters, scallops, crab meat, or squid)
- 2 tablespoons chopped fresh parsley, for garnish

Directions

- In a Dutch oven over medium heat, heat the olive oil. Add the garlic, onion, shallot, celery, and carrot, and sauté until lightly golden, about 20 minutes.
- Add the tomato paste, saffron, basil, minced parsley, salt, and pepper. Mix well.
- Add the tomatoes, clam juice, and juice from the jar of oysters. Bring the pot to a boil, lower the heat, and simmer for 15 minutes.
- Add the oysters, whitefish, and seafood mix. Bring the pot back to a boil. Skim off any scum or fat. Lower the heat and simmer for 15 minutes.
- Garnish with the chopped parsley.

191 Lemon Halibut with Tomato

Prep time: 10 minutes | **Cook time:** 30 minutes | Serves 4

Ingredients

- 4 tablespoons unsalted butter
- Juice from 2 medium lemons
- Several dashes Tabasco sauce
- 4 (8-ounce / 227-g) halibut steaks Pinch salt
- Pinch pepper
- 1 small onion, peeled and chopped
- ½ large red bell pepper, seeded and chopped
- 3 large tomatoes, peeled, seeded, and chopped

Directions

- Heat oven to 400°F (205°C).
- Place a Dutch oven over medium heat. Add butter, lemon juice, and Tabasco sauce. Stir until butter has melted. Turn off heat.
- Season fish on each side with salt and pepper. Sprinkle onion and bell pepper over the bottom of the Dutch oven. Add fish and scatter tomatoes over the top.
- Bake 20 to 25 minutes or until the thickest part of fish is opaque. Spoon the pan juices over fish every 10 minutes. Remove fish from pan and spoon sauce over it to serve.

192 Roast Fish with Lemon

Prep time: 20 minutes | **Cook time:** 40 minutes | Serves 4

Ingredients

- 1 (4-pound / 1.8-kg) whole fish, such as snapper or sea bass, cleaned and scaled
- 1 tablespoon olive oil
- ½ teaspoon sea salt
- ½ teaspoon freshly cracked black pepper 2 medium lemons, sliced ⅛-inch thick
- 4 dill fronds
- 2 sprigs thyme
- 1 clove garlic, peeled and thinly sliced

Directions

- Heat oven to 450°F (235°C) and lightly spray an ovenproof 12- inch Dutch oven with nonstick cooking spray.
- Brush the outside of the fish with olive oil and season with salt and pepper. Open the fish slightly and fill the center with 3 slices of lemon, along with dill, thyme, and garlic slices.
- Place fish into the Dutch oven and top with a few slices of lemon. Roast 30 minutes, occasionally spooning juices in the bottom of the Dutch oven over fish. The fish is ready when the flesh flakes easily and reaches an internal temperature of 130°F (54°C). Let

fish rest 10 minutes, and then carefully transfer to a platter to serve.

193 Beer Catfish Fillet

Prep time: 25 minutes | **Cook time:** 15 minutes | **Serves** 8

Ingredients

- 2 pounds (907 g) catfish fillets, about 4 ounces (113 g) each
- 2 (12-ounce / 340-g) beers, lager or ale preferred
- Oil, for frying
- 1 cup all-purpose flour 1 teaspoon salt
- ½ teaspoon freshly cracked black pepper
- 2 large eggs, beaten
- 1 cup buttermilk
- 1 teaspoon hot sauce 1 cup yellow cornmeal
- 1 cup fine saltine cracker crumbs

Directions

- In a large bowl combine catfish fillets and beer. Refrigerate 1 hour, then drain well and pat the fillets dry.
- In a 6- or 8-quart deep Dutch oven add 3-inch oil, making sure there is at least a 3-inch air gap at the top of the pot. Heat oil to 350ºF (180ºC).
- In a large zip-top bag combine flour, salt, and pepper. Seal the bag and shake to mix. In a shallow dish combine eggs, buttermilk, and hot sauce. Whisk to combine. Finally, in a second large zip-top bag combine cornmeal and cracker crumbs. Seal and shake to combine.
- Working in batches, add a few fillets to flour and toss to coat. Remove from flour and tap off any excess. Dip fillets into egg mixture, allowing any excess to drip off. Finally, add fillets to cornmeal mixture and toss to coat. Transfer coated fillets to a wire rack to hold.
- Fry fillets 2 to 3 at a time until they are golden brown on both sides, about 3 minutes per side. While first batch is frying, heat oven to 175ºF (79ºC). Transfer cooked fillets to a wire rack over a sheet pan and place in warm oven to hold while you fry remaining fillets. Serve hot.

194 Cod Fillet with Beer

Prep time: 20 minutes | **Cook time:** 25 minutes | **Serves** 8

Ingredients

- 2 cups all-purpose flour 1 teaspoon salt
- ½ teaspoon freshly cracked black pepper
- ½ teaspoon smoked paprika
- ½ teaspoon garlic powder
- ¼ teaspoon onion powder 1 large egg, beaten
- 1 (12-ounce / 340-g) beer, lager preferred
- Oil, for frying
- 2 pounds (907 g) cod fillets, about 4 ounces (113 g) each

Directions

- In a large bowl combine flour, salt, pepper, paprika, garlic powder, and onion powder. Whisk to combine, then add egg and beer and whisk until a smooth batter forms. Allow to rest at room temperature for 1 hour.
- In a 6- or 8-quart deep Dutch oven add 3-inch oil, making sure there is a 3-inch air gap at the top of the pot. Heat oil to 350ºF (180ºC).
- Heat oven to 175ºF (79ºC). Pat the fish fillets dry. Working with one fillet at a time, dip into batter and immediately add to hot oil. Fry until fish is golden brown on both sides, about 5 to 6 minutes. Remove fillet from the oil and transfer to a wire rack over a sheet pan to drain, then transfer to warm oven to keep warm while you fry remaining fish. Serve hot.

195 Salmon Fillet with Lemon

Prep time: 10 minutes | **Cook time:** 30 minutes | **Serves** 4 to 6

Ingredients

- 1 tablespoon extra-virgin olive oil
- 1 (1½-pound / 680-g) skin-on salmon fillet
- 1 teaspoon salt

- ¼ teaspoon freshly ground black pepper
- 1 teaspoon dried dill
- 2 tablespoons melted butter 2 lemons, sliced, divided

Directions

- Preheat the oven to 400°F (205°C).
- In a Dutch oven over medium heat, heat the olive oil. Add the salmon, skin-side down, and let it sear for 5 to 10 minutes, so the skin gets crispy. Remove the pot from the heat, and sprinkle the salmon with the salt, pepper, and dill. Pour the melted butter evenly over the salmon. Place half of the lemon slices on top of the salmon.
- Cover and bake in the oven for 15 to 20 minutes, until the salmon flakes easily with a fork.
- Transfer the salmon to a serving dish. Throw away the cooked lemons and replace them with the fresh sliced ones before serving. Season with salt, if needed.

196 Arugula Cod with Cherry Tomato

Prep time: 5 minutes | Cook time: 15 minutes | Serves 4

Ingredients

- 4 (6-ounce / 170-g) cod fillets
- 1 teaspoon salt
- ½ teaspoon freshly ground black pepper
- 2 tablespoons extra-virgin olive oil
- 2 cups grape or cherry tomatoes 2 garlic cloves, chopped
- ⅓ cup Italian salad dressing
- 6 cups baby arugula

Directions

- Pat the fish dry with paper towels, and season with salt and pepper. In a Dutch oven over medium-high heat, heat the olive oil. Sear the fish for 2 to 3 minutes on each side, until browned. Transfer the fish to a plate to rest.
- Add the tomatoes and garlic to the pot. Cook for 3 minutes or until the tomatoes start to soften. Stir in the salad dressing. Add the arugula and toss well. Cook for 2 more minutes or until the arugula is wilted.
- Place the cod fillets on top of the greens and tomatoes. Spoon some of the sauce over the fish. Cover and cook for 2 to 3 more minutes, until the cod easily flakes with a fork.
- Serve the fish with the vegetables and sauce, all in one pot.

197 Olive Cod with Lemon

Prep time: 5 minutes | Cook time: 15 minutes | Serves 4

Ingredients

- 4 (6-ounce / 170-g) cod fillets
- Kosher salt and freshly ground black pepper, to taste
- 12 thin lemon slices
- ¼ cup pitted, chopped kalamata olives
- ¼ cup capers, drained and chopped
- 2 teaspoons chopped fresh rosemary leaves
- ¼ cup olive oil

Directions

- Arrange the fish fillets in a single layer in the Dutch oven and season with salt and pepper. Top each piece of fish with 3 lemon slices and then scatter the olives, capers, and rosemary evenly over the top. Drizzle the olive oil evenly over all of the fish. Place the lid on the pot.
- Place the Dutch oven on a bed of 10 hot coals and then place 24 hot coals on the lid. Cook for about 15 minutes, until the fish is cooked through. Serve hot.

198 Mussels with Bacon

Prep time: 10 minutes | Cook time: 15 minutes | Serves 4 to 6

Ingredients

- 2 to 3 tablespoons extra-virgin olive oil, plus more for garnish
- ½ cup bacon, diced

- 4 cloves garlic, thinly sliced
- 1 onion, chopped
- 1 cup dry white wine
- 2 teaspoons paprika
- 2 dozen mussels, cleaned and beards removed Cayenne pepper, for garnish
- Handful fresh oregano, chopped, for garnish

Directions

- In a Dutch oven over medium heat, heat the olive oil and cook the bacon. Once the bacon fat begins to render, 2 minutes, add the garlic and onion. Cook, stirring, until they are translucent.
- Add the wine and stir in the paprika.
- Add the mussels. Increase the heat to high, and cook for about 30 seconds, or until the alcohol has evaporated.
- Reduce the heat to medium-low. Cover the pot and steam for 5 to 8 minutes, until all the mussels have opened. Discard any mussels that haven't opened.
- Garnish with a drizzle of olive oil, a sprinkle of cayenne pepper, and chopped oregano.

199 Chives Mussels

Prep time: 25 minutes | **Cook time:** 20 minutes | Serves 6

Ingredients

- 6 tablespoons unsalted butter, divided
- 2 shallots, peeled and minced
- 2 cloves garlic, peeled and minced
- ½ teaspoon salt
- ½ teaspoon freshly cracked black pepper
- 3 cups white wine
- 3 pounds (1.4 kg) cultivated mussels, scrubbed and beards removed
- ¼ cup chopped fresh chives
- 1 tablespoon chopped fresh tarragon

Directions

- In a Dutch oven over medium heat add 2 tablespoons butter. Once butter melts and starts to foam add shallots and cook until tender, about 1 minute. Add garlic, salt, and pepper and cook until the garlic is fragrant, about 30 seconds.
- Add white wine and bring to a boil, then add mussels and stir to combine. Cover and cook 6 to 8 minutes. With a slotted spoon remove and discard any mussels that did not open. Transfer remaining mussels to a serving bowl.
- Bring the cooking liquid to a simmer and whisk in remaining butter and herbs. Pour liquid over the mussels and serve immediately

200 Shrimp and Mussels Paella

Prep time: 20 minutes | **Cook time:** 45 minutes | Serves 6 to 8

Ingredients

- 2 to 3 tablespoons extra-virgin olive oil
- 2 pounds (907 g) chicken thighs, skinned, boned, and cut into 2-inch pieces
- 5½ cups low-sodium chicken broth or stock
- ½ pound (227g) shrimp, peeled and shells reserved
- 1½ pounds (680g) paella rice, or any Spanish-style medium-grain rice
- ¼ teaspoon saffron
- 1 (15-ounce / 425-g) can cannellini beans, drained and rinsed
- 1 to 2 tomatoes (about ¾ pound), peeled, halved, seeded, and finely chopped
- 1 tablespoon smoked paprika 1 dozen mussels, scrubbed Sea salt, to taste

Directions

- In a Dutch oven over medium heat, heat the olive oil. Add the chicken pieces and sauté until golden. Using a slotted spoon, transfer the chicken to a platter. Pour off the fat from the pot.
- Return the pot to the heat, add the broth, and bring to a boil. Add the shrimp shells (reserving the shrimp), and simmer for 15 to 20 minutes. Remove the shells with a slotted spoon and discard. Stir in the rice and cook on medium heat for 10 minutes. Add the chicken pieces, saffron, cannellini beans,

tomato, and paprika. Cook, covered, for 10 minutes.
- Add the shrimp and mussels. Cook, covered, for 5 minutes, or until the mussels have opened.
- Season with salt.

201 Crab and Clam Cioppino

Prep time: 20 minutes | Cook time: 2½ hours | Serves 8 to 10

Ingredients

- ¼ cup unsalted butter or olive oil
- 2 medium onions, peeled and chopped
- 4 cloves garlic, peeled and minced
- ¼ cup parsley leaves
- ¼ cup oregano leaves
- 2 (28-ounce / 794-g) cans whole tomatoes, peel removed
- 2 (10-ounce / 283-g) cans of clams
- 2 bay leaves
- 2 tablespoons dried basil leaves 2 cups dry white wine
- 16 fresh clams
- 16 mussels
- 1½ pounds (680g) salmon, cut into bite-sized chunks
- 1 pound (454 g) fresh crab meat or imitation crab stick, cut into chunks
- 1½ pounds (680g) small bay scallops
- ½ teaspoon salt
- ¼ teaspoon freshly cracked black pepper

Directions

- Place a Dutch oven over medium heat. Once it's heated through add butter and onion. Cook 10 to 12 minutes. Add the garlic and stir continually 1 minute. Stir in parsley and oregano.
- Add juice from the tomatoes to the Dutch oven. Squeeze each tomato in your hand to break apart. Add to pan and press each tomato against the side to break it into smaller pieces. Pour clam juice into pan and refrigerate clams for later. Stir in dried herbs and wine.
- Cover with a lid, reduce the heat to low, and simmer 2 hours. (If necessary, you can complete this part up to 2 days ahead and refrigerate. Return it to the pan and bring to a boil before turning the flame to low.)
- Scrub clams and mussels with a bristle brush. Remove beards from mussels. Soak in cold water 20 minutes. Gently add shellfish and reserved canned clams to the pan. Stir them into the sauce.
- Stir in fish chunks, then crab meat. Stir in scallops. Cover and steam 5 to 8 minutes until clams and mussels have opened.
- Remove bay leaves and season dish with salt and pepper. Serve directly from the Dutch oven while hot.

202 Breaded Crab Fish Cheese Casserole

Prep time: 10 minutes | Cook time: 50 minutes | Serves 6

Ingredients

- 2 tablespoons unsalted butter
- 1 medium onion, peeled and minced 3 cloves garlic, peeled and minced
- 1 (16-ounce / 454-g) jar Alfredo sauce
- ½ pound (227g) fish fillets 3 tablespoons orange juice
- ½ cup ground almonds
- 1 cup shredded Havarti cheese
- ½ pound (227g) crab meat
- 1 cup soft whole-wheat bread crumbs
- 3 tablespoons grated Parmesan cheese
- 3 tablespoons unsalted butter, melted

Directions

- Heat oven to 350°F (180°C).
- In a Dutch oven melt butter over medium heat. Once melted add onion and garlic, and cook 5 minutes or until tender. Add Alfredo sauce and bring to a simmer. Add fish fillets and simmer 4 to 5 minutes, or until fish flakes. Stir to break up fish.
- Stir in orange juice and almonds and remove from heat. Add Havarti cheese and crab meat.

- In a small bowl, combine the bread crumbs, Parmesan cheese, and melted butter; mix well. Sprinkle over fish mixture. Bake 30 to 40 minutes, or until the bread crumbs have browned. Serve immediately.

203 Panko Shrimp Scampi

Prep time: 10 minutes | **Cook time:** 25 minutes | **Serves** 4

Ingredients

- ½ cup Panko bread crumbs
- 6 tablespoons salted butter, divided 1 shallot, peeled and minced
- 1 clove garlic, peeled and minced
- 1 tablespoon finely chopped fresh chives 1 teaspoon finely chopped fresh parsley
- ½ teaspoon finely chopped fresh dill
- ¼ teaspoon smoked paprika
- ¼ teaspoon salt
- ¼ teaspoon freshly cracked black pepper
- 1 pound (454 g) (23 to 30 counts) tail-on shrimp

Directions

- Heat oven to 350°F (180°C).
- In a small bowl add bread crumbs. Melt 2 tablespoons butter and toss until the crumbs are evenly coated. Set aside.
- In a Dutch oven over medium heat add remaining butter. Once it melts and starts to foam add shallots and cook until tender, about 1 minute. Add remaining ingredients except the shrimp and cook until fragrant, about 30 seconds. Remove the Dutch oven from heat
- Add shrimp and toss to coat, then sprinkle the bread crumbs over the shrimp and bake 15 to 20 minutes, or until the shrimp are cooked through and the bread crumbs are golden brown. Serve immediately.

204 Creamy Shrimp Mushrooms Stroganoff

Prep time: 15 minutes | **Cook time:** 15 minutes | **Serves** 8

Ingredients

- 4 tablespoons unsalted butter 2 shallots, peeled and minced
- 2 cloves garlic, peeled and minced 4 plum tomatoes, diced
- 1 pound (454 g) chanterelle mushrooms, separated into individual pieces
- 4 ounces (113 g) portobello mushrooms, finely chopped 1 cup dry white wine
- 1 cup heavy cream
- 3 pounds (1.4 kg) shrimp, peeled and deveined 1 tablespoon chopped fresh tarragon
- 1 cup sour cream, room temperature
- ½ teaspoon salt
- ¼ teaspoon freshly cracked black pepper

Directions

- Melt butter in a Dutch oven over medium-high heat. Add shallots and garlic and cook until just tender, about 2 minutes.
- Add diced tomatoes and cook an additional 2 minutes. Add mushrooms and cook, stirring frequently, until the mushrooms soften, about 5 minutes.
- Add white wine and heavy cream to mushroom mixture. Bring to a boil and stir well. Add shrimp and cook
- just until they begin to turn opaque, about 2 minutes.
- Remove the Dutch oven from heat; stir in chopped tarragon, sour cream, salt, and pepper. Serve immediately.

205 Oysters and Shrimp Cream Salad

Prep time: 10 minutes | **Cook time:** 30 minutes | **Serves** 8

Ingredients

- 1 pound (454 g) dried penne pasta
- 2 tablespoons peanut or vegetable oil 2 tablespoons all-purpose flour
- 1 large yellow onion, peeled and diced
- 1 teaspoon anchovy paste 1 cup milk
- 1 cup heavy cream

- ½ teaspoon hot sauce
- 1 teaspoon Worcestershire sauce Pinch dried thyme
- 2 pints small oysters, drained, liquid reserved
- 2 pounds (907 g) medium shrimp, cooked, peeled, and deveined
- ½ teaspoon salt
- ½ teaspoon freshly cracked black pepper 8 cups salad mix
- 8 green onions, chopped

Directions

- In a Dutch oven, cook penne according to package directions; drain, set aside, and keep warm.
- Wipe out the Dutch oven; add oil over medium heat. Once the oil is hot, stir in flour and cook until it begins to turn light brown, about 5 to 6 minutes. Add onion and sauté 3 minutes or until soft. Whisk in anchovy paste, milk, and cream.
- Bring to a simmer and stir in hot sauce, Worcestershire sauce, and thyme; simmer 10 minutes.
- Stir oysters and shrimp into the cream sauce. Simmer just long enough to heat the seafood, about 2 minutes, then stir in pasta. If pasta mixture is too thick, stir in a little extra milk, cream, or liquid drained from the oysters. Taste for seasoning and add salt and pepper if needed.
- To serve, spread 1 cup salad mix over the top of a plate, ladle pasta mixture over the salad greens, and garnish with chopped green onion.

206 Shrimp and Tomato Provençal

Prep time: 20 minutes | **Cook time:** 1 hour | **Serves** 6

Ingredients

- 1 tablespoon olive oil
- 3 tablespoons unsalted butter
- 2 medium onions, peeled and chopped
- 4 cloves garlic, peeled and minced
- 1 (14-ounce / 397-g) can diced tomatoes, undrained
- 1 (8-ounce / 227-g) can tomato sauce
- ¼ cup dry sherry, if desired
- ½ teaspoon fennel seeds
- 1 teaspoon sugar
- ½ teaspoon salt
- ⅛ teaspoon cayenne pepper
- 1 teaspoon dried thyme leaves
- 1½ pounds (680 g) raw medium shrimp, shelled 3 cups hot cooked brown rice
- ½ cup crumbled Goat cheese

Directions

- In large Dutch oven combine olive oil and butter over medium heat. Once butter melts add onion and garlic; cook 5 to 6 minutes or until tender.
- Add all remaining ingredients except shrimp, rice, and cheese. Bring to a simmer, stirring frequently. Reduce heat to low, partially cover, and simmer 50 minutes, stirring occasionally.
- Just before serving, stir in shrimp and cook until shrimp curl and turn pink, about 3 to 4 minutes. Serve over rice and sprinkle with cheese.

207 Lemony Salt Snapper

Prep time: 15 minutes | **Cook time:** 35 to 40 minutes | **Serves** 6 to 8

Ingredients

- 2 pounds (907 g) sea salt
- ¾ to 1 cup water Cooking spray, for frying
- 1 large orange, sliced, divided
- 1 large lemon, sliced, divided
- 1 large grapefruit, sliced, divided
- 1 (4-pound / 1.8-kg) whole red snapper, cleaned and scaled

Directions

- Preheat the oven to 375°F (190°C).
- In a large bowl, combine the salt and water, and stir until it forms a pastelike consistency.

- Coat a Dutch oven with cooking spray, then pour a 1-inch-thick layer of the salt mixture into the bottom of the pot. Layer half of the orange, lemon, and grapefruit slices on top of the salt. Place the red snapper on top of the slices. Press the remaining salt on top of the fish to form a thick crust. Top with the remaining fruit slices.
- Cover, place in the heated oven, and bake for 35 to 40 minutes, or until the fish is done and the salt is lightly browned.

208 Baked Salmon Fillet

Prep time: 10 minutes | **Cook time:** 20 minutes | **Serves** 4 to 6

Ingredients

- 1 teaspoon kosher salt
- 1 teaspoon chili powder
- 1 teaspoon cumin
- 4 (6-ounce / 170-g) salmon fillets, skin on 1 tablespoon extra-virgin olive oil

Directions

- Preheat the oven to 375°F (190°C).
- In a small bowl, combine the salt, chili powder, and cumin. Rub the salmon fillets with the spice mixture, coating them evenly.
- eat the olive oil in a Dutch oven over medium-high heat. Place the salmon fillets in the pot, skin-side up. Cook for 3 minutes, or until the tops are evenly browned. For medium-rare, flip and cook for 3 minutes. For medium to well-done, cover, place in the preheated oven, and bake for 5 to 10 minutes.

209 Lemon Halibut with Salsa

Prep time: 25 minutes | **Cook time:** 15 minutes | **Serves** 4 to 6

Ingredients

- 6 halibut fillets
- Juice and zest of 1 lemon
- 1 tablespoon roughly chopped fresh thyme leaves
- 1 tablespoon chopped fresh parsley
- 6 tablespoons extra-virgin olive oil, divided Salt and freshly ground black pepper, to taste
- 1 fennel bulb, sliced
- ½ teaspoon sea salt 1½ cups arugula
- ¼ cup fresh tarragon leaves
- ¼ cup chives, cut into ½-inch pieces
- ¼ cup fresh mint leaves
- ¼ cup fresh basil leaves Salsa verde, for garnish

Directions

- Season the halibut fillets with the lemon zest, thyme, and parsley. Cover and refrigerate for at least 4 hours.
- Remove the fish from the refrigerator 15 minutes before cooking to bring it to room temperature. Brush with 2 tablespoons of olive oil, and season with salt and pepper.
- Heat 1 tablespoon of olive oil in a Dutch oven over medium heat, and add the fish. Cook for 2 to 3 minutes, until it's nicely colored on the first side. Turn the fish over and cook a few minutes, until it's almost cooked through, and remove the pot from the heat (the fish will continue to cook).
- In a large bowl, toss the sliced fennel with the sea salt, the remaining 3 tablespoons of olive oil, and 1 tablespoon of lemon juice. Add the arugula, tarragon, chives, mint, and basil, and toss, then season with salt and pepper. Arrange the salad on a large platter, place the fish on top, and garnish each fillet with a spoonful of salsa verde.

210 Quick Swordfish Steaks

Prep time: 10 minutes | **Cook time:** 10 minutes | **Serves** 4

Ingredients

- 4 tablespoons extra-virgin olive oil, divided
- 2 teaspoons chili powder
- 2 teaspoons dried oregano, crumbled
- 1 teaspoon sea salt
- ½ teaspoon freshly ground black pepper

- 4 swordfish steaks, cut ¾-inch thick

Directions

- Mix 3 tablespoons of olive oil with the chili powder, oregano, salt, and pepper. Brush the swordfish steaks with the oil mixture.
- In a Dutch oven over medium heat, heat the remaining 1 tablespoon of olive oil. Add the swordfish steaks and cook for about 4 minutes. Turn and cook for a few minutes, until browned on both sides but still moist.
- It's best if the fish is slightly undercooked in the center, as it will continue to cook a bit after you've removed it from the heat.

211 Panko Crab Cakes

Prep time: 10 minutes | Cook time: 30 minutes | Serves 6

Ingredients

- 1 pound (454 g) crab meat
- ⅓ cup mayonnaise
- 1 teaspoon seasoned salt, plus more to taste
- ½ cup Panko bread crumbs
- 1 egg, beaten
- ½ cup roasted red bell peppers, finely chopped
- 2 to 3 tablespoons extra-virgin olive oil
- Freshly ground black pepper, to taste

Directions

- In a medium bowl, mix together the crab meat, mayonnaise, seasoned salt, Panko crumbs, egg, and roasted red peppers. Divide the mixture and use your hands to form 6 patties. Place the patties a plate, cover with plastic wrap, and chill in the refrigerator for 30 minutes.
- Heat enough oil to coat the bottom of a Dutch oven over medium heat. Gently add the crab cakes to the pot, and cook for 5 to 6 minutes on each side, until the cakes are cooked through and golden brown. You may want to do this in batches, as all the crab cakes will probably not fit in the pot at once. Add another tablespoon of oil to the pot, if needed, for the second batch.
- Season with seasoned salt and pepper before serving—on buns with sauce, if using.

212 Mango Shrimp

Prep time: 5 minutes | Cook time: 10 minutes | Serves 4

Ingredients

- 2 tablespoons cooking oil
- 1 large onion, chopped
- 2 medium mangos, cubed
- ¼ cup soy sauce Juice of 2 limes
- 2 pounds (907 g) peeled and deveined shrimp

Directions

- Heat the oil in the Dutch oven set over a bed of 10 hot coals. Add the onion and cook, stirring, until soft and beginning to brown, about 5 minutes.
- Add the mango, soy sauce, lime juice, and shrimp and cook, stirring occasionally, until the shrimp are cooked through, about 5 more minutes. Serve hot.

213 Savory Calamari

Prep time: 15 minutes | Cook time: 20 minutes | Serves 2 to 3

Ingredients

- 1 pound (454 g) frozen calamari, cleaned
- ¼ cup fine cornmeal
- 2 tablespoons cornstarch
- 2 teaspoons seafood seasoning, such as Old Bay
- ½ teaspoon salt
- 1-quart canola or safflower oil

Directions

- Thaw calamari. Slice off the tentacles. Slice the tubes into ½- inch-wide rings. Pat dry with paper towels.
- Combine cornmeal, cornstarch, seasoning, and salt in a plastic bag. Add calamari to the bag and shake until coated evenly.
- Heat oven to 175ºF (79ºC). Place a wire rack over a baking sheet in the middle of the oven.

- Place 2-inch oil in a Dutch oven over medium-high heat. Once oil reaches 350°F (180°C), carefully add a handful of calamari pieces. Cook 2 to 3 minutes or until they're lightly golden brown.
- Remove cooked calamari with a slotted spoon or wire skimmer and place on wire rack in warm oven to drain.

214 Buttery Tomato Shrimp

Prep time: 5 minutes | **Cook time:** 15 minutes | **Serves** 4 to 6

Ingredients

- ¼ cup (½ stick) unsalted butter
- 2½ pounds shrimp, peeled and deveined
- 6 garlic cloves, minced
- Juice of 1 large lemon
- ¼ cup white wine (or substitute broth or water)
- 1 cup chopped tomatoes
- ½ teaspoon kosher salt
- ½ teaspoon freshly ground black pepper

Directions

- Melt the butter in the Dutch oven place on a bed of 6 hot coals. Add the shrimp, garlic, lemon juice, wine (or broth or water), tomatoes, salt, and pepper and cover the pot.
- Add 20 hot coals to the lid and bake for about 10 minutes, until the shrimp are cooked through. Serve hot.

Vegetarian recipes

215 Zucchini and Corn Chowder

Prep time: 10 minutes | **Cook time:** 35 minutes | Serves 4 to 6

Ingredients

- 1 ½ tbsp butter
- ½ cup white onions, diced
- 1 celery stalk, diced 1 carrot, diced
- 3 potatoes, diced
- 1 zucchini, diced
- 1 ¼ cups fresh corn
- 2 cloves garlic, crushed
- 1 tsp jalapeno, diced
- 2 cups chicken stock A pinch dried thyme
- ½ cup heavy cream Salt to taste

Directions

- In a Dutch oven, add butter, onions, celery, and carrots and cook for 5 minutes until the vegetables are softened.
- Add potatoes garlic, and jalapenos and cook for 5 more minutes.
- Add chicken stock and thyme and bring it to boil.
- Let the stock simmer for 8 minutes.
- Add corn kernels and zucchini and let it cook for 8-10 more minutes.
- Once all the vegetables are cooked through, blend the mixture using a hand blender.
- Bring the soup to boil and reduce the heat.
- Add heavy cream and let it simmer for 5 more minutes.
- Season and serve hot.

216 Butternut Squash Soup

Prep time: 10 minutes | **Cook time:** 20 minutes | Serves 4 to 6

Ingredients

- 1 large butternut (2 pounds in weight), peeled, de-seeded and sliced
- 1 onion, chopped
- 2 inches ginger root, chopped
- 3 cloves garlic, chopped
- A bunch of cilantro, chopped
- 1 ¾ cup coconut milk, unsweetened
- 2 tbsp. olive oil
- 3 tsp salt
- ¼ tsp red chilli flakes

Directions

- In a large Dutch oven, add olive oil and onion and cook for 5 minutes until translucent.
- Add garlic, ginger and chili flakes and continue to cook for 3 minutes.
- Add butternut squash, coconut milk, salt and 2 cups water.
- Bring the soup to a boil and reduce the heat to low and let it simmer for 15- 20 minutes.
- Once the butternut squash is soft, shift the mixture to a blender and blend until you get a smooth consistency.
- Pour the soup back in the cleaned Dutch oven and cook on medium speed for 5 minutes.
- Serve hot.

217 Lentil Coconut Soup

Prep time: 10 minutes | **Cook time:** 50 minutes | Serves 4 to 6

Ingredients

- 1 ½ cup red lentils, split 1 ½ cup frozen spinach
- 2 cups coconut milk, unsweetened
- ¾ cup shredded coconut, unsweetened
- 2 cups tomatoes, crushed
- 1 onion, chopped
- 6 cloves garlic, chopped
- 3 inches ginger root piece, chopped
- ¾ tsp cayenne powder 2 tbsp curry powder
- 1 tbsp salt
- 2 ½ tbsp coconut oil 6 cups of water

Directions

- In a large Dutch oven, add coconut oil and onions and cook for 5 minutes until they become translucent.
- Add chopped garlic and ginger and continue stirring for 4 minutes.

- Add curry and cayenne powder and cook for a minute.
- Add coconut milk and stir until the spices are mixed completely.
- Now add red lentils, shredded coconut, salt and 6 cups of water.
- Bring the mixture to boil and reduce the heat to let it cook for 30 minutes on low heat.
- Chop the thawed frozen spinach and add in the soup along with tomatoes.
- Mix well and let it cook for another 5 to 7 minutes.
- Pour the soup in a bowl and enjoy while hot.

218 Italian White Bean Soup

Prep time: 10 minutes | **Cook time:** 30 minutes | **Serves** 4

Ingredients

- 1 potato, medium, peeled and cut into cubes
- 2 ribs of celery, chopped
- 2 carrots, medium and chopped
- 1 zucchini, chopped
- 1 tsp jalapeno, chopped
- ¾ cup tomato sauce
- 2 cups chicken stock
- 1 ½ cup white beans, boiled
- ½ tsp dried thyme
- 2 tsp dried parsley
- Salt to taste
- 1 tbsp. olive oil

Directions

- In a Dutch oven, add oil, potatoes and carrots and cook for 3-4 minutes.
- Now add onion, zucchini, celery, and jalapeno and cook for 4 minutes.
- Add the remaining ingredients and bring to boil,
- Let the broth simmer on low heat for 15-20 minutes until the vegetables are soft.
- Serve hot.

219 Vegetarian Chili

Prep time: 10 minutes | **Cook time:** 25 minutes | **Serves** 4

Ingredients

- ¼ cup chopped onion
- ¼ cup chopped green pepper
- 1 clove garlic, chopped
- ½ cup Mexican stewed canned tomatoes, undrained
- ¾ cup pinto beans, boiled
- ¾ cup kidney beans, boiled
- ½ cup corn kernels, boiled
- ¼ cup rice, uncooked 1 ½ cup water
- 1 tsp canola oil
- ½ tsp chilli powder
- ¼ tsp cumin powder Salt to taste

Directions

- In a Dutch oven, add onion, garlic and green pepper and sauté for 5 minutes until tender.
- Add the rest of the ingredients and bring the mixture to boil.
- Reduce the heat and cover the pot for 20 minutes until the rice are cooked properly.
- You can adjust the consistency of the chilli according to your liking by adding more water.

220 Quinoa Veggies Bowl

Prep time: 30 minutes | **Cook time:** 1,30 h | **Serves** 4

Ingredients

- 1 cup quinoa
- 2 tablespoons extra virgin olive oil
- 1 onion, chopped
- 2 garlic cloves, minced
- 1 celery rib, diced
- 2 carrots, peeled and diced
- 15 oz. Cremini mushrooms
- 1 cup butternut squash, diced
- 5 broccoli florets, cut into quarters
- 2 small Zucchini, cut into rounds
- 4 cups vegetable broth

- 1 cup dry white wine
- 1 tablespoon tomato paste
- Sat and pepper, to taste

Directions

- Cook quinoa according to package instructions.
- Heat extra virgin olive oil over medium heat in a Dutch oven.
- Add onion and cook until lightly golden. Add in garlic cloves, celery, and carrots, and cook for an additional 8 to 10 minutes over medium heat.
- Stir in butternut squash, mushrooms, broccoli, and zucchini. Cover and cook for 15 minutes, stirring occasionally.
- Blend with wine, and when the wine evaporates, add in vegetable broth and tomato paste.
- Stir well and bring to a boil. Cover, reduce the heat and simmer for 25 minutes.
- Stir in quinoa and season with salt and pepper.

221 Vegetable Stew

Prep time: 30 minutes | **Cook time:** 1 h | **Serves** 4

Ingredients

- 1 onion, chopped
- 3 garlic cloves, minced
- 3 tablespoons extra virgin olive oil
- 1 small red bell pepper, seeded and diced
- 1 small yellow bell pepper, seeded and diced
- 1 small green bell pepper, seeded and diced
- 1 eggplant, diced 10 oz. tomato sauce 1 teaspoon paprika
- ½ teaspoon chili powder (optional)
- 1 teaspoon tomato paste
- Salt and pepper, to taste
- 1 tablespoon dried herbs, to taste

Directions

- Heat extra virgin olive oil in a Dutch oven over medium heat. Add the onion and cook until lightly golden. Add in garlic and cook for an additional minute or two.
- Stir in bell peppers, eggplant, and zucchini.
- Cook for 5 minutes and pour in tomato sauce, tomato paste and powders. Season with salt and pepper.
- Cover and cook for 45 minutes over medium-low heat, stirring occasionally.

222 Bean Basil Bowl

Prep time: 30 minutes | **Cook time:** 2,10 h | **Serves** 4

Ingredients

- 1 lb dried black beans Water
- 1 onion, chopped
- 1 shallot, chopped
- 1 jalapeno, minced
- Tomato sauce, to cover the beans
- 1 – 2 teaspoons tomato paste
- 10 fresh basil leaves, chopped
- 1 teaspoon dried oregano
- 1 tablespoon parsley, chopped
- Salt and pepper, to taste

Directions

- Place dry beans in a large bowl and cover them with water. Cover and leave overnight.
- Drain the beans and rinse them under warm running water.
- Heat extra virgin olive oil in a Dutch oven over medium heat and add in chopped onion and shallot.
- Cook for about 4 minutes, until lightly golden.
- Add in the rest of the ingredients, stir well and cover.
- Cook for approx. 2 hours over low heat or until the beans are cooked through.

223 Vegetarian Pasta e Fagioli with White Beans and Basil

Prep time: 30 minutes | **Cook time:** 45 minutes | **Serves** 4

Ingredients

- 4 cups water
- 1/2 tsp. salt, divided
- 1/2 cups small shell or bow tie pasta
- 2 cans great northern beans
- 3 tbsp. olive oil 1 onion, diced
- 3 cloves garlic, minced
- 2 tsp. fresh basil, chopped
- 1 tsp. dried oregano
- 1/2 tsp. pepper
- 1/2 tbsp. paprika 1 cup tomato sauce

Directions

- Gather the ingredients.
- Cook the pasta in the water with 1
- teaspoon of salt.
- Turn off the heat and drain almost all the water, reserving about 1/4 to 1/3 cup of the cooking water, then add the beans.
- Cover and set aside.
- In a separate skillet, add the olive oil and saute the diced onions, minced garlic, fresh chopped basil, oregano and remaining 1/2 teaspoon of salt and pepper for 3 to 5 minutes, until the onions are soft.
- Add the onions and spices to the beans and pasta pot and place over low heat.
- As the mixture is heating over low heat, add the paprika and tomato sauce and stir until well blended and heated through. (You can add a little bit more liquid, if you prefer a "soupier" dish, or heat it a little bit longer to cook off some more moisture if you find it too liquidly.)
- 8. Serve your vegetarian pasta fagioli hot and top it off with some Parmesan cheese or nutritional yeast to keep it vegan.

224 Oven Roasted Cauliflower

Prep time: 10 minutes | **Cook time:** 40 minutes | **Serves** 4

Ingredients

- 1 cauliflower head, medium
- 2 Tbsp apple cider vinegar
- 2 tbsp Dijon mustard
- 1 tsp onion powder 1 tsp garlic powder
- 1 tbsp dried oregano
- 1 tsp dried chives
- ½ tsp chili flakes
- ½ tsp black pepper powder
- 1 tsp salt
- ¼ cup olive oil

Directions

- Trim the leaves and stem and place the cauliflower head in a Dutch oven.
- Combine all ingredients in a bowl and mix well.
- Pour the spice mixture over the cauliflower head until it covers the cauliflower head completely.
- Cover the Dutch oven with lid and place it in pre-heated oven for 35 minutes.
- Remove the lid and broil for an additional 5 minutes until it gets a golden color.
- Remove from the Dutch oven and serve hot.

225 Beans with Chard

Prep time: 15 minutes | **Cook time:** 26 minutes | **Serves** 2

Ingredients

- 1 bunch red or rainbow chard 2 to 3 tablespoons olive oil
- ½ small onion, chopped 2 garlic cloves, chopped Kosher salt, to taste
- ¼ cup dry white wine
- medium tomato, seeded and diced
- tablespoons diced or puréed sun-dried tomatoes
- ¼ teaspoon red pepper flakes

Directions

- (14-ounce / 397-g) can cannellini beans, drained and rinsed
- Rinse the chard and cut the leaves from the stems. Dice enough of the stems to make ½ cup; reserve the rest for another use or discard. Stack the leaves up and cut into ½-inch ribbons.
- Place the Dutch oven over medium heat and add the olive oil. Heat until the oil shimmers and then add the onion, garlic, and chard stems. Season with salt and cook, stirring, for 5 to 6 minutes, or until the onion pieces have separated and the chard has softened.
- Add the wine and bring to a simmer. Add the diced tomato, sun-dried tomatoes, and red pepper flakes.
- Add the chard leaves by big handfuls, stirring to wilt. When all the chard is added, bring to a simmer and cover the Dutch oven. Cook for about 15 minutes, or until the chard is very soft. Taste and adjust the seasoning, adding more salt or red pepper flakes if necessary. Add the beans and cook for another 5 minutes, or until the beans are heated through.

226 Savory Beans Rice

Prep time: 15 minutes | **Cook time:** 21 minutes | **Serves** 2

Ingredients

- 2 to 3 tablespoons olive oil
- ½ small onion, chopped (about ⅓ cup)
- 1 large garlic clove, minced
- 1 small jalapeño pepper, seeded and chopped (about 1 tablespoon)
- ½ cup long-grain white rice
- 3 tablespoons red salsa
- 2 tablespoons tomato sauce
- ¾ cup vegetable stock
- ¼ teaspoon ground cumin
- ½ teaspoon kosher salt

Directions

- (14-ounce / 397-g) can pinto beans, drained and rinsed 1 tablespoon chopped fresh parsley
- Preheat the oven to 350°F (180°C).
- Place the Dutch oven over medium heat. Add enough oil to coat the bottom of the pot and heat until the oil shimmers. Add the onion, garlic, and jalapeño and cook, stirring, for 4 to 5 minutes, or until the onion pieces have separated and the vegetables have softened. Add the rice and stir to coat. Cook for about 1 minute.
- Add the salsa, tomato sauce, vegetable stock, cumin, salt, and beans and stir to combine. Bring the liquid to a strong simmer and cover the Dutch oven.
- Place the pot in the oven and cook for 18 minutes. Remove from the oven and let sit, covered, for 15 minutes. Remove the lid and add the parsley. Gently toss the rice with two large forks to fluff the rice and mix in the parsley.

227 Corn and Bean Succotash

Prep time: 15 minutes | **Cook time:** 40 minutes | **Serves** 2

Ingredients

- 2 to 3 tablespoons olive oil
- 1 garlic clove, minced
- ½ medium green bell pepper, seeded and diced (about ½ cup)
- ½ small onion, chopped
- ⅓ cup long-grain rice
- ⅔ cup frozen lima beans, thawed
- ⅔ cup fresh or frozen (thawed) corn kernels 1 bay leaf
- ¼ teaspoon cayenne pepper
- ½ teaspoon Old Bay seasoning
- ⅔ cup low-sodium vegetable stock
- ¼ teaspoon kosher salt
- 1 large tomato, seeded and chopped
- ¼ cup chopped fresh parsley or basil, or a combination

Directions

- Preheat the oven to 350°F (180°C).
- Place the Dutch oven over medium heat. Add enough oil to coat the bottom of the pot and heat until the oil shimmers. Add the garlic, bell pepper, and onion and cook, stirring, for 4 to 5 minutes, or until the onion pieces have separated and softened. Add the rice and stir to coat with oil. Cook for about 1 minute. Stir in the lima beans, corn, bay leaf, cayenne, and Old Bay seasoning.
- Add the vegetable stock and salt and stir to combine. Bring the liquid to a strong simmer and cover the Dutch oven. Place the pot in the oven and cook for 18 minutes.
- Remove the pot from the oven and rest, covered, for 15 minutes. Taste the rice to make sure it's done. Fluff the rice mixture and stir in the tomatoes and parsley or basil. Rest for a few more minutes to warm the tomatoes through.

228 Panko Eggplant

Prep time: 15 minutes | **Cook time:** 40 minutes | **Serves** 2

Ingredients

Eggplant:

- 1 medium eggplant (about 1 pound / 454 g), sliced about ½-inch thick
- Kosher salt, to taste
- ⅓ cup all-purpose flour
- 1 egg, whisked with
- 1 tablespoon water or milk
- ⅔ cup Panko bread crumbs
- ½ teaspoon dried Italian herbs (or a mix of thyme, basil, and oregano)
- ½ cup grated Parmigiano-Reggiano or similar cheese, divided Vegetable oil, for frying
- ¼ cup shredded whole milk Mozzarella cheese (or more)

Sauce:

- 2 tablespoons olive oil
- ½ small onion, chopped
- 1 large garlic clove, minced
- 1 (14-ounce / 397-g) can diced tomatoes, with their juice
- 2 tablespoons diced sun-dried tomatoes (optional)
- ¼ teaspoon dried Italian herbs
- ¼ teaspoon kosher salt

Directions

- Place the eggplant slices on a rack set over a sheet pan. Season heavily with salt. Carefully turn the slices over and salt the other side. Set aside for 15 minutes while you prepare the breading.
- 2. In a shallow bowl, place the flour; in another shallow bowl, place the egg. In a third bowl, stir together the Panko, Italian herbs, and
- ¼ cup of grated Parmigiano-Reggiano.
- 3. Place the Dutch oven over medium-high heat. Add enough oil to form a ½-inch layer in the bottom of the pot and heat until the oil reaches about 360°F (182°C).
- 4. While the oil heats, rinse off the eggplant slices with water and blot dry on both sides with paper towels. Working with a few slices at a time, dredge both sides of the eggplant slices in the flour, then coat with the egg. Place slices in the Panko mixture and coat both sides.
- 5. When the oil is hot, carefully place the slices in the oil and fry for 2 to 3 minutes or until golden brown. Turn the slices over and cook for 2 minutes or until the second side is browned. Work in batches until all slices are browned. As the slices finish frying, move them to a rack placed over a sheet pan.
- 6. Preheat the oven to 375°F (190°C).
- 7. Pour the frying oil out of the Dutch oven (no need to wipe it out).
- 8. For the sauce, place the pot over medium heat and add the olive oil. Heat until the oil shimmers, and then add the onion and garlic. Cook, stirring, for 4 to 6 minutes, or until the onion pieces have separated and softened and the garlic is very fragrant.
- 9. Add the canned tomatoes with their juice, the sun-dried tomatoes (if using), and Italian

herbs; bring to a simmer. Add the salt (slightly more if you're not using the sun-dried tomatoes) and stir. Bring to a simmer and cook for about 10 minutes. Using a potato masher or the back of a spoon, crush the tomatoes to form a smooth sauce. Taste and adjust the seasoning. Remove about ½ cup of the sauce.

- 10. Remove from the heat and use tongs to place the eggplant slices on top of the tomato sauce. Depending on the size of your Dutch oven and the number of slices, you may need to overlap them slightly. Drizzle the reserved sauce over the eggplant slices and sprinkle with the Mozzarella and the remaining ¼ cup of Parmigiano-Reggiano.
- 11. Place the pot in the oven, uncovered, and bake for 12 to 18 minutes, or until the sauce is bubbling and the cheese is melted.

229 Navy Beans and Zucchini

Prep time: 20 minutes | **Cook time:** 30 minutes | **Serves** 2

Ingredients

- Kosher salt, to taste
- 1 medium zucchini, sliced ½-inch thick 2 to 3 tablespoons olive oil
- ½ small onion, sliced (about ⅔ cup)
- 2 garlic cloves, minced or pressed
- ½ small green bell pepper, seeded and cut into ½-inch chunks (about ½ cup)
- ½ small red bell pepper, seeded and cut into ½-inch chunks (about
- ½ cup)
- 2 small tomatoes, seeded and diced
- 1 cup canned navy beans, drained and rinsed
- ½ teaspoon dried oregano
- ¼ teaspoon freshly ground black pepper
- 2 tablespoons minced fresh basil

Directions

- Very liberally salt one side of the zucchini slices. Place the slices salted-side down on a rack placed over a baking sheet. Salt the other side. Let the slices sit for 15 to 20 minutes, or until they start to exude water (you'll see it beading up on the surface of the slices and dripping down into the sheet pan). Rinse the slices and blot them dry. Cut the zucchini slices in half.
- Place the Dutch oven over medium heat. Add enough oil to coat the bottom of the pot and heat until the oil shimmers. Add the zucchini slices in a single layer and cook without moving for 3 to
- 5 minutes, or until browned. Turn and brown the other sides, about 3 minutes. Remove to the rack or a plate.
- Add the onion and garlic to the Dutch oven and season with a pinch of salt. Cook, stirring, until the onions just begin to brown, about 3 minutes.
- Add the bell peppers and cook for about 3 minutes, or until they just start to brown. Add the zucchini, tomatoes, beans, oregano, and black pepper. Bring to a simmer and cover. Reduce the heat to medium-low and simmer for 15 to 20 minutes, or until the vegetables are soft. If there is too much liquid in the pot, simmer uncovered for a few minutes until it is reduced.
- Garnish with the basil and serve.

230 Butternut Squash Risotto

Prep time: 15 minutes | **Cook time:** 1¼ hour | **Serves** 2

Ingredients

- 1 (8-ounce / 227-g) container butternut squash, peeled and diced
- 3 to 4 tablespoons olive oil
- Kosher salt, to taste
- 1 large shallot, finely chopped
- ¾ cup Arborio or Carnaroli rice
- ¼ cup dry white wine Pinch dried sage
- 2½ cups water
- 1 cup vegetable stock, divided
- ¼ teaspoon freshly ground black pepper
- 2 tablespoons unsalted butter
- ¼ cup grated Parmigiano-Reggiano or similar cheese, plus more for garnish

Directions

- Preheat the oven to 400°F (205°C).
- Add the butternut squash cubes to the Dutch oven and drizzle with enough olive oil to coat the squash completely. Season with salt. Place the pot in the oven, uncovered, and roast the squash for about 15 minutes, then gently stir. Return the pot to the oven for another 15 minutes and stir again. Return to the oven and roast until tender with some crisp edges, probably another 10 to 15 minutes. Remove the squash from the Dutch oven and set aside.
- Place the Dutch oven over medium heat. Add enough oil to coat the bottom of the pot and heat until the oil shimmers. Add the shallot and cook, stirring, for 3 to 4 minutes, until softened. Add the rice and stir to coat with the oil. Cook for about a minute; move the rice and shallots to the perimeter of the Dutch oven.
- Add 3 or 4 cubes of the squash to the center of the pot and smash with a potato masher or the back of a spoon until they form a coarse paste. Add the wine and the sage and stir the rice into the squash. Bring to a simmer and cook until the wine is mostly absorbed.
- While the wine is reducing, mix the water and stock and heat in a saucepan or a heat-proof bowl in the microwave. Pour ½ of the water-stock mixture into the Dutch oven and stir vigorously. Bring to a simmer and cover the Dutch oven.
- Place the pot in the oven and bake for 15 minutes. Uncover and stir vigorously once more. The rice should be fairly soupy; if it seems at all dry, pour in another ½ cup of the water-stock mixture. Cover the pot and return to the oven. Bake for another 10 to 15 minutes, or until most of the liquid is absorbed and the rice is barely tender.
- Place the Dutch oven over low heat on the stovetop and add ¼ cup of the water-stock mixture. Stir the risotto for 3 to 5 minutes, or until the liquid is mostly absorbed, then stir in the pepper, butter, and half the cheese. Gently stir in as much of the reserved roasted squash as you like and let the risotto sit for a few minutes to warm the squash through.
- Spoon into bowls and top with the remaining cheese and additional pepper, if desired.

231 Cheese Mushrooms Bake

Prep time: 20 minutes | **Cook time:** 30 minutes | **Serves** 2

Ingredients

- 4 portobello mushrooms, about 3 inches across
- 4 tablespoons sherry vinegar
- 4 teaspoons minced fresh oregano or 2 teaspoons dried
- 4 garlic cloves, minced or pressed, divided
- 1 teaspoon Dijon mustard
- ½ teaspoon kosher salt, plus more for seasoning
- ½ cup plus 2 to 3 tablespoons extra-virgin olive oil, divided
- ⅔ cup julienned green bell pepper (about ½ a small pepper)
- ⅔ cup julienned red, yellow or orange bell pepper (about ½ a small pepper)
- 1 small onion, sliced thin
- ¼ teaspoon red pepper flakes
- 2 ounces (57 g) Gruyère or Emmenthal cheese (about ½ cup), shredded

Directions

- Prepare the mushrooms by removing the stem and scraping out the gills with a small spoon.
- In a small bowl, whisk together the vinegar, oregano, half the garlic, mustard, and salt. Slowly whisk in ½ cup of olive oil. Pour the marinade into a sealable plastic bag and add the mushrooms, turning the bag over to coat all the mushrooms. Let them marinate for 1 to 2 hours at room temperature, turning the bag every 15 minutes or so.
- Preheat the oven to 375°F (190°C).
- While the mushrooms are marinating, place the Dutch oven over medium heat. Add enough of the remaining oil to coat the bottom of the pot and heat until the oil

shimmers. Add the bell pepper slices and stir to coat with the oil. Cook without stirring for 2 to 3 minutes, or until the slices just start to brown.

- Add the onion and remaining garlic, and cook, stirring, until the onion slices start to brown, 2 to 3 minutes. Add the red pepper flakes and salt. Transfer the sofrito mixture to a small bowl.
- Add another coat of oil to the Dutch oven and let it heat until shimmering. While the oil heats, remove the mushrooms from the marinade and pat dry. Add to the pot, under-side down and cook for 1 to 2 minutes, or until slightly browned. Depending on the size of your Dutch oven, you may need to do this in batches.
- Turn the mushrooms over, under-side up. Divide the sofrito stuffing evenly among the mushrooms and top with the cheese.
- Place the mushrooms back in the pot. Place in the oven and bake for 10 minutes or until the cheese has melted and the mushrooms are cooked through.

232 Cream Mushroom Pasta Bake

Prep time: 15 minutes | **Cook time:** 45 minutes | **Serves** 2

Ingredients

- Kosher salt, to taste
- 6 ounces penne, farfalle, or other short pasta
- ½ pound (227g) cremini or white button mushrooms
- 3 tablespoons extra-virgin olive oil
- 1 large garlic clove, minced
- ¾ cup heavy cream
- ½ cup fresh Ricotta
- 5 ounces (142 g) Fontina cheese, grated (1¼ cups)
- ¼ teaspoon freshly ground black pepper
- 2 ounces (57 g) aged Parmigiano-Reggiano or similar cheese, grated (½ cup)

Directions

- Add 8 cups of water to the Dutch oven and place over high heat. Add about 2 teaspoons kosher salt and bring the water to a boil. Add the pasta and cook according to the package directions. (If you prefer, you can use a separate pot to cook the pasta while you prepare the mushrooms.) Drain, reserving at least a cup of the hot pasta water. Cover the reserved water with a lid or plate to keep warm, and set both the water and the pasta aside.
- While the water heats and the pasta cooks, wash the mushrooms and trim the stems. Quarter the mushrooms if small to medium; cut into eighths if they are large. Set aside.
- Preheat the oven to 375°F (190°C).
- When the pasta is done cooking, add the mushrooms to the Dutch oven and cover with enough water to make the mushrooms float. Pour in the oil and season generously with salt.
- Place the pot over high heat and bring to a boil. Continue boiling until the water has evaporated and you can hear the mushrooms begin to sizzle. Add the garlic and cook, stirring the mushrooms occasionally, until brown on all sides, about 5 minutes.
- Pour the cream into the Dutch oven. Cook for about 3 minutes, or until the cream has reduced by about one-third.
- Pour the reserved hot pasta water over the cooked pasta to loosen it up, then add the pasta to the cream and mushrooms in the pot. Stir in the Ricotta, fontina, and pepper and toss gently to coat. Sprinkle the Parmigiano-Reggiano cheese over the top of the pasta and place the pot in the oven. Bake for 10 minutes, or until the top is browned and the pasta is bubbling.

233 Tomato and Peas Korma

Prep time: 20 minutes | Cook time: 20 minutes | Serves 2

Ingredients

- ⅔ cup canned diced tomatoes, drained (about half a 14-ounce / 397- g can)
- ½ small onion, cut into chunks
- 1 small jalapeño pepper, seeded and cut into chunks
- 1 teaspoon grated fresh ginger
- 2 medium garlic cloves, smashed 1 teaspoon ground coriander
- ½ teaspoon ground cardamom
- ½ teaspoon ground cinnamon
- ¼ teaspoon ground turmeric
- 1 teaspoon kosher salt
- ¼ teaspoon freshly ground black pepper 2 to 3 tablespoons vegetable oil
- 2 cups mixed frozen "stir-fry" vegetables, thawed
- ½ cup frozen peas, thawed
- ¼ teaspoon red pepper flakes (optional)
- ¼ cup whole-milk yogurt

Directions

- Place the tomatoes, onion, jalapeño, ginger, garlic, coriander, cardamom, cinnamon, turmeric, salt, and pepper in a blender or small food processor and blend to a smooth paste (or use an immersion blender and a deep sturdy cup to blend).
- Place the Dutch oven over medium heat. Add enough oil to coat the bottom of the pot and heat until the oil shimmers. Add the puréed tomato mixture and bring to a simmer. Cook for about 15 minutes, or until the sauce has thickened slightly and is very fragrant.
- Add the thawed mixed vegetables and peas and bring back to a simmer. Cook for about 5 minutes, or until the vegetables are heated through. Taste and add the red pepper flakes if you want a spicier sauce. Stir in the yogurt and bring back to just a simmer. Serve over steamed basmati rice.

234 Rice with Kale and Lentils

Prep time: 15 minutes | Cook time: 25 minutes | Serves 2

Ingredients

- ½ cup brown lentils
- 2 to 3 tablespoons olive oil
- ½ medium onion, chopped
- 2 garlic cloves, minced Kosher salt, to taste
- ⅓ cup long-grain rice
- 1 teaspoon ground cumin
- ½ teaspoon ground coriander
- ¼ teaspoon cayenne pepper
- ⅛ teaspoon ground cinnamon
- 3 cups low-sodium vegetable stock
- 2 cups chopped kale or other sturdy greens
- 2 tablespoons chopped toasted pistachios

Directions

- Rinse the lentils and then place them in a small bowl. Cover with water and let them soak while you chop and cook the onion and garlic.
- Place the Dutch oven over medium-high heat. Add enough oil to coat the bottom of the pot and heat until the oil shimmers. Add the onion and cook, stirring, for 6 to 8 minutes, or until browned. Add the garlic and season with salt. Cook for a minute or so, or until the garlic is fragrant.
- Add the rice and stir to coat with the oil. Cook, stirring, for 2 to 3 minutes, or until the rice smells nutty. Add the cumin, coriander, cayenne, and cinnamon and stir to coat the rice with the spices.
- Cook for a minute, then add the stock and ¼ teaspoon of salt.
- Drain the lentils and add to the Dutch oven. Stir to combine. Bring the liquid to a simmer and stir again. Cover and reduce the heat to low. After cooking for 15 minutes, stir gently. Taste the rice and lentils; they should be a bit firm in the center but almost done. Add the kale and press into the rice and lentil mixture.

- Cover and cook for an additional 8 to 10 minutes, or until the kale, rice, and lentils are all tender.
- Ladle into bowls and top with the pistachios.

235 Lentils and Tomato over Rice

Prep time: 25 minutes | **Cook time:** 35 minutes | **Serves** 2

Ingredients

- 1 medium onion
- 4 garlic cloves
- 2 to 4 tablespoons vegetable oil
- 1 jalapeño pepper or serrano chile, seeded and diced
- 1 cup dried red lentils, rinsed
- 3½ cups water
- ½ teaspoon ground turmeric
- ¼ teaspoon ground cumin
- 1 bay leaf
- 1 teaspoon kosher salt
- 1 cup canned diced tomatoes, drained
- 2 tablespoons coarsely chopped fresh cilantro

Directions

- Slice half the onion, and dice the other half. Slice two cloves of garlic and mince or press the other two. Set aside the diced onion and the minced garlic.
- Place the Dutch oven over medium heat. Add enough oil to coat the bottom of the pot and heat until the oil shimmers. Add the sliced onion and garlic. Stir to coat the onion and garlic slices with the oil, then let them sit in a single layer until browned, about 4 minutes. Don't stir until you can see them browning. Stir them to expose the other side to the heat and repeat. The onion and garlic should be browned, but still slightly firm. Remove the mixture from the pan and set aside.
- Add more oil if necessary to coat the bottom of the Dutch oven. When it's hot, add the chopped onions, minced garlic, and jalapeño; cook, stirring, for 2 minutes, or until softened slightly and fragrant. Add the lentils, water, turmeric, cumin, bay leaf, and salt, and bring to a simmer. Cover and cook for 15 minutes, stirring once or twice.
- Add the tomatoes. Simmer, uncovered, for another 5 to 8 minutes, or until the lentils are tender.
- When the lentils are done, stir in the reserved onion-garlic mixture and simmer for another minute or two, or until the onions are warmed through. Garnish with the cilantro and serve plain or over rice.

236 Tofu with Cashews and Spinach

Prep time: 12 minutes | **Cook time:** 23 minutes | **Serves** 2

Ingredients

Tofu:

- ½ pound (227g) extra-firm tofu Vegetable oil for frying
- 5 to 6 ounces fresh baby spinach
- ½ cup cornstarch
- 1 tablespoon minced garlic (about 3 cloves)
- 2 teaspoons minced ginger
- 3 scallions, minced
- ¼ cup roasted unsalted cashews

Sauce:

- 1 tablespoon soy sauce
- 2 tablespoons rice vinegar
- ¼ cup water or vegetable stock
- 2 teaspoons Asian chile-garlic sauce, like Sriracha (or more)
- ¼ teaspoon freshly ground black pepper
- 1 teaspoon cornstarch
- 1 teaspoon granulated sugar
- 2 teaspoons sesame oil

Directions

- Slice the tofu into ½-inch-thick slices. Place on a layer of paper towels and cover with another layer. Press lightly to dry the slices. Uncover and let air-dry for 15 minutes while you prepare the sauce and aromatics, and cook the spinach.
- For the sauce, whisk all the ingredients together in a small bowl. Keep the whisk

handy, as you'll need to whisk the sauce again right before using.

- Place the Dutch oven over medium heat. Add enough oil to coat the bottom of the pot and heat until the oil shimmers. Add the spinach and toss just to wilt. Remove from the Dutch oven and wipe the pot dry.
- To make the tofu, increase the heat to high, and pour in enough oil to form a layer about 1-inch deep. Heat to 365ºF (185ºC). While the oil is heating, cut the tofu slices into bite-size pieces, about 1 inch by 1½ inches. Pour the cornstarch into a small bowl and toss the tofu pieces in the cornstarch until they are coated heavily.
- Use a slotted spoon or spider to remove about half the tofu from the cornstarch and add to the hot oil. Cook for 4 to 5 minutes or until golden brown and crisp. Use the spoon or spider to remove the pieces to a rack placed over a sheet pan, and let the oil heat back up to 365ºF (185ºC). Repeat with the remaining tofu. (Depending on the size of your Dutch oven, you may have to cook three batches; don't crowd the pan).
- Pour off all but a light coating of the oil. Return the pot to medium-high heat and add the garlic, ginger, and scallions. Cook, stirring, for a minute or two, or until fragrant and just slightly browned. Whisk the sauce to combine, and add to the Dutch oven. Bring to a simmer and let cook for 2 to 3 minutes, or until thickened. Add the tofu, spinach, and cashews, and toss gently to coat with the sauce. Serve with or without steamed rice.

237 Kidney Bean and Tomato Pasta Soup

Prep time: 5 minutes | **Cook time:** 40 minutes | **Serves** 4 to 6

Ingredients

- 1 tablespoon extra-virgin olive oil
- 1 small yellow onion, chopped
- 1 (14-ounce / 397-g) can diced fire-roasted tomatoes
- 8 cups vegetable broth
- 2 cups uncooked small elbow pasta
- 1 pound (454 g) frozen soup vegetables
- 1 (15-ounce / 425-g) can red kidney beans, drained and rinsed Salt and freshly ground black pepper, to taste

Directions

- In a Dutch oven over medium-high heat, heat the olive oil. Add the onion and sauté for 5 minutes or until translucent. Add the tomatoes and vegetable broth and cook over medium heat for 5 to 10 minutes, until the liquid comes to a boil.
- Add the pasta, soup vegetables, and beans. Bring to a boil, reduce the heat to low, cover, and simmer for 20 to 25 minutes, until the pasta is tender. Season with salt and pepper before serving.

238 Peas and Carrot Fried Rice

Prep time: 25 minutes | **Cook time:** 15 minutes | **Serves** 4

Ingredients

- 3 tablespoons butter, divided
- 1 (10-ounce / 283-g) package frozen peas and carrots
- 3 cups leftover cooked rice, cold
- 3 tablespoons low-sodium soy sauce (gluten-free if needed), plus
- more for serving
- 2 eggs, beaten
- Freshly ground black pepper, to taste

Directions

- In a Dutch oven over medium-high heat, heat 1 tablespoon of the butter. Add the frozen peas and carrots. Sauté for about 5 minutes, until the peas and carrots are soft.
- Increase the heat to high, add the remaining 2 tablespoons of butter, and stir until melted. Immediately add the rice and soy sauce, and stir until combined. Continue cooking, stirring constantly, for 3 more minutes to fry the rice.
- Push the fried rice to one side of the pot, and add the eggs to the other side. Stir well so the

eggs are scrambled while cooking. Mix the cooked eggs into the rice.
- Remove from the heat. Season with pepper and more soy sauce before serving.

239 Cabbage Noodles

Prep time: 10 minutes | **Cook time:** 35 minutes | Serves 6

Ingredients

- 1 (16-ounce / 454-g) package egg noodles
- 1 tablespoon extra-virgin olive oil
- 3 tablespoons butter
- 1 medium onion, peeled and chopped
- 6 cups shredded cabbage (about half a head)
- 3 garlic cloves, crushed
- Salt and freshly ground black pepper, to taste

Directions

- Fill a Dutch oven with water, and bring to a boil over medium-high heat. Cook the egg noodles for 8 minutes or according to the package directions. (Different thicknesses of egg noodles will have different cooking times.) Drain and set aside.
- In the pot over medium heat, heat the olive oil. Add the butter and cook for a minute or two, until melted. Add the onion and cook until softened, about 5 minutes. Add the cabbage and garlic. Cook until tender, 10 to 15 minutes, and give it a few good stirs.
- Stir in the noodles, and season with salt and pepper. Cook, stirring often, for another 3 minutes or until the pasta is heated through.

240 Asparagus Peas Risotto with Cheese

Prep time: 15 minutes | **Cook time:** 55 minutes | Serves 6

Ingredients

- 5 cups vegetable broth, divided, plus more if needed
- 1 cup frozen peas
- ½ pound (227g) asparagus, trimmed and cut into bite-size pieces
- 1½ cups arborio rice
- 1 cup freshly grated Parmesan cheese
- 3 tablespoons salted butter, cut into pieces Salt and freshly ground black pepper, to taste

Directions

- Preheat the oven to 350ºF (180ºC).
- Pour 4 cups of the vegetable broth into a Dutch oven. Turn the heat to medium-high and cook until the broth comes to a boil, 5 to 10 minutes. Stir in the peas, asparagus, and rice, and mix well.
- Cover the pot, transfer it to the oven, and bake for 40 minutes or until most of the liquid is absorbed and the rice is tender.
- Remove the risotto from the oven. Microwave the remaining cup of vegetable broth for 2 minutes. Stir the heated broth, Parmesan cheese, and butter into the pot. Continue to stir vigorously for 2 to 3 minutes, until the rice is very creamy. (You can add extra warm broth to thin the risotto if necessary.) Season with salt and pepper before serving.

241 Cheesy Spinach Ziti Bake

Prep time: 5 minutes | **Cook time:** 45 minutes | Serves 6

Ingredients

- 1 (16-ounce / 454-g) box ziti pasta 3 cups marinara sauce
- 1 (10-ounce / 283-g) package frozen chopped spinach, thawed Salt and freshly ground black pepper, to taste
- 2 cups Ricotta cheese
- 3 cups shredded Mozzarella cheese, divided

Directions

- Preheat the oven to 350ºF (180ºC).
- Fill a Dutch oven with water, and bring to a boil over high heat. Add the ziti and cook until al dente, according to the package instructions. Drain the pasta and keep warm.
- In the Dutch oven over medium-high heat, heat the marinara sauce. Add the spinach and cook for 10 minutes or until the mixture

comes to a simmer. Season with salt and pepper, then remove the pot from the heat.

- Add the drained pasta to the pot, and mix in the Ricotta cheese and 2 cups of the Mozzarella cheese. Make sure everything is well mixed. Sprinkle the remaining cup of Mozzarella cheese on top.
- Cover the pot, transfer it to the oven, and bake for about 20 minutes, until the pasta is bubbling. Remove the lid and bake for 5 more minutes, until the cheese melts and starts to turn golden. Remove the pot from the oven, and let it cool slightly before serving.

242 Chickpeas Pasta with Cheese

Prep time: 10 minutes | Cook time: 30 minutes | Serves 6

Ingredients

- 1 (16-ounce / 454-g) box penne pasta
- 2 tablespoons extra-virgin olive oil
- 1 (15-ounce / 425-g) can chickpeas, drained and rinsed
- 10 to 12 ounces (283 to 340 g) baby greens, such as spinach
- 2 cups marinara sauce
- ⅓ cup grated Parmesan cheese, plus more for serving
- Salt and freshly ground black pepper, to taste

Directions

- Fill a large Dutch oven with water, and bring to a boil over medium-high heat. Add the pasta and cook for 10 to 12 minutes (or per package directions), until al dente. Drain in a colander, reserving ½ cup of pasta water, and keep warm.
- In the pot over medium heat, heat the olive oil. Add the chickpeas and greens. Cook for about 5 minutes or until the greens are wilted.
- Add the cooked pasta, marinara sauce, and reserved pasta water. Reduce the heat to low and cook for another 5 to 10 minutes, until the sauce is thickened and bubbly.
- Transfer the pasta mixture to a large bowl, and mix in the Parmesan cheese. Season with salt and pepper. Serve with extra Parmesan cheese on top.

243 Cheesy Butter Pasta

Prep time: 10 minutes | Cook time: 25 minutes | Serves 6

Ingredients

- 1 (16-ounce / 454-g) box medium pasta shells
- 3 tablespoons butter
- ⅓ cup all-purpose flour
- 4 cups low-fat milk 1 teaspoon salt
- 8 ounces (227 g) mild Cheddar cheese, shredded
- 8 ounces (227 g) smoked Gouda cheese, shredded

Directions

- Fill a Dutch oven with water, and bring to a boil over medium-high heat. Add the pasta shells and cook according to package instructions for al dente (about 6 to 8 minutes). Drain well and keep warm.
- Add the butter to the pot, and melt it over medium heat. Stir in the flour, and keep stirring to form a thick paste. Mix with a wire whisk, and slowly add the milk and salt. Cook over medium heat for about 10 minutes, until the sauce is thickened and simmering. Make sure to constantly stir to remove any lumps in the sauce.
- Add both cheeses, a handful at a time, and mix well until the sauce is smooth and thick.
- Stir in the cooked pasta, and combine well until the pasta is well coated with the cheese sauce. Cook for another 5 minutes, until the pasta is heated through and the sauce has thickened. Serve warm in bowls.

244 Spaghetti with Cheese

Prep time: 10 minutes | **Cook time:** 20 minutes | **Serves** 6

Ingredients

Salt, to taste

- 1 (16-ounce / 454-g) box thick spaghetti
- 1 teaspoon freshly ground black pepper
- 4 tablespoons butter
- ½ cup freshly grated Parmesan cheese, plus more for serving
- 2 tablespoons extra-virgin olive oil
- Small handful chopped fresh basil or parsley

Directions

- Fill a Dutch oven with salted water, and bring to a boil over high heat. Add the spaghetti and cook for 9 minutes or until al dente. Reserve 1 cup of pasta water, then drain the pasta.
- Add the pepper to the Dutch oven, and toast it over medium heat for 30 seconds. Add the butter and cook for 1 to 2 minutes, until melted.
- Add the reserved pasta water and the Parmesan cheese. Mix well, so the cheese melts into the pasta water. Add the pasta and toss vigorously, until it is well coated with the cheese sauce. Mix in the olive oil, and season with salt.
- Sprinkle and toss with the fresh herbs right before serving. Serve with additional Parmesan cheese, if desired.

245 White Bean and Tomato Chili

Prep time: 10 minutes | **Cook time:** 35 minutes | **Serves** 4 to 6

Ingredients

- 2 tablespoons extra-virgin olive oil 1 medium onion, chopped
- 3 medium sweet potatoes, peeled and cubed
- 1 to 2 tablespoons chili powder (depending how much spice you like)
- 1 (28-ounce / 794-g) can diced tomatoes with chiles
- 2 cups vegetable broth
- 2 (15-ounce / 425-g) cans white cannellini beans, drained and rinsed Salt and freshly ground black pepper, to taste

Optional Toppings:

- Shredded Cheddar cheese Sour cream
- Chopped scallions, white and green parts
- Sliced avocado Chopped fresh cilantro

Directions

- In a Dutch oven over medium-high heat, heat the olive oil. Add the onion and cook for 5 minutes or until translucent.
- Add the sweet potatoes, chili powder, tomatoes, and broth. Cook, stirring constantly, for 5 minutes, then let the mixture come to a boil. Reduce the heat to low, cover, and simmer for 10 minutes, until the sweet potatoes are tender.
- Stir in the beans and cover the pot. Cook for 10 to 15 minutes more, until the beans are tender and the chili is to your desired thickness. If it gets too thick, add a little water to thin it out.
- Season with salt and pepper. Serve hot, with optional toppings as desired.

246 Baked Cheese Pizza

Prep time: 15 minutes | **Cook time:** 40 minutes | **Serves** 4

Ingredients

- 1 pound (454 g) pizza dough
- 1 tablespoon extra-virgin olive oil
- 1 cup marinara sauce
- 2 cups shredded Mozzarella cheese, divided

Directions

- Preheat the oven to 450°F (235°C). Place your Dutch oven (uncovered) on the lowest rack in your oven so it also preheats.
- Roll half the pizza dough out to a 10- to 12-inch disk (about the size of the bottom of your Dutch oven). Transfer the dough to a piece of parchment paper, and let it rest for about 10 minutes. If it starts to shrink, roll it out a bit more.

- When the dough is ready, brush it with the olive oil, then spread
- ½ cup of the sauce on top of the dough. Top with 1 cup of the cheese. Slide the pizza, paper and all, onto a cutting board or pizza paddle to bring it to the oven. Carefully place the pizza in the Dutch oven by holding onto the edges of the parchment paper and gently dropping it into the pot. The parchment paper will still be under the pizza.
- Bake for about 15 to 20 minutes, until the crust is golden brown and the cheese is melted. Remove the Dutch oven from the oven, and use the parchment paper to lift the pizza out and onto a board. Cool for 5 minutes before slicing.
- While you're eating the first pizza, repeat everything for the second pizza.

247 Rice and Quinoa Stuffed Pepper

Prep time: 10 minutes | **Cook time:** 35 minutes | **Serves** 4

Ingredients

- 2 tablespoons olive oil, divided
- 4 medium bell peppers, red, green, or yellow, tops removed and cored
- 1 medium onion, peeled and chopped
- 1 clove garlic, peeled and minced
- 1 (14½-ounce / 411-g) can diced tomatoes, drained
- ¼ teaspoon cumin
- ¼ teaspoon salt
- ¼ teaspoon freshly cracked black pepper
- 1 cup cooked brown rice
- 1 cup cooked quinoa

Directions

- Heat oven to 375°F (190°C).
- Lightly brush bell peppers inside and out with 1 tablespoon olive oil. Place peppers into a Dutch oven and roast 8 to 10 minutes, or until peppers are just starting to become tender. Remove from oven and set aside.
- Heat the Dutch oven over medium heat add remaining olive oil. Once oil shimmers add onion and cook until tender, about 5 minutes. Add garlic, tomato, cumin, salt, and pepper and cook until tomatoes are heated and the garlic is fragrant, about 3 minutes. Fold in rice and quinoa, then turn off heat.
- Divide rice mixture evenly among peppers and clean out the Dutch oven, then return the peppers to the Dutch oven and bake, uncovered, for 10 to 15 minutes or until peppers are very tender and filling is hot.

248 Barley Butternut Squash Risotto

Prep time: 10 minutes | **Cook time:** 1¾ hour | **Serves** 8

Ingredients

- 1 butternut squash, peeled and cut into ½-inch cubes
- 3 tablespoons olive oil, divided
- 1 teaspoon salt, divided
- 1 teaspoon freshly cracked black pepper, divided
- 6 cups vegetable broth
- 1 medium onion, peeled and finely chopped
- 1 clove garlic, peeled and minced
- 1½ cups pearl barley
- ½ cup white wine
- 2 tablespoons finely chopped fresh parsley

Directions

- Heat oven to 400°F (205°C).
- In a large bowl combine butternut squash, 1 tablespoon olive oil,
- ¼ teaspoon salt, and ¼ teaspoon pepper. Toss to thoroughly coat squash, then transfer to a baking sheet and roast until squash is tender, about 25 to 30 minutes. Remove from the oven and set aside to cool.
- In a medium saucepan bring vegetable broth to a simmer.
- In a Dutch oven over medium heat add remaining olive oil. Once it shimmers add onion and cook, stirring often, until tender, about 5 minutes. Add garlic and remaining salt and pepper, and cook until the garlic is fragrant, about 30 seconds.

- Add barley and cook, stirring frequently, until barley is coated in oil and is lightly toasted, about 5 minutes. Add white wine and cook, stirring constantly, until wine is absorbed, about 2 minutes.
- Begin ladling in vegetable broth ½ cup at a time, stirring frequently, allowing broth to be absorbed by barley after each addition, about 45 to 50 minutes.
- Once all the broth is absorbed fold in roasted squash and chopped parsley. Serve immediately.

249 Barley and Mushroom Casserole

Prep time: 10 minutes | **Cook time:** 1¼ hour | **Serves 6**

Ingredients

- 2 tablespoons unsalted butter
- 1 medium onion, peeled and chopped
- 3 cloves garlic, peeled and minced
- 2 cups sliced cremini mushrooms
- 1 cup sliced button mushrooms
- 1½ cups pearl barley
- ½ cup chopped celery 1 teaspoon salt
- ¼ teaspoon pepper
- 1 teaspoon dried thyme leaves
- 3½ cups vegetable broth
- ¼ cup chopped flat-leaf parsley
- ½ cup grated Parmesan cheese

Directions

- Heat oven to 350°F (180°C).
- In a Dutch oven melt butter over medium heat. Add onion and garlic, and cook until just softened, about 3 minutes. Add mushrooms and cook 4 minutes longer.
- Add barley and cook 5 to 6 minutes, stirring often, until barley is lightly browned. Add celery, salt, pepper, thyme, and broth and bring to a simmer.
- Bake 50 to 65 minutes, or until barley is tender. Mix in chopped parsley and cheese and serve.

250 Corn and Black Bean Couscous

Prep time: 10 minutes | **Cook time:** 25 minutes | **Serves 8**

Ingredients

- 2 tablespoons olive oil
- 1 (10-ounce / 283-g) bag frozen whole kernel corn 1 medium onion, peeled and finely chopped
- 1 medium red bell pepper, seeded and finely chopped
- 2 cloves garlic, peeled and minced
- ¼ teaspoon chili powder
- ¼ teaspoon salt
- ¼ teaspoon freshly cracked black pepper
- 1 cup pearl or Israeli couscous
- 1½ cups vegetable broth
- 1 (14½-ounce / 411-g) can low-sodium black beans, rinsed and drained
- 2 Roma tomatoes, seeded and chopped

Directions

- In a Dutch oven over medium heat add olive oil. Once oil starts to shimmer add corn. Cook, stirring often, until corn starts to brown, about 10 minutes. Add onion and bell pepper and cook until they soften slightly, about 5 minutes. Add garlic, chili powder, salt, and pepper and cook until fragrant, about 1 minute.
- Add couscous and stir well to mix with the vegetables. Add vegetable broth, bring to a boil, then reduce heat to low and cover with the lid. Cook until couscous has absorbed all the liquid, about 10 to 15 minutes.
- Once couscous has absorbed the liquid remove the lid and fluff with a spoon. Fold in black beans and tomatoes. Serve warm or at room temperature.

251 Roast Chickpeas and Zucchini

Prep time: 10 minutes | Cook time: 20 minutes | Serves 6

Ingredients

- 4 medium zucchini, cut into ½-inch-thick slices
- 1 (15-ounce / 425-g) can chickpeas, drained and rinsed
- 1 medium onion, peeled and roughly chopped
- 3 tablespoons olive oil
- 1 tablespoon fresh lemon juice
- ½ teaspoon curry powder
- ¼ teaspoon salt
- ¼ teaspoon freshly cracked black pepper
- 2 tablespoons chopped fresh parsley

Directions

- Heat oven to 400°F (205°C).
- In a Dutch oven combine all ingredients expect chopped parsley. Toss until everything is evenly coated.
- Roast 20 minutes, stirring halfway through the cooking time, or until zucchini and onion are tender. Garnish with chopped parsley. Serve immediately.

252 Lentils with Carrot and Turnip

Prep time: 30 minutes | Cook time: 1 hour | Serves 8

Ingredients

- 2 medium carrots, peeled and cut into ½-inch pieces
- 1 medium turnip, scrubbed and cut into ½-inch cubes
- 1 medium beet, peeled and cut into ½-inch cubes
- 1 medium sweet potato, peeled and cut into ½-inch pieces
- 2 tablespoons olive oil, divided
- 1 tablespoon honey
- ½ teaspoon salt
- ½ teaspoon freshly cracked black pepper
- 2 cups green lentils
- 4 cups water
- 1 clove garlic, peeled and smashed
- 2 sprigs fresh thyme
- 1 bay leaf
- 2 tablespoons fresh chopped parsley

Directions

- In a large bowl add carrot, turnip, beet, sweet potato, 1 tablespoon olive oil, honey, salt, and pepper. Toss to coat, then let stand at room temperature 30 minutes.
- Heat oven to 425°F (220°C).
- Spread vegetables out on a baking sheet in a single layer. Roast until vegetables are tender, about 25 to 30 minutes. Remove from oven and let cool.
- In a Dutch oven combine lentils, water, garlic, thyme, and bay leaf. Bring mixture to a simmer over medium heat, then reduce the heat to medium-low and cook lentils at a bare simmer until they are tender, adding additional water if needed to keep them covered, about 30 minutes. Drain lentils, discard garlic, thyme, and bay leaf, and return lentils to the Dutch oven.
- Add remaining olive oil and roasted vegetables to lentils and toss to combine. Garnish with chopped parsley. Serve warm or room temperature.

253 Cauliflower with Chickpeas

Prep time: 10 minutes | Cook time: 15 minutes | Serves 6 to 8

Ingredients

- 1 medium white onion, peeled and chopped
- 1 tablespoon olive oil
- 5 tablespoons yellow or black mustard seeds
- 1 head cauliflower, divided into florets
- Pinch salt
- 1 (15-ounce / 425-g) can chickpeas, drained and rinsed
- ¼ cup white wine

Directions

- Place a Dutch oven over medium heat. Once the Dutch oven is heated add onion, olive oil, and mustard seeds. Stir frequently and let

onion cook until it starts to turn brown, about 8 minutes.
- Add the cauliflower florets to the Dutch oven with a sprinkle of salt.
- Stir to combine and cook 4 minutes. Add chickpeas to the Dutch oven with white wine. Stir to combine.
- Cover the Dutch oven and cook 3 to 4 minutes. Remove the lid and let liquid evaporate. Serve when cauliflower is fork tender.

254 Spinach and Mushroom Curry

Prep time: 10 minutes | **Cook time:** 30 minutes | **Serves** 4

Ingredients

- ¼ cup jarred green curry paste
- 2 cups vegetable broth
- 1 large sweet potato, peeled and cut into ½-inch cubes
- ¼ pound (113 g) green beans, stems removed
- 8 ounces (227 g) sliced button mushrooms
- 8 ounces (227 g) fresh spinach leaves Juice from 1 medium lime
- 1 (14-ounce / 397-g) can coconut milk

Directions

- Place a Dutch oven over medium heat. Once it is heated, add curry paste and vegetable broth and stir to combine.
- Stir in sweet potato cubes, cover, and cook 15 to 20 minutes or until you can pierce them with a fork. Stir the contents occasionally to keep them from sticking.
- Turn heat to medium-high and remove the lid. Add remaining vegetables and cook 5 to 7 minutes, stirring frequently.
- Once liquid has reduced, lower the heat to medium-low and add lime juice and coconut milk. Keep coconut milk from boiling and cook 2 to 3 minutes. Serve.

255 Okra Corn and Tomato Stew

Prep time: 15 minutes | **Cook time:** 30 minutes | **Serves** 4

Ingredients

- 3 tablespoons oil or unsalted butter
- 1 medium onion, peeled and finely diced
- 1 small green bell pepper, seeded and finely diced
- 1 stalk celery, finely diced
- 2 cloves garlic, peeled and minced
- 2 cups sliced okra
- 2 cups diced ripe tomatoes
- 2 cups fresh corn kernels
- 1 cup water or vegetable broth
- ¼ teaspoon cayenne 1 green onion, sliced
- 2 tablespoons minced fresh parsley
- ½ teaspoon salt
- ¼ teaspoon freshly cracked black pepper

Directions

- In a Dutch oven, heat oil or butter over medium-high heat. Add onion, green pepper, celery, and garlic, and cook until tender, about 5 minutes.
- Add okra and cook, stirring constantly, 3 minutes or until okra begins to release thick liquid.
- Add tomatoes, corn, and water or broth. Bring to a boil then reduce heat to medium-low and simmer, stirring often and adding more liquid if needed, 20 minutes, or until corn is tender.
- Stir in cayenne, green onion, parsley, salt, and pepper. Remove the Dutch oven from heat. Serve.

256 Ratatouille with Tomato

Prep time: 15 minutes | **Cook time:** 25 minutes | Serves 4 to 6

Ingredients

- 1 medium eggplant, diced
- 2 teaspoons salt, divided
- 2 tablespoons olive oil
- 1 small onion, peeled and diced
- 1 large green bell pepper, seeded and diced
- 3 cloves garlic, peeled and minced
- 1 large zucchini, diced
- 2 medium yellow squash, diced
- 4 ounces (113 g) white mushrooms, quartered
- 1 (28-ounce / 794-g) can crushed tomatoes
- 1 teaspoon dried Italian seasoning mix
- ¼ teaspoon freshly cracked black pepper
- ¼ cup chopped fresh basil leaves

Directions

- Sprinkle eggplant with 1½ teaspoons salt and leave in a colander 1 hour.
- Rinse eggplant well and pat dry with paper towels.
- In a Dutch oven heat olive oil over medium-high heat. Once oil shimmers add onion, bell pepper, and garlic. Cook until just tender, about 3 minutes.
- Add eggplant, zucchini, squash, and mushrooms to the Dutch oven. Pour in crushed tomatoes and Italian seasoning, then reduce heat to medium and simmer 10 to 15 minutes or until eggplant is tender.
- Season with remaining salt and pepper and then stir in fresh basil. Remove the Dutch oven from the heat and allow to stand 5 minutes before serving.

Dessert

257 Quick and Easy Pop Brownies

Serves 8 | Prep. time 10 minutes | Cooking time 45 minutes

Ingredients

- 1 box brownie mix
- 1 can soda pop
- ¾ pound chocolate chips

Directions

- Line the Dutch oven with parchment paper.
- Add the brownie mix and soda to a mixing bowl. Mix well until you get a smooth mixture.
- Pour the batter over the parchment paper. Sprinkle the chocolate chips on top.
- Heat to 350°F (175°C) and bake for 45–60 minutes until well set. Check by inserting a toothpick; it should come out clean. If not, cook for a few more minutes.
- Slice and serve warm.

258 Chocolate Chip Cookies

Serves 24 | Prep. time 10 minutes | Cooking time 8–10 minutes

Ingredients

- 1 cup butter, softened
- ¾ cup granulated sugar
- ¾ cup packed brown sugar
- 1 egg
- 1 teaspoon vanilla
- ½ teaspoon of sea salt
- 1 teaspoon baking soda
- 2¼ cups flour
- 1–2 cups semisweet chocolate chips

Directions

- Add the butter and both sugars to a mixing bowl. Mix well.
- Beat the eggs in another bowl. Add the vanilla. Mix well.
- Add the sea salt, baking soda, and flour; mix again.
- Combine the mixtures until smooth.
- Mix in the chocolate chips.
- Divide into 24 balls.
- Line the Dutch oven with parchment paper and lightly grease it with cooking spray.
- Arrange the balls on the bottom.
- Cover and cook for 6 minutes. If cookies have turned light brown, take them out. If not, cook for 2–4 more minutes. Do not overcook.
- Let cool for a while.
- Serve warm.

259 Dutch Oven Brownies

Serves 9 | Prep time 10 minutes | Cooking time 30 minutes

Ingredients

- 1 box brownie mix
- ½ cup melted butter
- 2 large eggs
- 3 tablespoons water
- 1 cup of chocolate chips
- 1 teaspoon vanilla extract

Directions

- Add the brownie mix to a large mixing bowl and stir in the melted butter, eggs, and water, and chocolate chips until just combined, being careful not to over-mix the batter.
- Line the Dutch oven with a piece of parchment paper and pour in the brownie mixture.
- Bake at 350°F (180°C) for 25–30 minutes.
- Let the brownies cool slightly and then cut into squares and serve.

260 Double Chocolate Cake

Serves 8 | Prep time 10 minutes | Cooking time 30 minutes

Ingredients

- 1 box chocolate cake mix
- ⅓ cup vegetable oil
- ¼ cup whole milk
- 1 cup of chocolate chips
- 2 cups heavy whipping cream
- 3 tablespoons powdered sugar
- 1 teaspoon vanilla extract

Directions

- Add the cake mix to a large mixing bowl and stir in the vegetable oil, milk, and chocolate chips until just combined, being careful not to over-mix the batter.
- Line the Dutch oven with a piece of parchment paper and pour in the chocolate cake mixture.
- Bake at 350°F (180°C) for about 30 minutes.
- Remove the cake from the Dutch oven and place it on a cooling rack. Let it cool completely.
- Add the whipping cream, powdered sugar, and vanilla extract to a large mixing bowl and beat with a hand mixer.
- Cut the chocolate cake in half to create two layers. Spread half of the whipped cream on one layer, cover with the second layer and decorate the whole cake with whipped cream.
- If desired, sprinkle with more chocolate chips for better presentation.

261 Cinnamon Rolls

Serves 8 | **Prep time** 10 minutes | **Cooking time** 30 minutes

Ingredients

- 8 canned cinnamon rolls
- 2 cups powdered sugar
- 5 ounces cream cheese, softened
- 1 teaspoon vanilla extract
- Zest of 1 orange

Directions

- Place a piece of parchment paper in the Dutch oven and arrange the cinnamon rolls on it.
- Bake at 350°F (180°C) for 30–35 minutes until golden brown.
- Add the softened cream cheese to a medium mixing bowl and mix it well with the powdered sugar, vanilla extract, and lemon zest.
- Make sure that the mixture is pourable. If it's too thick, add a little bit of water.
- Spread the cream cheese mixture on top of the cinnamon rolls while they are still warm.
- Let cool slightly and then serve with a cup of coffee or chocolate milk.

262 Verry Berry Swirl

Serves 6 | **Prep time** 10 minutes | **Cooking time** 30 minutes

Ingredients

- 1 (14-ounce) pizza dough
- 3 cups frozen or fresh mixed berries
- ¾ cup granulated sugar
- ½ teaspoon cinnamon
- 2 tablespoons all-purpose flour
- ¼ cup powdered sugar for dusting

Directions

- Roll out the pizza dough into a ¼-inch-thick square.
- Sprinkle the mixed berries, granulated sugar, cinnamon, and all-purpose flour on top. Ensure that every berry is coated with flour, so a nice thick sauce will form during baking.
- Roll up the dough with the berries inside and cut diagonally with a sharp knife.
- Carefully twist both parts of the dough together to make one long braid.
- Shape the braid into a circle and place it in the Dutch oven on top of a piece of parchment paper.
- Bake at 350°F (180°C) for 30–40 minutes.
- Let cool slightly and then dust with powdered sugar when ready to serve.

263 Upside Down Peach Cake

Serves 4 | **Prep time** 15 minutes | **Cooking time** 15 minutes

Ingredients

- 1/2 cup butter
- softened
- 1/4 cup oil Canola or vegetable
- 3/4 cup brown sugar
- 1 cup sugar
- 3 eggs

- 2 cups all purpose flour
- 1 teaspoon baking soda
- 1 teaspoon baking powder
- 1 teaspoons salt
- 1 teaspoon cinnamon
- 1 cup buttermilk

For base layer:

- 1/4 cup butter
- 1/2 cup brown sugar
- 3 cups or 4 peaches, peeled and sliced

Directions

- Prepare a 12 inch Dutch Oven for cooking, wipe out, spray inside lightly with cooking oil.
- Heat up about 25 coals for cooking (the recipe calls for 19, but I always heat up extras). This will take approximately 30 minutes. While the coals are heating up, prepare the cake. The coals will be white when ready.
- Cream butter, oil and sugars together in a bowl. Beat until smooth.
- Add eggs and beat until smooth and fluffy about 1 minute.
- Add flour, soda, powder, salt and cinnamon. Pulse until the flour disappears and is mixed
-
- Leaving the mixer on low, add the buttermilk a little at a time until all of the buttermilk is added to the mixture in the bowl. Mix for one additional minute or until all ingredients are incorporated.
- Create base layer by melting butter in the bottom of the Dutch Oven. Add the brown sugar and peaches and spread the peaches out into a single layer in the bottom of the Dutch oven.
- Pour the cake mix over the peaches, place the lid on top of the Dutch Oven.
- Place 12 hot coals on top of the Dutch Oven and 7 under the Dutch Oven.
- Set a timer for 12 minutes. The cake will take 10-15 minutes to cook. When the cake has baked for 12 minutes, remove so the Dutch Oven is not over the coals. Continue baking with coals on top for a few more minutes.
- Serve with whipped cream or vanilla ice cream.

264 Cherry Grunt

Serves 4 | **Prep time** 10 minutes | **Cooking time** 25 minutes

Ingredients

- 1 cup canned red cherries, pitted with juice
- ¾ cup of water
- 6 tbsp sugar
- 2 tbsp butter
- ½ cup all-purpose flour
- ¾ tsp baking powder
- 2 ½ tbsp milk
- ¼ tsp vanilla extract

Directions

- In a Dutch oven, add cherries along with juice, 4 tbsp sugar, 1 ½ tbsp butter, and let it simmer for 5 minutes.
- In a bowl, add flour, remaining sugar, salt, and baking powder and mix well.
- In a pastry blender, add milk, butter, vanilla essence, and dry mixture and blend to make a dough.
- For dumplings from the dough and place them over the cherry mixture in the Dutch oven.
- Cover and let the mixture simmer for 20 minutes until the dumplings are cooked through.
- Serve with ice-cream.

265 S'mores Cookie Cake

Serves 4 | **Prep time** 15 minutes | **Cooking time** 60 minutes

Ingredients

- 3 grams cracker sheets
- 1 cup sugar cookie mix
- ¼ cup softened salted butter
- 1/2 egg, beaten
- ¾ cup milk choco chips

- 1 ½ cup mini marshmallows

Directions

- Line aluminum foil at the bottom of the Dutch oven to make the shape of a baking tray.
- Crush the gram crackers in a zip-lock bag. Add cookie mix, egg and butter and mix well to form a dough.
- Spread the dough on the baking pan made from aluminum.
- Place the Dutch oven in a pre-heated oven at 300 F for an hour until the edges turn golden.
- Remove the Dutch oven from heat and sprinkle marshmallows and choco chips on the cooked dough.
- Cover the lid and let it stay until the chocolate melts.
- Lift the pan out of the Dutch oven and cut into equal pieces.

266 Dutch Baby Mixed Berry

Serves 4 | **Prep time** 10 minutes | **Cooking time** 20 minutes

Ingredients

- 1 ½ cup all- purpose flour
- 1 ½ cup milk
- 6 eggs
- 2 tbsp sugar
- 6 tbsp butter
- 1 tbsp vanilla extract
- 1 tsp cinnamon powder
- 3 cups mix berries, fresh
- A pinch salt

Directions

- In a bowl, add milk and eggs and mix well.
- Add flour, sugar, cinnamon, vanilla extract, and salt and mix until the mixture turns smooth.
- Add melted butter and mix well.
- Pour the mixture in the hot Dutch oven, add berries on the top.
- Place the Dutch oven in a pre-heated oven at 400 F for 20 minutes until the edges are golden in color.
- Remove from the Dutch oven, chill, and serve with a scope of ice- cream or whipped cream.

267 Fruity Pebbles Doughnuts

Serves 4 | **Prep time** 15 + 90 resting in time | **Cooking time** 10 minutes

Ingredients

- 1 ¾ cup all- purpose flour
- 1 tbsp warm milk
- ¾ tsp active yeast
- ½ cup whole milk
- 4 tbsp unsalted butter
- 2 egg yolks
- 1 tbsp sugar
- 1 tsp salt
- ¼ tsp vanilla extract
- ¼ cup confectioners' sugar
- Oil for frying

Directions

- In a small bowl add warm water and yeast and let it sit for 6 minutes.
- In a separate bowl, add flour, butter, milk, egg yolks, sugar, salt, and yeast mixture. Mix with hands until it forms a dough.
- Continue to knead the dough for 5 minutes and cover it with plastic wrap.
- Let it sit for 1 ½ hour.
- Take out a portion of dough and roll it with the help of a pin.
- Cut shapes with a doughnut cutter and poke a hole in the center.
- Heat 2 cups of oil in a Dutch oven.
- Once the oil is hot, add the doughnuts into the Dutch oven and fry them from both sides for 2-3 minutes until they turn golden brown.
- Place the doughnuts on a paper towel and dust confectioners' sugar.

268 Peach Cobbler

Serves 4 | Prep time 10 minutes | Cooking time 50 minutes

Ingredients

- 4 tbsp butter, unsalted
- 4 large peaches
- 4 tbsp honey
- 1 ½ tbsp corn starch
- ½ tsp vanilla extract
- ½ tsp cinnamon powder

For Topping:

- 4 tbsp wheat flour
- 4 tbsp all-purpose flour
- ½ cup of sugar 6 tbsp milk
- 1 tsp baking powder
- ¼ tsp salt

Directions

- Add peaches in boiling water. Boil for a minute and remove peaches and place in an ice bath.
- Remove the skin and cut peached into slices.
- In a bowl, add peach slices, corn starch, honey, cinnamon and vanilla extract. Mix well and set aside.
- In a Dutch oven, melt butter and set aside.
- In a bowl, mix wheat flour, all-purpose flour, sugar, salt and baking powder.
- Add milk to the mixture and mix well.
- Add peaches and then this mixture to the Dutch oven without stirring.
- Place the Dutch oven in preheated oven for about 50 minutes at 425 °F (220°C).
- Serve hot with an ice cream scoop.

269 Chocolate Cake

Serves 4 | Prep time 25 minutes | Cooking time 40 minutes

Ingredients

- 1 cup canola oil
- 1 cup buttermilk
- 3 large eggs
- 1 cup almond milk
- 2 1/3 cups flour 1 ½ cups sugar

Directions

- Preheat your oven to 350°F and grease Dutch oven and place parchment paper.
- In a mixing bowl combine canola oil, buttermilk, eggs, rum aroma, and a few drops of vanilla extract.
- In another bowl, combine dry ingredients.
- Mix dry ingredients into liquid ingredients, and whisk until you get a smooth and lump-free mixture.
- Bring almond milk to a boil, remove from the heat, and pour into the mixture. Mix well to combine.
- Pour cake batter into a Dutch oven, cover, and bake for approx. 40 minutes.

270 Cheesecake

Serves 4 | Prep time 20 minutes | Cooking time 1h

Ingredients

- 10 oz. vanilla cookies
- ½ teaspoon cinnamon
- 5 oz. butter, melted 8 oz. cream cheese
- 1 cup sugar
- 3 tablespoons flour
- 1 tablespoon vanilla
- 1 cup sour cream
- 4 large eggs Cooking spray Strawberry jam

Directions

- Preheat oven to 350°F. Grease the Dutch oven or line it with parchment paper.
- Make cookie crumb crust by mixing vanilla cookie crumbs, cinnamon, and melted butter.
- Press it gently against the bottom of the Dutch oven.
- Bake it for 8 minutes.
- In the meantime, add sugar, flour, sour cream, and cream cheese in a mixing bowl.
- Mix well to combine.
- Add in the eggs and whisk until you get a homogeneous mixture.

- Pour it over the cookie crust and bake for approx. 40 minutes.
- Remove from the heat and let it cool.

271 Mud Cake

Serves 4 | **Prep time** 10 minutes | **Cooking time** 40 minutes

Ingredients

- 1 ½ cup all-purpose flour
- 2 tsp baking powder
- 1 cup of sugar
- ½ cup milk, non-fat
- ½ cup of water
- 6 tbsp oil
- 1 tsp vanilla extract
- 2 eggs
- For Mud and Toppings
- ½ cup of cocoa powder
- 1 cup hot water
- 1 ½ cup brown sugar
- 1 tsp cinnamon powder
- 1 tsp vanilla extract
- ½ cup pecans

Directions

- In a large bowl, mix all dry ingredients and then add milk, water, eggs, and vanilla extract and mix well.
- Pour this mixture into a Dutch oven.
- In another bowl, mix ingredients for mud except for pecans.
- Pour this batter over the cake batter and sprinkle pecans on the top.
- Place it in a preheated oven for 30-40 minutes at 425 °F (220 °C).
- Stick a toothpick into the cake and check if it comes clean.
- Remove from the oven and serve hot with whipped cream.

272 Buttermilk Cherry Clafoutis

Prep time: 15 minutes | **Cook time:** 35 minutes | **Serves** 6

Ingredients

- Unsalted butter, for preparing the Dutch oven
- 1 pound (454 g) sweet black cherries
- 4 large eggs
- ½ cup granulated sugar
- ¼ cup packed light brown sugar
- 1 cup buttermilk
- 2 teaspoons vanilla extract
- ¼ teaspoon salt
- ¾ cup all-purpose flour Powdered sugar, for dusting
- Vanilla ice cream, for serving (optional)

Directions

- Preheat the oven to 375ºF (190ºC). Coat the Dutch oven with butter.
- Prepare the cherries. Stem and pit the cherries, then place them in the Dutch oven.
- Whisk the other ingredients. In a medium bowl, whisk the eggs, granulated sugar, brown sugar, buttermilk, vanilla, salt, and flour until smooth. Pour the filling over the cherries.
- Bake for 10 minutes. Lower the oven temperature to 350ºF (180ºC) and bake for about 25 minutes more, until the top swells and is springy to the touch. Dust with powdered sugar and serve warm with vanilla ice cream (if using). Cover and refrigerate leftovers for up to 3 days.

273 Pearl Tapioca Pudding

Prep time: 5 minutes | Cook time: 15 minutes | Serves 6

Ingredients

- 1½ cups whole milk
- 1 (14-ounce / 397-g) can full-fat coconut milk Pinch salt
- ½ cup small pearl tapioca, or large pearl tapioca
- ¼ cup sugar
- 1 large egg yolk
- Dried coconut flakes, for garnish

Directions

- Hydrate the tapioca pearls. In a Dutch oven, stir together the milk, coconut milk, salt, and tapioca pearls. Let sit to hydrate for 30 minutes.
- Cook the tapioca pudding. Add the sugar to the tapioca mixture and bring to a boil over medium-high heat. Immediately reduce the heat to medium-low to maintain a low simmer. Cook for 7 minutes, stirring often to prevent sticking, until the tapioca is soft and fully cooked.
- Add the egg yolk. Turn off the heat and let the pudding cool for about 5 minutes. Whisk in the egg yolk until well combined.
- Chill to thicken. Transfer the pudding to small serving dishes. Cover each with plastic wrap (aluminum foil will not create a tight enough seal to prevent a "skin" from forming), pressing it onto the surface of the pudding, and refrigerate for at least 2 hours or until the pudding is thick and set.
- Toast the coconut flakes and serve. In a medium skillet over medium heat, toast the coconut flakes for about 4 minutes, stirring frequently, until golden. Sprinkle over the tapioca puddings to serve. Refrigerate leftovers for up to 4 days.

274 Butter Brownie Pudding

Prep time: 10 minutes | Cook time: 1 hour | Serves 8

Ingredients

- 1 cup (2 sticks) cold unsalted butter
- ¼ cup semisweet chocolate chips
- ¾ cup cocoa powder
- ½ cup all-purpose flour
- ½ teaspoon salt
- 4 large eggs
- 2 cups sugar
- 2 teaspoons vanilla extract Coffee ice cream, for serving

Directions

- Preheat the oven to 325°F (163°C).
- Melt the butter. In a Dutch oven over low heat, combine the butter and chocolate chips. Heat for about 5 minutes, just until melted, then turn off the heat. Set the Dutch oven inside a baking pan (large enough to fit the Dutch oven and hold 2 inches of water).
- Mix the dry ingredients. In a medium bowl, whisk the cocoa powder, flour, and salt. Set aside.
- Mix the wet ingredients. In another medium bowl, whisk the eggs, sugar, and vanilla until very smooth, thick, and light yellow. Pour the egg mixture into the cooled Dutch oven and stir to combine with the melted chocolate. Add the flour mixture and stir again just until combined.
- Bake. Place the baking pan with the Dutch oven in it on the center oven rack. Add just enough of the hottest tap water to the baking pan to come 2 inches up the sides of the Dutch oven. Bake for 1 hour. You want the edges of the pudding to be slightly firmer than the center, which should appear under cooked. Transfer the Dutch oven to a cooling rack for 15 minutes, then serve warm with coffee ice cream. Refrigerate leftovers for up to 4 days.

275 Baguette Butter Pudding

Prep time: 15 minutes | Cook time: 2 hours | Serves 8

Ingredients

- 1 day-old French baguette
- 8 tablespoons (1 stick) unsalted butter, melted
- ½ vanilla bean, split, seeds scraped, pod discarded
- 3 tablespoons spiced rum
- 5 large eggs 1¾ cups sugar
- ¼ teaspoon salt
- 4 teaspoons poppy seeds
- 4 cups half-and-half

Directions

- Preheat the oven to 325°F (163°C).
- Make the bread pudding. Remove any hard crust from the ends of the baguette, then cut the bread into ½-inch-thick cubes. Put the bread in a Dutch oven and pour the melted butter over the top. In a large bowl, whisk the vanilla bean seeds and rum to break up the clumps of seeds. Add the eggs, sugar, and salt and whisk well to combine. Stir in the poppy seeds and half-and-half, then pour the mixture over the bread. Press down lightly so all the bread soaks up the custard. Cover and refrigerate overnight, or for at least 3 hours to allow the bread to absorb the liquid.
- Bake, uncovered, for about 2 hours or until the top and edges are very brown. The center will appear tall and puffy right out of the oven but will settle a bit as it cools. Let cool, then refrigerate overnight so the custard-like base has time to set completely. To serve, reheat each slice in a 375°F (190°C) oven for about 10 minutes, until just warmed through. Refrigerate leftovers for up to 5 days.

276 Strawberry and Oats Crumble

Prep time: 15 minutes | Cook time: 50 minutes | Serves 6

Ingredients

- 6 rhubarb stalks, sliced
- 8 ounces (227 g) strawberries, stemmed and halved
- ½ cup granulated sugar
- 5 teaspoons cornstarch
- 2 teaspoons vanilla extract
- ½ teaspoon salt, divided
- ¾ cup all-purpose flour
- 6 tablespoons (¾ stick) unsalted butter, cubed
- 1 cup old-fashioned rolled oats
- ½ cup packed light brown sugar

Directions

- Preheat the oven to 360°F (182°C).
- Mix the filling. In a Dutch oven, stir together the rhubarb, strawberries, granulated sugar, cornstarch, vanilla, and ¼ teaspoon of salt, stirring and tossing the fruit until it's coated well. Set aside.
- Mix the topping. In a medium bowl, whisk the flour and the remaining ¼ teaspoon of salt to combine. Add the butter. Using a fork, smash and work the butter into the flour until the butter pieces are no larger than peas. Stir in the oats and brown sugar, using your hands to squeeze some of the crumble mixture together to form some larger clumps for texture. Spread the crumble over the fruit.
- Bake for 40 to 50 minutes, until the top is golden brown and the fruit is bubbling. Let cool for 10 minutes, then serve. Refrigerate leftovers for up to 4 days.

277 Peach Butter Cobbler

Prep time: 20 minutes | **Cook time:** 40 minutes | **Serves** 8

Ingredients

- 9 tablespoons (1 stick plus 1 tablespoon) unsalted butter, divided
- 1½ cups pastry flour
- ½ teaspoon salt
- ⅓ cup ice water
- ¼ cup sugar
- 1 teaspoon vanilla extract
- 14 fresh, ripe peaches, quartered and pitted

Directions

- Preheat the oven to 375°F (190°C).
- Make the crumble. Cut 8 tablespoons of butter into small cubes and put them in a medium bowl. Sift the flour and salt over the butter. Using 2 forks or a pastry cutter, mash the butter into the flour. You want the mixture to resemble wet sand. When no large clumps of butter remain, add the ice water, one tablespoon at a time, just until the dough sticks together. Gather the dough into a ball, without kneading, and refrigerate while you work on the filling.
- Make the filling. In a Dutch oven over medium heat, melt the remaining 1 tablespoon of butter. Stir in the sugar and vanilla to combine, then turn off the heat and add the peaches. Toss well to coat.
- Assemble and bake. Using your fingers, break the dough into crumbles and sprinkle a thick layer of pastry crumbles over the peaches. Bake for about 40 minutes, until bubbly. Using a large spoon, scoop the cobbler into serving bowls. Serve warm with a scoop of vanilla ice cream, if desired. Refrigerate leftovers for up to 3 days.

278 Buttery Chocolate Chip Cookie

Prep time: 10 minutes | **Cook time:** 35 minutes | **Serves** 8

Ingredients

- 1 cup (2 sticks) unsalted butter 1 cup packed light brown sugar
- ½ cup granulated sugar
- 1 teaspoon vanilla extract
- 2 large eggs
- 2 cups plus
- 2 tablespoons all-purpose flour
- 1 teaspoon baking soda
- ½ teaspoon salt
- 1½ cups semisweet chocolate chips

Directions

- Preheat the oven to 325°F (163°C).
- Melt the butter. In a Dutch oven over medium heat, melt the butter. Add the brown sugar and granulated sugar. Turn off the heat and stir well until smooth. Let cool completely. Stir in the vanilla and eggs until well mixed.
- Mix the dry ingredients. Stir in the flour, baking soda, and salt. Fold in the chocolate chips, then press the dough down into the bottom of the Dutch oven to form a flat layer.
- Bake for 28 to 35 minutes, until the edges are golden brown, more or less, depending on whether you want the center to be really soft or firmer. Transfer the Dutch oven to a wire rack to cool for 5 minutes, then serve the cookie warm. Refrigerate leftovers for up to 4 days.

279 Fluffy Butter Cheesecake

Prep time: 20 minutes | **Cook time:** 55 minutes | **Serves** 8

Ingredients

- 1 cup cream cheese
- 4 tablespoons (½ stick) unsalted butter
- 7 tablespoons whole milk
- 2 teaspoons vanilla extract
- 1½ tablespoons freshly squeezed lemon juice
- 6 large eggs, separated
- ¾ cup sugar, divided
- ¾ cup cake flour
- 2½ tablespoons cornstarch
- ¼ teaspoon salt

Directions

- Preheat the oven to 400°F (205°C). Set a Dutch oven inside a 12-by-15-inch baking pan (large enough to fit the Dutch oven and hold 2 inches of water).
- Melt the cream cheese. In a medium microwave-safe bowl, combine the cream cheese, butter, and milk. Microwave for about 1 minute on high power, just until soft and partly melted. Whisk to remove any lumps. Whisk in the vanilla, lemon juice, egg yolks, and ¼ cup plus 2 tablespoons of sugar until smooth.
- Sift the flour. Set a fine-mesh sieve over the cream cheese mixture and sift the cake flour, cornstarch, and salt into it. Whisk and set aside.
- Beat the egg whites until stiff peaks form. In the bowl of a stand mixer fitted with the whisk attachment, or in a large bowl using a handheld electric mixer, whip the egg whites on medium-high speed until foamy. Gradually add the remaining ¼ cup plus 2 tablespoons of sugar while beating. Beat for about 3 minutes, until the egg whites are fluffy, have a nice shimmer, and form stiff peaks. Gradually fold the egg white foam into the cream cheese mixture until combined.
- 5. Bake the cheesecake inside the water bath. Pour the cheesecake batter into the Dutch oven. Place the baking pan with the Dutch oven in it on the bottom oven rack. Add just enough of the hottest tap water to the baking pan to come 2 inches up the sides of the Dutch oven. Bake for 18 minutes. Reduce the oven temperature to 325°F (163°C) and bake for 12 minutes more. Turn off the oven and open the door slightly. Let the cheesecake sit in the warm oven for 25 minutes. Remove and let cool completely before serving. Refrigerate leftovers for up to 3 days.

280 Rhubarb and Strawberry Oats Crisp

Prep time: 20 minutes | **Cook time:** 35 to 40 minutes | **Serves** 6 to 8

Ingredients

- 6 tablespoons butter, plus extra for greasing
- 3 cups sliced rhubarb
- 3 cups sliced strawberries
- ¾ cup sugar
- 1 tablespoon cornstarch
- ¾ cup flour
- ¾ cup brown sugar
- ½ cup rolled oats
- ½ teaspoon cinnamon

Directions

- Preheat the oven to 350°F (180°C).
- Grease a Dutch oven with butter.
- In a large bowl, combine the rhubarb, strawberries, sugar, and cornstarch. Place the fruit mixture in the Dutch oven.
- Combine the flour, the brown sugar, and the remaining 6 tablespoons of butter, and use two forks to blend until the mixture resembles coarse crumbs. Add the oats and cinnamon. Mix again. Spoon the topping over the fruit mixture.
- Cover the pot and bake for 35 to 40 minutes, or until the top is lightly browned and crisp.

281 Cherry and Almond Oats Crumble

Prep time: 20 minutes | **Cook time:** 35 to 40 minutes | **Serves** 4 to 6

Ingredients

- 1 cup rolled oats
- ¾ cup sugar, divided 1 cup almond flour
- ¼ teaspoon baking soda
- 2 pinches salt, divided 3 tablespoons butter
- ½ cup chopped almonds (preferably Marcona)
- 3 cups fresh cherries, pitted
- ½ teaspoon ground cinnamon

Directions

- Preheat the oven to 350°F (180°C).
- In a food processor, combine the oats, ¼ cup of sugar, almond flour, baking soda, and 1 pinch of salt. Pulse. Add the butter, and pulse until combined. Mix in the chopped almonds. In a Dutch oven, spread the crumble mixture evenly.
- In a large bowl, combine the remaining ½ cup sugar, cherries, cinnamon, and the remaining 1 pinch salt. Spread the cherry mixture on top of the crumble mixture in the Dutch oven.
- Cover, place in the preheated oven, and bake for 35 to 40 minutes, or until the fruit is bubbly and the crust golden.

282 Chocolate Bread Pudding

Prep time: 20 minutes | **Cook time:** 1 to 1¼ hours | **Serves** 4 to 6

Ingredients

- Butter, for greasing
- 8 cups sweet bread (such as challah or brioche), cut into 1-inch cubes
- ¼ cup melted unsalted butter
- 1 cup sugar
- ½ cup cocoa powder
- 2 teaspoons cinnamon
- 1 teaspoon vanilla extract
- ½ teaspoon almond extract
- ¼ teaspoon salt
- 3 cups whole milk
- 4 large eggs
- ½ cup chocolate chips, divided

Directions

- Preheat the oven to 350°F (180°C).
- Generously grease a Dutch oven with butter.
- Toss the bread cubes in the melted butter, and arrange in the Dutch oven. Bake for 8 to 10 minutes, or until light golden brown.
- In a large bowl, combine the sugar, cocoa powder, cinnamon, vanilla, almond extract, and salt. Add the milk and eggs, and whisk until blended. Add the bread cubes and fold until evenly moistened. Let sit for 15 to 20 minutes, folding once or twice, until the bread cubes have absorbed most of the liquid.
- Return half of the bread mixture to the Dutch oven. Sprinkle with ¼ cup of chocolate chips. Pour in the rest of the bread mixture, and top with the remaining ¼ cup chocolate chips.
- Cover, return the pot to the oven, and bake for 1 to 1¼ hours, or until the top is puffed and a knife inserted near the center comes out mostly clean.

283 Brandy Banana Flambé

Prep time: 10 minutes | **Cook time:** 10 minutes | **Serves** 6 to 8

Ingredients

- 5 tablespoons unsalted butter
- 6 bananas, thinly sliced
- 4 teaspoons brown sugar
- ¾ cup brandy (or cognac)

Directions

- In a Dutch oven over medium-high heat, melt the butter. Sauté the bananas, sprinkling them with the brown sugar and stirring until they are slightly caramelized.
- In a small saucepan, warm the brandy.
- Pour the just-warmed brandy over the bananas.

- Strike a match, stand back, and carefully and ignite the alcohol in the pot. Shake the pot slightly so that the flame dies down, and serve directly from the Dutch oven. Top with whipped cream or ice cream.

284 Apples with Caramel Sauce

Prep time: 15 minutes | **Cook time:** 20 to 25 minutes | **Serves** 6

Ingredients

- 1 stick (8 tablespoons) butter, divided
- 6 apples, peeled and cored (preferably Fuji)
- ½ cup granulated sugar, divided
- 1½ teaspoons cinnamon
- 1¼ cups brown sugar
- 3 tablespoons water

Directions

- Preheat the oven to 325ºF (163ºC).
- Grease a Dutch oven with 1 tablespoon of the butter.
- Trim a small amount off the bottom of each apple to create a flat surface. Place the apples, cut side down, in the Dutch oven. Cut 3 tablespoons of the butter in half, and place 1 piece on top of each apple.
- In a small bowl, combine the granulated sugar and the cinnamon, and sprinkle over the apples. Cover and bake until the sugar is melted, 15 to 20 minutes. Arrange the apples on serving plates.
- In the Dutch oven, combine the brown sugar, the remaining 8 teaspoons granulated sugar, and the water. Bring to a boil over a medium heat, and cook until thick, about 5 minutes, stirring often. Whisk in the remaining butter. Drizzle the caramel sauce over each apple.

285 Almond Butter Cake

Prep time: 10 minutes | **Cook time:** 30 minutes | **Serves** 6 to 8

Ingredients

- 8 tablespoons unsalted butter, at room temperature, plus extra for greasing
- 7 ounces (198 g) almond paste
- 3 large eggs
- 1 tablespoon rum or amaretto
- 2 drops almond extract
- ⅓ cup all-purpose flour
- ½ teaspoon baking powder

Directions

- Preheat the oven to 350ºF (180ºC).
- Grease a Dutch oven with butter.
- In a bowl, combine the almond paste, the remaining 8 tablespoons butter, the eggs, rum, and almond extract, and blend together, using a spatula.
- Fold the flour and the baking powder into the cake batter. Spoon into the Dutch oven.
- Cover, place the pot in the preheated oven, and bake for 30 minutes, or until the top of the cake is golden and a knife inserted into the center comes out almost clean.

286 Berry Cream Bake

Prep time: 10 minutes | **Cook time:** 50 minutes | **Serves** 4 to 6

Ingredients

- Butter, for greasing
- 3 eggs
- 1 cup milk
- ¼ cup heavy cream
- ½ cup flour
- 1 teaspoon vanilla extract
- ½ cup sugar
- 2 cups mixed berries

Directions

- Preheat the oven to 350ºF (180ºC).
- Grease a Dutch oven with butter.
- In a stand mixer, combine the eggs, milk, cream, flour, vanilla, and sugar, and blend on high for 30 seconds.
- Pour 1 cup of batter into the Dutch oven. Cover, place in the preheated oven, and bake for 5 to 7 minutes.

- Remove from the oven and arrange the berries on top. Pour the remaining batter over the fruit.
- Return to the oven, and bake for 45 minutes, or until golden and a knife inserted in the center comes out almost clean.

287 Pears with Orange Peel

Prep time: 10 minutes | **Cook time:** 30 minutes | **Serves** 4

Ingredients

- 1 (750 ml) bottle Riesling 1 teaspoon whole cloves
- 1 teaspoon cardamom pods
- 2 cinnamon sticks
- 2 strips orange peel,
- ½ inch wide by 2 inches long
- 4 pears, stems and peels removed, cut in half

Directions

- In a large Dutch oven, bring the Riesling, cloves, cardamom, cinnamon, and orange peel to a simmer over medium-high heat.
- Add the pears. Put a plate over the top of them as a weight to keep them submerged in the liquid.
- Reduce the heat to medium-low. Simmer until the pears are tender, about 25 minutes.
- Serve the pears with the poaching liquid (minus the spices and orange peel) spooned over the top.

288 Apple and Cashew Toffee Crisp

Prep time: 15 minutes | **Cook time:** 1¾ hours | **Serves** 12

Ingredients

- 7 large Granny Smith apples, peeled, cored, and sliced into ¼-inch- thick slices
- 2 tablespoons lemon juice
- ¼ cup apple juice
- ½ cup sugar
- 2½ cups brown sugar, divided
- 2 cups plus 2 tablespoons all-purpose flour, divided
- 1 teaspoon cinnamon
- ¼ teaspoon nutmeg
- 2 cups quick-cooking oatmeal
- ½ teaspoon baking soda
- 1 cup butter, melted
- 1 cup English toffee bits
- ½ cup chopped cashews

Directions

- Heat oven to 350ºF (180ºC).
- Place apples in a medium bowl with lemon juice, apple juice, sugar, ½ cup brown sugar, 2 tablespoons flour, cinnamon, and nutmeg and toss to coat.
- In a large bowl, combine oatmeal, 2 cups brown sugar, 2 cups flour, and baking soda and mix well. Add melted butter and mix until crumbs form. Stir in toffee bits and cashews.
- Place half of oatmeal mixture in an ovenproof Dutch oven. Top with apple mixture, then remaining oatmeal mixture. Bake 45 to 55 minutes or until topping is browned and apples are tender when pierced with a fork. Let cool 1 hour, then serve.

289 Apple Cream Crumble

Prep time: 15 minutes | **Cook time:** 50 minutes | **Serves** 8

Ingredients

- 2 cups sugar, divided
- 2 tablespoons water
- 2 tablespoons light corn syrup
- ¾ cup heavy cream
- 4 tablespoons unsalted butter
- 1½ teaspoons sea salt
- 8 Granny Smith or Pink Lady apples, peeled, cored, and cut into ½- inch wedges
- ¼ cup cornstarch
- 1 teaspoon vanilla
- ½ teaspoon cinnamon
- ¼ teaspoon nutmeg
- 1 cup all-purpose flour

- 8 tablespoons (1 stick) unsalted butter, cubed

Directions

- In a medium saucepan with deep sides add 1 cup sugar, water, and corn syrup. Place the pot over medium heat and, swirling but never stirring, bring mixture to a boil. Brush the sides of the pan with a wet pastry brush if any sugar crystals cling to the edge of the pot. Allow mixture to boil until it is a deep amber color and smells like dark caramel, about 6 minutes.
- Remove pot from the heat and, very carefully as it will bubble up, whisk in heavy cream, butter, and salt. Once butter is melted let caramel cool to room temperature.
- In an ovenproof Dutch oven combine apples, cornstarch, vanilla, cinnamon, and nutmeg until all apples are evenly coated. Pour in ½ cup salted caramel sauce and mix to combine. Set aside.
- Heat oven to 350°F (180°C).
- In a medium bowl combine remaining sugar, flour, and butter. With your fingers rub butter into the flour and sugar until mixture is crumbly and well combined. Spread mixture evenly over apples and bake 30 to 40 minutes, or until apples are fork tender and crumble topping is golden brown.
- Cool 10 minutes before serving. Drizzle each serving with a little of remaining caramel sauce.

290 Apple and Cranberry Stew

Prep time: 10 minutes | **Cook time:** 30 minutes | **Serves** 4

Ingredients

- 2 Granny Smith apples, peeled, cored, and diced
- 2 Fuji or McIntosh apples, peeled, cored, and diced
- 1 cup dried sweetened cranberries
- ½ cup sugar
- 1 teaspoon cinnamon
- 1 cup apple or cranberry-apple juice

Directions

- Combine all ingredients in a Dutch oven. Stirring constantly, bring to a boil over medium-high heat. Reduce heat to low and simmer 20 minutes or until apples are tender.
- Let mixture stand at least 10 minutes then serve.

291 Marshmallow Casserole with Chocolate Chips

Prep time: 10 minutes | **Cook time:** 45 minutes | **Serves** 10

Ingredients

- 1¼ cups graham cracker crumbs
- 1½ sticks unsalted butter, melted, divided
- 2 large eggs
- 1 cup sugar
- 1 teaspoon vanilla
- ½ cup all-purpose flour
- ⅓ cup Dutch-processed cocoa powder
- ¼ teaspoon salt
- 1 cup semisweet chocolate chips
- 1 (10-ounce / 283-g) bag miniature marshmallows

Directions

- Heat oven to 350°F (180°C) and lightly spray an ovenproof and broiler proof 10-inch Dutch oven with nonstick cooking spray.
- In a medium bowl combine graham cracker crumbs with ½ cup melted butter. Mix until graham cracker crumbs are completely coated, then press into the bottom of the Dutch oven. Bake 10 minutes, then set aside to cool.
- In a small bowl combine remaining butter with eggs, sugar, and vanilla. Mix until thoroughly combined.
- In a medium bowl combine flour, cocoa powder, and salt. Whisk to combine.

- Pour wet ingredients into dry ingredients and mix until dry ingredients are just moistened, about 12 strokes. Fold in chocolate chips, then pour batter over the graham cracker base.
- Bake 25 to 30 minutes, or until filling is just set around the edges.
- Pour marshmallows over the top of chocolate filling. Heat the broiler and broil until marshmallows are golden brown and puffed. Cool 10 minutes before serving.

292 Red Wine Pears

Prep time: 5 minutes | **Cook time:** 30 minutes | **Serves** 6

Ingredients

- 3 Bosc pears
- 2 cups red wine, such as Cabernet or Merlot
- 1 teaspoon vanilla extract
- 2 teaspoons sugar
- 2 star anise pods (optional)

Directions

- Prepare the pears. Peel the pears and halve them lengthwise. Remove the seeds and core. Set the pear halves in the Dutch oven and pour the red wine on top. Add the vanilla, sugar, and star anise (if using).
- Poach. Bring the wine to a low simmer over medium heat. Cover the pot, leaving the lid slightly ajar. Cook for 8 minutes, checking frequently to ensure the liquid is bubbling only slightly. Flip the pears and cook for about 8 minutes more, until a skewer pierces the pear flesh very easily. Transfer the pears to shallow serving bowls.
- Reduce the wine. With the lid off, bring the liquid to boil. Cook for about 15 minutes, just until the sauce thickens enough to coat the back of a spoon. Drizzle a large spoonful of sauce over each pear and serve. Refrigerate leftovers with the sauce for up to 3 days.

293 Apple with Vanilla Ice Cream

Prep time: 20 minutes | **Cook time:** 30 minutes | **Serves** 6

Ingredients

- Grated zest and juice of 1 lemon
- 2 pounds (907 g) Granny Smith apples
- 2 pounds (907 g) sweet red apples, such as Gala
- ⅓ cup packed light brown sugar
- 3 tablespoons unsalted butter
- 1½ teaspoons ground cardamom
- ¼ teaspoon salt
- Vanilla ice cream, for serving

Directions

- Prepare the apples. In a Dutch oven, combine the lemon zest and lemon juice. Peel, core, and roughly chop the apples. Add the apples to the pot, stirring to coat them in the lemon juice, which will help prevent them from turning brown.
- Cook the apples. Turn the heat to medium-low. Stir in the brown sugar, butter, cardamom, and salt. Cover the pot and simmer for about 30 minutes, until the apples release their juices and become very tender. Using a wooden spatula, stir vigorously, breaking up larger pieces. Serve warm with a scoop of vanilla ice cream on top. Refrigerate leftovers in the Dutch oven for up to 5 days.

294 Cookies and Cream Ice Cream Cake

Prep time: 30 minutes | **Cook time:** 0 minutes | **Serves** 8

Ingredients

- 1 gallon cookies and cream ice cream
- 1 (19-ounce / 539-g) package chocolate sandwich cookies
- 4 tablespoons (½ stick) unsalted butter, melted
- 1 (16-ounce / 454-g) jar fudge topping
- 1 (8-ounce / 227-g) container frozen whipped topping, thawed

Directions

- Soften the ice cream. Set the ice cream on the counter for 30 minutes to soften.
- Chop the cookies and make the crust. You need about 36 sandwich cookies for this recipe. Using a chef's knife, chop the sandwich cookies well. Reserve 1 cup of the chopped cookies for topping the cake; put the remaining cookies in a Dutch oven with the melted butter. Stir to combine, then press down to form a crust.
- Layer the cake. Using a spatula, spread the softened ice cream over the cookie crust. Cover the pot and freeze for 2 hours. Pour the fudge sauce over the ice cream layer and freeze for 1 hour more. Spread the whipped topping over the fudge layer and top with the reserved chopped cookies. Freeze overnight or for at least 8 hours.
- Serve. Remove the Dutch oven from the freezer at least 20 minutes before serving. Once the cake has thawed slightly, use a spatula to slice it and serve. Tightly wrapped to prevent freezer burn, the ice cream cake can be frozen for up to 1 month. Thaw on the counter for 20 minutes for easy slicing.

295 Cherry Pie Cake

Prep time: 5 minutes | Cook time: 1 hour | Serves 12

Ingredients

- 2 (20-ounce / 567-g) cans cherry pie filling
- 1 (15¼-ounce / 432-g) package yellow cake mix
- 8 tablespoons (1 stick) butter, sliced

Directions

-
- Heat oven to 350°F (180°C) and lightly spray an ovenproof 10- or 12-inch Dutch oven with nonstick cooking spray.
- In the prepared Dutch oven add cherry pie filling. Sprinkle cake mix over filling then lay butter slices over cake mix.
- Bake 50 to 55 minutes, or until top is browned and filling is bubbling. Cool 20 minutes before serving.

296 Raisins Rice Pudding

Prep time: 10 minutes | Cook time: 1 hour | Serves 8

Ingredients

- 3 large eggs
- 1 large egg yolk
- 2 cups whole milk
- 1 cup half-and-half
- 1 cup sugar
- ½ teaspoon fresh grated nutmeg Pinch of cinnamon
- 3 cups cooked rice
- ½ cup raisins

Directions

- Heat oven to 375°F (190°C).
- In a medium bowl whisk together eggs and egg yolk until well combined. Add milk, half-and-half, sugar, nutmeg, and cinnamon. Mix in rice and then pour into an ovenproof Dutch oven. Stir in raisins.
- Bake 45 to 50 minutes, or until the center of rice pudding jiggles slightly when the Dutch oven is moved and a paring knife inserted into the center comes out clean. Cool 20 minutes before serving.

297 Chocolate and Walnuts Brownies

Prep time: 15 minutes | Cook time: 30 minutes | Serves 10

Ingredients

- ½ cup all-purpose flour
- ½ cup cocoa powder
- 1 teaspoon baking powder
- ¼ teaspoon salt
- ½ cup butter
- 1 cup chocolate chips, divided
- 1 cup sugar
- 1 teaspoon vanilla

- 2 large eggs
- 2 tablespoons honey
- 1 cup chopped walnuts or pecans

Directions

- Heat oven to 350°F (180°C) and lightly spray an ovenproof 10-inch Dutch oven with nonstick cooking spray.
- In a large bowl combine flour, cocoa powder, baking powder, and salt. Set aside.
- In a microwave-safe bowl combine butter with ½ cup chocolate chips. Microwave for 30 second intervals, stirring after each interval, until the butter and chips are melted and smooth.
- Transfer chocolate mixture to a medium bowl along with sugar, vanilla, eggs, and honey. Whisk until smooth and well combined.
- Pour the wet ingredients into the dry and mix until just combined, about 10 strokes, then add remaining chocolate chips and nuts and fold to combine, about 3 to 4 strokes more.
- Pour batter into the prepared Dutch oven and bake 25 to 35 minutes or until the brownies are set around the edges and slightly jiggly in the center. Enjoy warm from the Dutch oven, or cool completely and cut into wedges.

298 Butterscotch Crumble Cake

Prep time: 20 minutes | **Cook time:** 30 minutes | **Serves** 10

Ingredients

- 1½ cups all-purpose flour, divided
- 1¼ cups packed light brown sugar, divided
- ½ teaspoon baking powder
- ½ teaspoon baking soda
- ¼ teaspoon salt
- 2 large eggs
- ½ cup buttermilk
- ⅓ cup vegetable or coconut oil
- 1 teaspoon vanilla
- 1 (12-ounce / 340-g) package butterscotch chips, divided
- 4 tablespoons unsalted butter

Directions

- Heat oven to 350°F (180°C) and lightly spray an ovenproof 10-inch Dutch oven with nonstick cooking spray.
- In a large bowl combine 1 cup flour, ¾ cup sugar, baking powder, baking soda, and salt. Whisk until well combined.
- In a medium bowl combine eggs, buttermilk, oil, and vanilla. Whisk until smooth.
- Pour the wet ingredients into the dry and mix until just combined, about 8 strokes, then add half the butterscotch chips and fold to combine, about 3 to 4 strokes more. Pour batter into the prepared Dutch oven.
- In a medium bowl combine remaining flour, sugar, and butter. With your fingers rub butter into flour and sugar until mixture is crumbly and well combined. Spread mixture evenly over cake batter, then sprinkle remaining butterscotch chips over top.
- Bake 25 to 35 minutes, or until the cake springs back in the center when gently pressed and a toothpick inserted into center of cake comes out clean. Cool to room temperature before serving.

299 Pineapple Rings and Cherry Cake

Prep time: 25 minutes | **Cook time:** 50 minutes | **Serves** 12

Ingredients

- 1 cup butter, melted, divided
- 1⅔ cups packed light brown sugar, divided
- 1 (14-ounce / 397-g) can pineapple rings, drained, juice reserved Maraschino cherries, to put in the center of the pineapple rings
- 1½ cups all-purpose flour
- 1½ teaspoons baking soda
- ½ teaspoon salt
- ¾ cup milk
- 1 large egg

Directions

- Heat oven to 350°F (180°C) and lightly spray an ovenproof 10-inch Dutch oven with nonstick cooking spray.
- Pour ⅓ cup melted butter into the prepared Dutch oven, then sprinkle 1 cup of the brown sugar evenly into butter. Lay pineapple rings into the Dutch oven, as many as will fit in one layer, and place a cherry in the center of each ring. Set aside.
- In a medium bowl combine flour, baking soda, and salt. Whisk to combine.
- In a separate bowl add remaining butter, remaining sugar, ¼ cup reserved pineapple juice, milk, and egg. Mix until smooth. Pour the wet ingredients into the dry ingredients and mix until batter is well combined, about 20 strokes. Small lumps are okay.
- Carefully pour batter over pineapple rings. Spread so it is even. Bake 50 to 55 minutes, or until the cake springs back when gently pressed and the sides of the cake are starting to pull away from the sides of the Dutch oven.
- Immediately turn cake out onto a heatproof serving plate, allowing butter and brown sugar sauce to drip over the cake. Be careful, the cake and Dutch oven are very hot. If any of the pineapple rings or cherries stick, loosen them with a fork and place them back on cake. Serve warm or at room temperature.

300 Mango Sushi Rice

Prep time: 10 minutes | **Cook time:** 40 minutes | **Serves** 6

Ingredients

- 1½ cups sushi rice
- 1 (14-ounce / 397-g) can full-fat coconut milk
- ⅓ cup sugar
- ¼ teaspoon salt
- 2 mangoes
- 1 tablespoon toasted sesame seeds

Directions

- Rinse the rice. Pour the rice into a fine-mesh sieve and set it over a medium bowl. Fill the bowl with water and slosh the rice around with your hand for several minutes. Let sit for 3 hours, then drain.
- Steam the rice. Set the sieve with the rice over a Dutch oven of simmering water. Cover the pot and steam the rice for 30 to 40 minutes, until tender. Check the water level in the pot occasionally and add more if it gets low. Transfer the cooked rice to a bowl and cover with a plate.
- Make the coconut milk sauce. While the rice cools, in a small saucepan over medium-high heat, combine the coconut milk, sugar, and salt. Cook, stirring occasionally, for 1 minute. Turn off the heat and leave to thicken while you cut the mangoes.
- Cut the mangoes and serve. Peel the mangoes. Cut on either side of the pit, which is in the middle, then thinly slice the flesh. To serve, scoop and press the rice into a measuring cup to mold. Turn it onto a serving plate and drizzle the coconut milk sauce over the rice. Fan the mango slices on top and sprinkle with toasted sesame seeds. Refrigerate leftovers for up to 2 days.

Printed in the USA
CPSIA information can be obtained
at www.ICGtesting.com
LVHW060925301124
798009LV00005B/172